# Simple Christianity vs. Churchianity:

## The Way Forward Is Back to Basics

## by Stan Paregien

D1472841

Forewords by

Dr. David R. Langford, Ph.D.
Dr. Perry C. Cotham, Ph.D.

# Acknowledgements

Copyrighted 2021 – by Stan Paregien
ISBN: 979-8594035072
Published by Paregien Enterprises
1127 48th Ave. East, Bradenton, FL
Processed and distributed by Amazon KDP and other fine retailers.

Topics: Titus 3:1-8, Churchianity, simple Christianity, priesthood of all believers, evangelism, gospel, salvation, grace, faith, repentance, baptism.

## Credits:

We have tried to carefully document our sources. Most of the materials and photos, unless otherwise specified, are in the Public Domain or the Fair Use Domain. **Please note:** I hereby give permission for anyone to use the graphics I have created for this book (my name will be on them in small print). I enjoyed creating them, and I will be pleased if others can use them. All graphics in this paperback are in black and white due to the high cost of full-color printing. However, all graphics are in full-color in my **eBook** version.

# Bible Citations

Unless otherwise noted, all Scripture citations are from the **Easy-to-Read Version** (ERV). Copyright © 2006 by Bible League International. Used with permission.

**Amplified Bible** (AMP). La Habra, CA: The Lockman Foundation, 2015. Used with permission. Similar in style to **The Expanded Bible**.

**The Contemporary English Version** (CEV). Tulsa, OK: American Bible Society, Copyright © 1991, 1992, 1995. Used with permission.

**The English Standard Version** (ESV; The Holy Bible, English Standard Version). Wheaton, IL: Crossway Bibles, a publishing ministry of Good News Publishers, 2001. Used by Permission.

**The English Standard Version Anglicised** (ESVUK). Wheaton, IL: Crossway Bibles, a division of Good News Publishers, 2001. Used by permission.

**The Evangelical Heritage Version** (EHV). Sturtevant, WI: Wartburg Project, Inc., 2019. Used with permission.

**The Expanded Bible** (EXB). Nashville, TN: Thomas Nelson, Inc., 2011. Used with permission. Similar in style to **The Amplified Bible**.

**Good News Translation** (GNT). Philadelphia, PA: American Bible Society, 1992. Used with permission.

**The Holman Christian Study Bible**. Nashville, TN: Holman Bible Publishers, 2017. Used with permission.

**J.B. Phillips New Testament**. (PILLIPS). England: Archbishops' Council of the Church of England, 1960, 1972. Used by permission.

**Jubilee Bible 2000** (JUB). Written by Russell Stendal of Ransom Press International, 2013 and 2020. Available online for free.

**The Lexham English Bible** (LEB). Bellingham, WA: Logos Bible Software, 2012. Used with permission.

**The Living Bible**. Carol Stream, IL: Tyndale House Foundation, 1971. Used by permission.

**The Message (MSG).** Colorado Springs, CO: NavPress, a division of The Navigators, 1993, 2002, 2018. Written by Eugene H. Peterson. Used by permission.

**The Modern English Version** (MEV). Charisma House & Military Bible Association, 2014. It is a literal translation ("formal correspondence translation") based on ancient manuscripts as well the King James Version. Used by permission.

**The New Century Version** (NCV). Nashville, TN: Thomas Nelson, Inc., 2005. It is an English translation related to the ERV, but with more fluent style and longer sentences. Used by permission.

**The New King James Version** (NKJV). Nashville, TN: Thomas Nelson Publishers, 1982. Used by permission.

**The New Life Version** (NLV). Uhrichsville, Ohio: Barbour Publishing, Inc., copyrighted 1969, 2003. Used with permission.

**The New Living Translation** (NLT). Carol Stream, IL.: Tyndale House Publishers, Inc., Copyrighted 1996, 2004, 2015. Used by permission.

**The New Revised Standard Version Bible**. (NRSV) Washington, DC: Division of Christian Education of the National Council of the Churches of Christ in the United States of America. Copyright © 1989. Used by permission.

**The New Revised Standard Version Bible, Catholic Edition.** (NRSVCE) Based on the NRSV but includes the deuterocanonical books. Adapted for and approved by the Catholic Church. Based on the British style of English. Various publishers. 1989, 1993, 1995. Used with permission.

# Dedication

**To the late G.B. Shelburne, Jr., my Bible teacher at the Amarillo Bible Training Work in Amarillo, Texas, and to his four sons who followed him into the preaching ministry: B. Shelburne, Gene Shelburne, Curtis W. Shelburne, and Jim Shelburne.**

# First Foreword

### By Dr. David R. Langford, Ph.D.

I have known David Langford since he was about knee-high to a Texas grasshopper. And I knew, loved and appreciated his late father, Dr. Thomas Langford, and his mother Nellie. David Langford serves as both a minister and an elder with the Quaker Avenue Church of Christ in Lubbock, Texas. He has received the Master's degree in Communication and the Ph.D. in Marriage and Family Therapy from Texas Tech University. He also earned a Masters in Ministry from Lubbock Christian University, where he has also served as a Bible Professor. He and his wife, Lisa Gomez, have lived in Lubbock for decades.

Dr. Langford has several well-written books to his credit. Among them are ***Navigating the Winds of Culture***; ***The Influential Christ: Why was Jesus so Influential?***; ***Questioning Jesus: Questions Jesus Asked and Answered***; ***A Curse, a Cradle and a Cross: Reflections on the Christmas Story***; ***The Divine Dilemma: And Other Reflections on the Cross***; and ***A Troubled Faith for a Troubled World***. He is also a consulting editor and writer for a magazine titled, ***Christian Appeal***.

I sometimes refer to myself as a "unity brat." My father was active in the unity efforts among members of the Restoration Movement from late '50s. Consequently, I was drug to unity conferences as long as I can remember. The first I remember was the Consultation on Christian Unity in Denver, CO in 1961. While brethren were consulting on unity, I was outside splashing in the hotel fountain with other "unity brats." Over the years I attended multiple unity meetings from Bethany, WV to Nashville, TN, to Los Angeles, CA. As I listened to brethren plead for unity, I began to have religious heroes from across the movement, Don DeWelt, Edward Fudge, Leroy Garrett, Perry Gresham, Monroe Hawley, Carl Ketcherside, Victor Knowles, Robert Myers, Roy Osborne, Gene Shelburne, Rubel Shelly, Ervin Waters and James Woodroof to mention a few.

I first became aware of Stan Paregien from his 1971 book, **Thoughts on Unity,** which he compiled to help promote unity among Restoration churches. The book is a collection of many voices (including my father's) encouraging greater unity. Over the years I've come to appreciate Stan's multiple contributions to spiritual growth both through his thoughtful books on biblical themes and his delightful contributions to the heritage of cowboy poetry and stories. Both literary heritages are seen in **Simple Christianity vs Churchianity** as Stan combines his Bible knowledge with his own colorful "rhetorical style."

Stan continues the Restoration Movement's rich tradition of calling us to be "Christians only but not the only Christians" and to overcome the unfortunate sectarian tendency of our heritage. The tragic irony of the Restoration Movement is its legacy of division despite its original plea of unity. Stan calls us back to the vision of Elder Thomas Campbell, that "division among Christians is a horrid evil." He challenges us to appreciate and respect the diversity of honest interpretation that has existed among believers since the first century.

**Alister McGrath**, in his book, **Christianity's Dangerous Idea**, notes "the idea that lay at the heart of the 16th century Reformation which brought Protestantism into being, was that the Bible is capable of being understood by all Christian believers and that they all have the right to interpret it and to insist upon their perspective being taken seriously." One can hardly disagree that we all should have the freedom to interpret the Bible, but the consequence of such freedom is our inevitably different interpretations and visions of how to reform the Church. Such differences need not be so dangerous however if we follow, as Stan encourages, the counsel of Thomas Campbell so eloquently expressed in the 6th Article in his "Declaration and Address."

> Although inferences and deductions from Scripture premises, when fairly inferred, may be truly called the doctrine of God's holy word, yet they are not formally binding upon Christians farther than they perceive the connection; for their faith must not stand in the wisdom of men, but in the power and veracity of God.

Typically, when we baptize believers into Christ, we don't require them to give answers to all the questions about what we may believe or practice. There is in fact only one answer to one question we believe ultimately important. The question is "What do you believe about Jesus Christ." The answer is "I believe that Jesus Christ is the Son of God." To believe in Christ is to acknowledge him as Lord of our life, to submit to and be conformed into his image. A young Christian is not aware of and certainly unable to understand all the doctrines that Christians differ about. There is much he or she will need to learn in coming years. But that new believer will never be any more a part of God's family than he is at that moment, because at that moment he is God's child. And wherever our Father has a son or daughter, we have a brother or sister.

Throughout history we've tried to determine our brethren by their "correct" answers to various Bible questions. Biblical instruction is vitally important, but history is clear. It has been notoriously hard for believers to agree on everything. Which is perhaps why Paul speaks of two kinds of unity in Ephesians 4. There is a unity of the Spirit given to us when we are baptized into Christ, a unity for us to maintain, guard and preserve (Ephesians 4:3).

That unity is based on seven basic truths, each one related to Christ. There is one Father of whom Christ is the Son. There is one Lord, Christ. There is one body, the body of Christ. There is one hope, the hope of Christ's return. There is one baptism, baptism into the name (authority) of Christ. There is one faith, faith in Christ's work on the cross. There is one Spirit, the Spirit of Christ. This understanding of Christ is the basis of our unity and Paul pleads with us to guard this unity.

But in that same chapter, Paul speaks of another unity, a unity in the faith we are to attain, to eventually arrive at, to come to (vs 13). The first is a unity given to us when we begin the journey; the second is a unity always ahead of us until we finish the journey. This is the same distinction referred to in another phrase popular in our Restoration heritage. "In faith unity…" (the first unity). "In opinion liberty…" (until we reach the second unity). And until that 2nd unity is fully reached, "In all things love."

Stan's instruction is designed to help us increase our unity of the faith, but never at the expense of our unity in the Spirit. As you read it, you will be blessed and challenged. Challenged because you may not agree with every conclusion. I suspect Stan might be disappointed if you did. And you will be blessed as you travel through the Scriptures and learn more of Stan's vision of "simple Christianity" that helps us avoid the troublesome "Churchianity."

I don't believe God wants our church life
To be centered on buildings and service.
Instead, God wants our churches to be
focused on active discipleship, mission,
and the pursuit of unity.

Francis Chan & Robert Sprinkle

# Second Foreword

## By Dr. Perry C. Cotham, Ph.D.

NOTE: Perry Cotham and I were classmates at Lipscomb University in Nashville, Tenn. That belies the fact that we barely knew one another back then. I was married and we were sole-supporters of my educational efforts, so I preached at small, country congregations on the weekends and I usually held some other part-time job on top of that. So I flat-out did not have much time for socializing. However, he and I reconnected in late 2019 by Facebook and emails. Soon we discovered we had similar views on many things, though we still have not been able to sit down face to face. –SP.

Dr. Cotham is a son of the late and well-known Perry B. Cotham who spent his life preaching for congregations of the Church of Christ. Cotham received his B.A. from Lipscomb University in Nashville, with a minor in Biblical Studies. He earned both his M.A. and Ph.D. in Speech Communication from Wayne State University. In addition, he studied theology at Vanderbilt University and psychology at Middle Tennessee State University.

He taught Speech, Political Science and Bible for a time at his *alma mater*, Lipscomb University. Then he taught at and retired from Middle Tennessee State University in Murfreesboro. He and his wife Glenda are enjoying retirement at their home in Brentwood, Tenn.

Dr. Cotham is the author of several books, including **Marriage in the Fast Lane**; **The Heart & Soul of Business: A Christian Perspective**; **From Pilgrim Pulpit to the Electronic Era**; **American Rhetorical Excellence**; **Toil, Turmoil, and Triumph: A Portrait of the Tennessee Labor Movement**; **Christian Social Ethics** (Editor); **Harsh Realities, Agonizing Choices: Making Moral Decisions in a Morally**

**Complex World**; **One World, Many Neighbors: A Christian Perspective on Worldviews**; **Please Don't Revive Us Again!: The Human Side of the Church of Christ**; and, **Ceasefire: Ending Worship Wars through Sound Theology and Plain Common Sense**.

When a person has spent a lifetime in service to others, especially in public speaking and teaching, but also in writing all kinds of literature, then for what kind of message would that person most want to be remembered?

As a writer myself, I am aware of two realities: First, one never knows when his or her last book, last essay, or last poem will be written. And second, any writer of sound mind and available time feels compelled to keep writing. Such seems woven into a writer's DNA. Just as an artist will keep painting portraits even when no one seems interested in buying and framing them, a writer will keep writing—whether books, essays, poetry, or just humor and nonsense—even if no one seems interested in buying or reading them.

We writers of sound mind, even if our bodies are not as sound as they once were, must express ourselves in words. And there comes a moment in our personal history in which we pay homage to our personal legacy. We make a grand statement, a kind of summary exposition of all the relevant truths and wise insights that we sincerely believe to be most important. Once our statement is completed, however long or brief it may be, then we say to ourselves: "If all else about me is forgotten, these ideas and insights are what I most want to be remembered."

Having given **Simple Christianity vs. Churchianity** a careful reading, that is what I sense about my friend and colleague Stan Paregien. I sense he primarily does not care if you know where he lives, how long he has been married, what political ideologies he holds, or what his favorite hobbies, stories, or jokes happen to be. Of course, as I know Stan, he will be plenty glad to tell you about any of those matters and even answer almost any question. What I sense here is that Stan, in his twenty-fifth book (for which he deserves congratulations, of course), deeply desires to share with readers of all backgrounds and all faiths (or little or even no faith) a clear, understandable, and highly interesting statement and discussion of the truths that have been foundation for his God-centered life.

Stan and my backgrounds are similar in many ways. By the time I left what was known then as David Lipscomb College as a Bible and Preaching major, I felt I had most, if not all, the answers I needed for my vocation. My college major reinforced what I had learned as young boy and teenager:

- The Bible is the Word of God.
- All biblical verses are equally inspired.
- We can know truth absolutely.
- There is a five-step plan of salvation.
- There are five ordained acts of worship.
- There is one true church and it is not a denomination.
- The New Testament gives a clear pattern for the entire Christian life and worship.
- All Scripture can be harmonized, even verses that seem contradictory at first reading.
- All sincere students of Scripture can understand the Bible alike.
- Church worship attendance is the most important command in the Bible.
- Communion is the most important act of worship.

The first few years after that undergraduate education became so intellectually challenging. Serving a congregation as a full-time minister and then attending graduate classes at a large, public university all combined to raise questions continually in mind. Often late at night, I lay awake with the fear I was actually serving "the wrong church" or that I might be actually "losing my faith." Either outcome would have been distressing to the point of causing major alarm to my parents, to former Bible teachers, and to some of my best friends. Issues of intellectual honesty became paramount.

After reading Stan's **Simple Christianity vs. Churchianity**, oh how I wish I could have read that book during those formative years. This book would have reassured me that my questioning was normal for a thinking person and that conclusions I was reaching were reasonable and sensible. Or, as Stan states it, this book would "destroy some of the myths of our early indoctrination." I so empathized with Stan's youthful spiritual condition. "As a young man I was so narrow-minded," he confesses, "you could not see my head if you looked straight at me."

Stan does not claim to know all the answers to our deepest religious questions. He simply calls himself "one sin-prone Christian saved by Jesus." Topics Stan then discusses are matters of utmost importance to him, and it is a compliment to readers of all ages and backgrounds that he seeks to share commonsense insights. Writing a book with substance and relevance is no easy challenge. And the breadth of this study is as wide as the entire Christian life.

"Churchianity" is more slang than an actual word found in dictionaries. Stan sees it as "a disease of the heart." Most of us will know what "churchianity" means. The word represents commitment to institutionalism. To seeing church membership as an end in itself. Robot-style compliance to some institutional authority. Mechanical rule-keeping. Seeing non-conformists as enemies of the "truth." Emphasis on the externals. "Churchianity" becomes a form of onerous compliance and conformity, and true believers seek a way out of such a web of institutional rules and outward requirements—all in the hope of finding genuine Christian life and meaningful relationships.

Many features of this book impress me. The author maintains such an open attitude toward all seekers of God and seekers of truth. Stan is not in the condemnation business. He is willing to address adherents of other world faith traditions. At times he will cite some author or fellow preacher from his own tradition, but then he also finds inspiration in the life and the words of saints such as Mother Teresa. At times his little detours are so interesting, for example his reporting Jon Meacham's interview experience with George H. W. Bush while writing the latter's biography or his reporting his visit to "Ark Encounter" in Williamstown, Kentucky.

May I state the feature that strikes me as both rare and valuable? This book demonstrates that profound truth can be stated and explained in the most casual and informative format. I love Stan's style. It kept me reading when I was tempted to "pull off" and go watch the NFL playoff series (yes, I could have managed a way to see the games on tape delay). Imagine this: A Bible scholar and skilled teacher is sitting across a table from you while you both enjoy a meal or your favorite beverage and he is answering and explaining some of the deepest concepts of the Christian faith in language that you immediately understand, and that at times brings a wide smile to your face, then this is how Stan writes.

This book is a "theology," in one sense of the word. This treatise encompasses all biblical scripture. It is thorough. All major themes of biblical doctrine and practical Christian life are treated. But it is a theology not intended simply for Bible scholars and Bible majors in Christian schools—it is theology for ordinary, down-to-earth people. The book is so readable, so interesting, so sensible! There's a "ton" of Scriptural citation, quite often long passages are quoted—always from an understandable, plain and modern English translation.

I confess that I am human enough even to enjoy the slang in this book, an oral style that employs words such as "yep," "heck," "gonna," "crap," "wanna," and "ain't." I must caution that the slang is that of "the greatest generation" and "Baby Boomers," and not of "Millennials" and "Generation-Xers." Stan notes at one time he was "telling God he is doggoned lucky we were on his side." And then there are expressions that may or may not be found in dictionaries: "None, Zip, Nada," "bamboozled," "yikes," and "raising seven kinds of hell." Stan does not worry about political correctness when describing "mankind wandering in sin like a pig knee-deep in slop." Scholars in theology and other academic types may disdain this folksy style. Ordinary readers who are veterans of "church wars" and "worship wars," but still seeking insights for spiritual growth, will appreciate the straight-talk and simplicity.

Stan notes that lifestyles under COVID-19 have necessarily impacted the way we "do church" as well as any other social function. Perhaps our realization in 2020 and 2021 that we do not need huge physical church facilities or mega-church membership rolls or high-salaried, multi-personnel church staffs to sustain the faith may be providential avenues leading us "simple church" once again—a kind of "back to the future" phenomenon. "Jesus did not call people to fill pews in fancy cathedrals," he rightly asserts.

Culture changes, for certain, yet some things do not change. This author's ultimate goal is unity of believers in the "one faith" with the desire that unity is also in the Spirit. There are so many religious topics and controversies that Christians need not agree on. Furthermore, the author notes, we certainly do not need to agree on politics or public policy issues to be Christian brothers and sisters in the same spiritual family. Why divide, distrust, and disband over matters that are irrelevant to our spiritual life and connection to God and his Son?

**Simple Christianity vs. Churchianity** contains enough content for groups to study and discuss for weeks. "After all," the author notes, "we are not living this thing as the Lone Ranger." I appreciate Stan always pointing readers to additional resources for those who seek to learn even more. Most of all, we simple Christians can appreciate this friend and author's attitude that undergirds a study of this breadth: "I am just an ordinary Christian with a deep desire to share the wonderful truths I have found in the Bible."

# Introduction

This book, my 25th , was especially challenging. This study took me several places I had no plans to go, and I was led to rethink matters on which I had firmly tied a neat, blue ribbon years ago.

Ultimately, through three years of reading, studying, and praying, I plowed some new ground. New to me, anyhow, if not to some of you. I alone am responsible for the conclusions I've expressed in this book. They are a fair snapshot-in-time of my theological ideas on January 10, 2021. Surely any honest searcher for truth will agree with my sentiment when I say here is what I think today, pending further study and leading of the Holy Spirit.

I want you to know I kicked around for years the idea of writing a book about salvation through grace by faith in Jesus Christ. When I finally started writing about it, the end result was my 2020 book, **The Gospel of Jesus in Simple English**. I kept my words as simple as possible and used for Bible references **The Easy-to-Read Version**. That little book (136 pages) is available on Amazon as a paperback and as a free eBook through Smashwords.com. That book was really aimed at those with little religious background and/or education. I wound up with an advanced education in writing with simple English. It just ain't that easy, as I learned.

However, that book only covered a small portion of what I wanted to write. It turned out to be a motivation for me to write a more comprehensive and extensive study of "The Basis of Salvation." As I spent countless hours reading and rereading large portions of Scripture (especially in the Old Testament), I began to reexamine a lot of my assumptions and misconceptions. Then I began to organize the major sub-topics. I started writing this book in August of 2017 and it simmered on the back burner while I wrote my **Gospel of Jesus** book.

So while the copyright date of his book is 2021, the idea took at least ten years from conception to publication. Some critics might say that it probably rolled around in my head for a long time like a BB in a railroad boxcar. Maybe so, but with my advanced age and such this is likely as good as I can do. Like physicians, all of us should seek to do no harm. My hope is many of you will find it helpful and will cause you to do your own investigation on the subject.

First, please allow me to share a few personal remarks. Consider them as just a frank discussion of things on our reality checklist. A few months ago, Peggy and I celebrated our 58th wedding anniversary. More than anyone else on ol' Planet Earth, she has been my rock and my inspiration. Often, I would see looming problems ahead of us . . . and she would see blooming opportunities. Most of the time she was right.

We live in beautiful Bradenton, Florida. But even here, the terrible Covid-19 Virus has impacted the availability of hospital beds and elective surgeries. And our stats statewide put us in one of the most dangerous states to live in right now. We have been ranked near the top of the five worst states for spread of the disease.

National experts on the Covid-19 Virus say that those who die from the virus often do so because of certain "pre-existing health problems." It comes as no surprise that both Peggy and I are in the ***Uno Numero*** bunch of folks at highest risk. Yep, that would be senior citizens, especially over age 65. Hey, we whizzed by that marker more than a decade ago. That is where we are on that score.

The next facet of our reality is that I personally score high on three other pre-existing health issues. So we have been under a "self-quarantine" since April. Like those three legendary monkeys, we "speak no evil," and the only other evils are only what we see and hear being broadcasted over the TV sets in our cave. Er, . . . I mean, our house.

Whatever happens next, I just wanted to say here and now that my life with Peggy has been far more interesting, productive, and blessed than I ever dreamed it would be. And one of my other blessings high on my list is having been able to share with you so many books on such diverse topics. Thank you, one and all.

Stan Paregien

January 15, 2021

# Contents

*Paregien*

# Chapter 1

# An Overview of this Book

The story is told of an old farmer sitting on his front porch with his wife during the Great Depression in the United States in the 1930s. His wife said she had gone to a political rally the day before and came home confused. "I tell ya, Elmer, this here feller talked long and hard, but I jest didn't understand much. He kept talkin' about somethin' called **'the status quo.'** Reckon what **'status quo'** means?" The farmer sipped his coffee a spell and said, "Lulu, the way I heared it, **'status quo'** is one of them fancy Latin phrases. Near as I kin figure, **'status quo'** is jest a way to say 'We are sure 'nuff in a big mess.'"

I "Amen!" the old farmer. And the reality is that today's brand of Christianity, sometimes called **Churchianity**, is sure 'nuff in a mess. A big mess. There was a boom time for mega churches when they were drawing in many thousands of people from a wide area, mostly attracting folks from small congregations and making them even smaller.

Now is a good time for me to clarify and define how I use the word "Churchianity" in this book. The word "churchianity" was coined in about 1837, with various meanings over the years. Here is how I use it:

**Churchianity** is a disease of the heart. It slowly robs its victims of their deep love for God, as well as their love for others. They no longer see the body of Christ as a fellowship of diverse believers but as an institution. They degrade it to the level of a political party or a Chamber of Commerce or a County Club. They neglect mutual ministry, evangelism of the lost and caring for the poor and abused. Instead, they

1

become proud of and protective of their sect, and seek to increase that institutional grown and power. Their focus is on using an array of gimmicks to add recruits to their "membership" roles and money to their treasury. Loyalty to the faction outweighs loyalty to Jesus and his teachings. The bureaucracy views non-conformists as traitors rather than brothers and sisters with alternative beliefs.

Rather than focusing on God's simple covenant of love (Matthew 22:37-30), they create traditions that become rules by which they critically judge others. Spirituality is supplanted by legalistic religiosity, secularism and dogmatism ("It is our way or no way."). Such people think of congregational activities as a spectator sport, where the final score is really what matters no matter the motivation or the methods. They had rather be seen on a religious stage rather than actually go down in the trenches to offer hope to the lost. Rather than evangelizing with the simple gospel of Christ, they stress the fringe benefits of "church membership" and they hawk a blatant "prosperity gospel" (Think Oral Roberts, Joel Osteen, Creflo Dollar, Reverend Ike, Joyce Meyer, Kenneth and Gloria Copeland, Jerry Duplantis, etc.).

Churchianity creates mean-spirited critics rather than reflective, forgiving believers. That is true whether the person's leanings are toward ultra-liberalism ("the left") or ultra-legalism ("the right"). Their organizational chart looks like one from Microsoft rather than the biblical style where Christ is head, and the elders and deacons serve as shepherds and servants. Instead, churchianity is tightly controlled by charismatic, domineering clergy. Churchianity is pseudo-Christianity at its worst and it is toxic to your spiritual health. (SEE: 1 Timothy 4:1, 2 Timothy 2:24; Matthew 6:2; Jude 20). Churchianity is pseudo-Christianity at its worst and it is toxic to your spiritual health.

It is an ugly picture, is it? The good news is changed by people devoted to that challenge no matter the slander, the abuse or the forced isolation. Wherever possible, we should emphasize the core beliefs of Christians that still draw people of faith together. Those are our belief in one body, one Spirit, one hope, one Lord, one faith, one God and Father of all (Ephesians 4:4-5). In other words, stress our many points of agreement rather than any points of disagreement.

Back to our discussion of how we got where we are.

Expansion and PR projects were on the top of their list. TV shows, celebrity appearances, big-name singers and musicians, podcasts with prominent politicians, and more.

Growth. Growth. Growth. Move 'em in. Pack 'em in. Stack 'em in.

Money, money, money. Get more. Spend more. Ask for more.

Please do not misunderstand me. While I favor smaller congregations and house churches, I am not necessarily against large congregations. After all, in Acts 2 we read where there were over 3,000 in the very first "congregation." And small congregations are not immune from the disease of churchianity; that's how some very large groups evolved. The heavenly antidote is unshakeable faith in Jesus and his sacrifice for our sins.

Well, nobody did big-church TV any classier than **Dr. David Jeremiah** and his Shadow Mountain Community Church in El Cajon, CA (the San Diego area). Their TV program is called, "Turning Point with Dr. David Jeremiah." I highly recommend the show, as I deeply appreciate Jeremiah's writing and speaking ability. Peggy, my wife, and I even got to hear him once here in Bradenton at a convention center.

A recent TV broadcast of his was pretty much standard procedure. I haven't actually counted the numbers, but I'm guessing that their choir, dressed all in black shirts, numbered 50 or more. They were sandwiched together on risers. Below them was a group of black-shirted and oh-so-talented musicians numbering about 25 or so. Flutes, clarinets, saxophones, violins, pianos, guitars galore. And they had a drummer and his set of drums in the isolation chamber, a plastic box of sorts. Gee, if only he had a volume knob on his amplifiers. Yeah, right. The sanctuary or auditorium there at Shadow Mountain was packed by an audience of maybe 2,000 or so.

Then the Corona-19 Virus came along in the spring of 2020.

Shazam! Wham, bam!

Life as we knew it for many generations suddenly changed.

Now, we might say that Dr. Jeremiah's isolated drummer in his plastic cave may have the best and safest seat in the whole church building. Yikes, what a difference a few months can make.

That pandemic created pandemonium in all social circles. We had to start wearing facemasks to protect ourselves and others, particularly the young and the old. We had to practice something called "social distancing," meaning not getting closer to any other human than 6' (but scientists were divided on whether that was far enough or not). We had to make sure we washed our hands for at least 20 seconds each time and to do it several times a day. Bottles of sanitizers and baby wipes became our sidekicks.

Just when we thought the United States was a land of abundance, we found ourselves running from store to store in a desperate search for rolls of . . . no, not money, more useful than that. Toilet paper. Yep, a simple thing like that suddenly became a scarce and often valuable commodity. A 12-roll pack of Charmin or AngelSoft toilet paper are now hoped-for gifts for birthdays, weddings and Bar Mitzvahs.

Worst of all, we all found ourselves retreating into the safety of our homes and away from other human contacts. Authorities closed the bars, the restaurants, theaters, beaches, sports stadiums, public schools, and university campuses. Then they highly restricted visits to close kin in the hospitals. They advised against shaking hands (Dr. Fauci of the CDC famously said he didn't care if he ever shook hands with anyone again). They ruled out hugs and substituted virtual elbow touches or fist touches.

Then came the big whammy.

They closed our houses of worship. It didn't matter whether the buildings would seat 5,000 or 50, they had to shut the doors. Ultimately, just to barely get along, churches could operate at 25% capacity as long as social distancing took place and everyone wore facemasks. Then some states legislated no singing in church, because it could spread the disease. No more potlucks or Sunday afternoon buffets at the pizza parlors. They forced larger churches, particularly the megachurches, to rethink and downsize everything as best they could.

Well, duh.

**Simultaneously, we slowly realized we had been presented with a tremendous opportunity for restoring simple Christianity.** Maybe even for bringing sanity and common sense back to the way we "do church."

Church without all the bureaucracy. Churches without walls, for Pete's sake. Praying without pastoral pre-approval. Neighbors spontaneously looking out for not only their neighbors but for homeless people. House churches for groups of ten or less. Christian men and women, some with little theological training, jumping in and teaching Bible topics through Zoom meetings, podcasts and YouTube postings. Small, intimate churches with no fancy equipment and no burdensome mortgage have started looking better and better to those who are tired of churchianity.

It also generated a lot of questions that should have been asked years ago. Do we actually need to have paid staff to do our witnessing for us in the community? Why are we jealous of congregations that have grand architectural cathedrals and massive construction and maintenance debt? Would we be better off operating as an independent congregation rather than being tightly controlled by some distant denominational headquarters? Do we really need such a crowded church calendar, one that requires folks to attend choir practice, teacher meetings, elders and deacons meetings, this thing and that thing? We like to say that the Bible is our guide and standard, but why do we require prospective members to state their agreement with our man-written denominational handbook, creed or discipline? Isn't the early church's simple confession of "Jesus is Lord" good enough for us?

Isn't it time to take another look at the role of women in the modern church and become proactive in righting some wrongs? How is it that the vast number of folks in our congregations look just like you and me? What should we be doing to show other congregations we want to cooperate with them? Does our worship music style always have to reflect the oldest, most vocal group (or wealthiest) in the congregation? Why do churches spend so much time and money to concoct gimmicks to get people inside the building, only to see them soon run out the back door and down the block to the next hot gimmick? Why do we treat God's "Good News" like anemic, powerless old-time history?

Come on, now. Let's get down to it.

There are people in your community who know they are saved and right with God. Others know for certain they are lost and alienated from God. And still others have no idea at all whether they are saved or not, and they don't know whether God really gives a flip one way or the other.

I am here to say, as one sin-prone Christian but saved by Jesus, that God absolutely cares about each one of us. His love for the people he created is so intense his heart breaks when we wallow in sin just like pigs wallowing in muddy slop.

Well, I grew up in a legalistic sect of Christianity. I learned our church's interpretations of scripture, though we bragged we did not interpret the Bible but "just read the Bible." That claim never flew very far. We put our creeds into the tracts we put in the foyer and into our church deeds, where we often legislate that if we should disband our congregation building then funds must go to the nearest church that agrees with our denominational peculiarities.

We held to our comforting, rock-solid belief we were the only ones going to heaven. That meant all those people outside of our sect, whether professed and active Christians or not, were hell bound. Heck, we saw a whole mission field right there among our heathen neighbors who were Presbyterians, Pentecostals, Catholics and pesky Baptists.

At the same time, I was not really sure at any given minute I was saved. In our self-satisfied, sanctimonious sect, we had to earn our way by always being "right" on various issues. We also had to confess our sins in prayer morning, noon, and bedtime. We were afraid we might die with a sin left on the balance sheet of justice, and that would send us sliding down that king-sized ramp to Satan's backyard barbeque.

What a depressing, hypocritical, joyless, and rabidly sectarian way to live. Yet we did so because we thought by being baptized (by immersion, of course) and memorizing scriptures and working hard we could go through the Pearly Gates doing high-fives and telling God he was doggoned lucky we were on his side.

Okay, maybe it was not quite that awful. Remember, my memory really is not what it never was. Still. Theologically, that lifestyle was more crooked than a dog's hind leg.

Since about 1968, I have tried to be a peacemaker within my own denomination and in the larger Christian community. Within five years after I made that commitment, a certain Christian journalist in our sect wrote me up as a heretic. His rebuke spilled over three issues of their widely-distributed magazine. He and the editor publicly gave me a good butt whuppin', then tarred and feathering me – all in the name of Jesus, of course.

The powerful editor absolutely refused to give me any space in his magazine to explain my views. That unethical and certainly unChristian tactic was an old editorial device, even then, but it still had the desired effect of silencing the offender and putting the fear of god (god being in this case, the editor) in the hearts of other "liberal digressives." I share that still painful story simply to alert all who think for themselves to be prepared for a day when you might be doing most of your thinking in isolation. It happens.

Let's get one thing absolutely clear from the start. You and I do not have to agree on an economic theory—capitalism, socialism, or communism—for us to be friends and to voice our ideas openly to one another. Nor do we have to agree on every political issue before we can have friendly relations and civil discussions about them.

Right?

Right.

And the same thing is true regarding our different philosophical opinions and foundational religious concepts. I am a free person in Christ, meaning I am able and eager to think for myself and reach my own conclusions (held pending further evidence). And to be as consistent as I am able, I encourage others to speak their minds freely.

Anything that I have written or will ever write is a reflection of that amazing freedom in the Lord. And within the Christian community, in order for us to work and worship together, we must start by loving Jesus with all our hearts. We must be committed to obeying whatever our Father God wants, as we become aware of and convinced of his will for each of us.

You see, God did not design us with a cookie cutter. We meet together as flawed people with remarkably different educations, work experiences and lifestyles. We are rich people and poor people, Ph.D.'s and only degrees from the School of Hard Knocks. We are executives and sanitary engineers (garbage haulers), 5$^{th}$ generation residents of small towns and new immigrants to giant cities. Some of us are constant world travelers, while others have never been much over 100 miles from where they were born. We are different. Very different. Wonderfully different, as I hope to show in this book.

Some of us were fortunate enough to be introduced to Jesus and the Bible when we were babies in our cribs. Our Christian parents read to us and sang Christian songs to us. But others grew up in families where God was only the first part of a curse word. These unfortunate souls were reared where the atmosphere was polluted with anti-religious thought, racial bigotry, and negative thinking and actions. So let us be kind and patient and merciful with one another as we consider several important topics.

I encourage you to study with an open mind and a receptive heart, which is the way I prayerfully wrote this book. On the coming Judgment Day, each of us will be judged by our own individual actions and attitudes. If God should ask why you seldom worshiped with other believers, he is not going to be impressed when you say: "Well, God, you remember I never kept my wife from going to Easter and Christmas services." And when he asks why you never read his love letters (the Bible) to you, he will frown deeply when you say: "Oh, sir, I covered that base. Yes, siree. I designated my brother-in-law, Willard Q. Dimmwitt, as my Bible reader."

What I am saying is this: You need to be responsible for your own spiritual life and for becoming a more mature Christian. Your brother-in-law cannot do it for you. Your mother or father cannot do it for you. And your husband or your wife cannot do it. It is the responsibility of one person, you. Yep,

**Y-O-U**. Now's a good time to start.

## Tips on Reading the Bible

Allow me to explain some basic tips on reading a modern text of the Bible. Please open to the "Contents" page at the front of your Bible. You will note two major divisions.

There is a group of 39 documents commonly called the books of the "**Old Testament**." The Old Testament is the original Hebrew Bible, the sacred scriptures of the Jewish faith, written at different times between about 1200 and 165 BC. It is the work of prophets, priests, kings, poets, and songwriters. These documents cover human history from the time of Adam and Even (estimated dates, uncertain) to about 165 BC.

And here comes the shocker, for many people. Nowhere in the documents now collected up and labeled "Old Testament" is there even a single reference to a "book" (called the Old Testament) having 39 documents. Nor is there any hint that this entire collection of 39 documents together constituted the "Mosaic Covenant" (i.e., the old covenant).

For example, in 1776 the Founding Fathers of the United States wrote an important legal document called "the constitution." It is very specific about the functions and limitations of the federal government and about the rights of the individual states. Today, in high schools and universities, they have a textbook on the history of the United States. That history book likely has a few songs, poems, and photos of people and of places like Mount Rushmore and the White House. But that history book is separate and far apart from the Constitution itself. Nor is the Constitution a history book, not even in the case of a book on the history of the constitution.

That same thing holds true regarding God's Covenant with the nation of Israel. Most of the "Old Testament" documents deal with the history of the Israelites as stated by various historians, poets and songwriters. **The Constitution (or Covenant) for Israel is confined to Exodus 20:1-17 and, therefore, literally to the 10 Commandments.** The first four commands deal with a vertical relationship between the Nation and God. The final six commands deal with the horizontal relationship between the people of Israel.

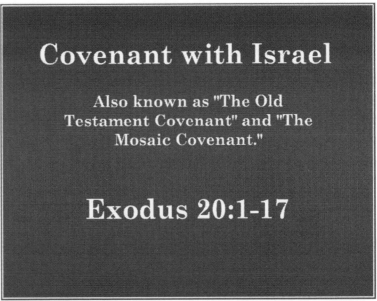

All those other pages of information about kings, judges, battles, romance, prophetic promises and warnings, and songs of praise may be interesting . . . but they are not – and never have been – the Mosaic Covenant. They certainly grew out of that covenant relationship between God and Israel but they do not constitute the Covenant itself.

Think of it this way: Nothing written before the 10 Commandments is a part of the covenant of law and nothing written after them is part of the covenant between God and Israel. Nuttin'. Zip. *Nada*. What was written immediately afterward, the requirements for the Tabernacle and the priests, the laws related to sex, cleanliness, dietary matters, etc., were not part of the Covenant. However, they reflected God's will for how people in the Covenant should behave.

More on that, later.

The other major division is commonly called the "**New Testament**." There are 27 letters or "books" in that group. They were all written between 45 A.D. and about 95 A.D. The authors of those documents wrote them in the common Greek language of the First Century. "The Gospels" (Matthew, Mark, Luke & John) tell about the life, ministry, death, and resurrection of Jesus Christ. Acts of the Apostles tells about the founding of the Christian Church or fellowship, with a focus on the missionary work of the apostle Paul.

Then there are personal letters to specific people on spiritual themes. It concludes with Revelation, a document filled with prophecies, allegories, and pretty doggoned strange and symbolic language about a future New World on earth and a final home in heaven. It was not until about 355 A.D. that there was a sufficient consensus among the churches as to which documents should be included in the first "canon" (collection, which later was labeled "New Testament"). Those documents are the ones that make up our New Testament today.

Well, here is the second major shocker for most of you. The documents in the New Testament speak of the New Covenant but they are not the covenant. The New Covenant between God and each individual cannot be chiseled onto tables of stone like the old one. The New Covenant cannot be printed and then sandwiched between covers of a book, but it can be imprinted and engraved on our minds. It was not written on paper, papyrus, or even on space age materials. This covenant is also stoneless because it was not written on stone tablets like the old one.

Under the Mosaic Law, the tablets of stone containing the Covenant with Israel were placed in a fancy container called the **Ark of the Covenant**. It was holy to the people and to the priests. They never got to see the tablets or touch them because the Ark of the Covenant, containing the Ten Commandments, was securely kept in the Holy of Holies in both the Tabernacle and much later in the first Temple in Jerusalem. The Ark of the Covenant, along with the tablets, disappeared in about 587 B.C. Scholars seem to think that the Babylonians destroyed it. The Ark never appeared in the second Temple.

Instead, the New Covenant is written on our hearts by the Holy Spirit himself. While God's glory, his **Shekinah**, formerly rested over the Ark . . . now his code of love, grace and knowledge is present in the heart of each Christian. Instead of God temporarily residing in a Tabernacle or a fancy Temple, he now lives in the temple of our earthly bodies. That makes our inner man a sort of holy of holies for Jehovah, the one and only true God. And the Holy Spirit also occupies our hearts and bodies.

What we have in the 27 documents we call the New Testament is not the Old Testament with fewer rules. It is not a rule book at all. If you think of it as a code of laws to be dissected and rigidly apply to all people of all time, then you will miss the essence of what early Christianity was all about. The mostly ordinary people who wrote those documents were simply sharing what they knew about Jesus Christ. Many of their documents sound like love letters to other family members, which is exactly what they were. There was no intent to impose legal codes but to reveal the love of God.

Some people have been duped into studying the Bible through sectarian glasses with the mindset of a Constitutional lawyer. They honestly believe – but are honestly wrong – that the New Testament is a "permanent pattern" or a "divine blueprint" or a "law book" which guided all of the first century Christians and is binding on all disciples today.

There are major flaws in that premise. For one thing, they miss the point that Jesus is the only pattern, blueprint, or example that matters (1 Peter 2:21). Our challenge is to conform to his image, not to conform to a set of codes.

Second, a large number of congregations never even read, much less had, any of those documents for years after the church of God was established in 33 A.D. in Jerusalem. In that ancient world, fewer than 20 % of the people could read anything. There were no copy machines or printing presses to run off convenient copies. Most of what they knew was from one person sharing the gospel and the New Covenant verbally, since both of those items were short and easily understood. It never occurred to the early Christian church they were missing any pattern or blueprint. And most only had a few documents even after many years.

Much more about that, later.

## Chapters and Verses

Please open your Bible to the first "book" in the Bible, "Genesis," I want you to notice something. You will see the manuscript starts off with Chapter 1 of Genesis and continues all the way through Chapter 50. The original Hebrew text had exactly ZERO chapters. Zip. **Nada.** None. Nor did it have any of the "subdivisions" called "Verses," usually written as Geneses 3:15, for example.

As a plain matter of convenience, Chapters and Verses were added to make it easy to refer to an event - say when Joseph was sold to Egyptians by his own brothers - by saying that it is in Genesis 3:1-6. This is much better than just digging through pages and pages of text.

For example, the writer of the Book of Hebrews in the New Testament had just such a problem. He wanted to include a quote into his document, but he could not recall exactly where it was found. So he told his readers, "Someone somewhere has testified . . ." and included that material. Today, a writer could easily quote the material and add that it is found in Palm 8:5-7 of the Latin version of the Hebrew text. No so in Bible times.

Well, a **Mr. Stephen Langton** was the smart fellow who added Chapters in all of the documents of the Latin Vulgate version of the Hebrew (Old Testament) scriptures way back in the 12th century. His aim was to mark off where one event (or idea) began and ended. He was rather good, but not perfect. Sometimes, to get the complete idea or event, you need to read two or three chapters at once (such as in Romans 9-11 in the New Testament).

A fellow named **Robert Estienne** was traveling through France in 1551. He had no game apps on his iPhone, so to pass the time, I guess in jest, he further divided each chapter into verses. His aim with "verses" was much like Langton's idea of chapters; only they acted sort of like a modern paragraph. When the Geneva Bible was published in 1560, it was the very first complete Bible with all documents divided into both chapters and verses. In most of the modern translations, each documents has x-number of paragraph groupings.

Well, the point of all that is just to remind you that none of those divisions and subdivisions were in the original documents. After all, when you write that next great America novel, it will not be sliced up into hundreds of verses. Chapters, yes, verses, no. And when you write a long letter to Grandma Gertie or a romantic letter to your lover, you are not going to format it like a law book with codes and sub-codes. Well, the writers in olden times did not do it that way, either.

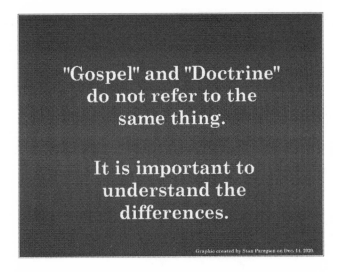

Here is another important idea to remember about the New Testament. That is the big difference between "gospel" and "doctrine." In the "books" by Matthew, Mark, Luke, and John we have extensive biographical information about Jesus – his history and heritage, his coming to earth, his teachings, his good deeds and miracles, his illegal trials, his death on a Roman cross, his resurrection from the grave, and his ascension back to heaven.

People often mistakenly believe the gospel is everything that is in the New Testament. Or they erroneously believe that the gospel in the New Testament and the doctrine in the New Testament are one and the same thing. But that is not the case.

It is crucial to your understanding of the New Testament to know that the "gospel" message makes up only a relatively small part of the four documents of Matthew, Mark, Luke, and John.

## Definition of Gospel

The gospel or good news (Greek, **kerugma**) is the declaration by God's authority that both eternal life and the remission of one's sins are available to every person by God's loving grace through their faith in Jesus as Lord. It is inseparably linked to the blood-sacrifice of Jesus on the cross to pay our debt and to his resurrection from the dead. The simple gospel story is spread by preaching (Greek, **euangelizō**) or evangelizing.

The gospel of Christ is actually *the faith* as opposed to *faith*. In other words, we can speak of **the faith** being one's trust or belief in the gracious and loving act of God the Father in letting his son die on a Roman cross for us. We accept in mind and heart the world-changing reality of his voluntary death for our salvation. That is the simple gospel.

The gospel centers on the life, death, and resurrection of Jesus and calls on those who believe that message to repent of their sins, to please God by being baptized and blessed by him. That message is always directed at non-believers or aliens, those who are not Christians. It is focused on persuading non-believers to become Christians. Preaching the gospel has been a strong emphasis from the beginning of God's church.

In the 5th book of the New Testament, the Book of Acts, we have in Chapter 2 **the very first time that the full gospel was preached**. They proclaimed God's love for them as proved by the life, sacrificial death, and the resurrection of Jesus. The audience heard the good news (*the faith*) and believed it. Then the apostles and others told these new adult believers to repent of bad deeds and to be baptized. Among the many benefits, was removal and forgiveness of their sins. But not all of the blessing were known by any given individual at the time of their baptism.

That theme is repeated many times in the Book of Acts, with people usually repenting and being baptized as soon as possible after they had their initial life-altering faith-experience. That was the gospel at work. Not another word was ever added to that basic gospel message. People could hear it and come to faith in Christ, repent of their sins and be baptized all within an hour or so. It is not that complicated. We may say that the good news for mankind is the fundamental truth regarding God's love for us, but that is certainly not all the truth about God.

On the other hand, the term *faith* speaks of our whole-hearted respect for the teachings of the New Testament (New Covenant). A person may accept **the faith** (i.e., the gospel) and be walking in fellowship with God and his other children, while at the same time he may be young in faith and mixed up on many faith matters. One may teach others the truth regarding many Bible subjects (the organization of the church, the role of women, the millennium, etc.) without mentioning the gospel.

So we may say that when a person hears the gospel message and then has faith in Jesus Christ, he is inducted into the Christian community. After his induction, then he studies Bible doctrines so he can mature in his knowledge, skills, and attitudes.

It is similar to what an 18-year old youth does who wants to be a solder. He is inducted into the army and goes through basic training. Then he goes on active duty and continues learning Army procedures and doctrines so he can be a better soldier. That effort at improving does not let up until his last day in the Army.

## Definition of Doctrine

People often mistakenly believe that the gospel in the New Testament and the doctrine in the New Testament are one and the same thing. But that is not the case.

Doctrine (Greek, *didachē*) literally refers to a **body of teaching** or **the act of teaching**. As a body of teaching material, Christian doctrine is made up of Spirit-inspired biblical teachings which are designed for the encouragement and edification of baptized adult believers – i.e., people who have the mental capacity to make an informed personal decisions It is sort of the raw truth of the word of God, without the burdensome overlays of denominational creeds and bylaws and traditions. All readers should understand doctrine in the New Testament is privileged information intended only for those who are part of the fellowship of Christians.

In fact, non-Christians may think all the doctrinal material is both odd and foolish. That is because, in a real sense they are reading somebody else's mail. Or it is like they have come into a theatrical play in the middle of the third act. They really can't begin to figure it out, because they don't know what went on before and led to those writings. In 1 Corinthians 1:18, Paul describes that situation this way: "For the message about Christ's death on the cross is nonsense to those who are being lost; but for us who are being saved it is God's power" (**Good News Translation** – GNT).

The books of Acts through Revelation were primarily aimed at a Christian audience. They focus on doctrines for Christian nurturing and growth (with Acts having examples of the preaching of the gospel). The four gospel documents – Matthew, Mark, Luke, and John – obviously focus on the message of the gospel of Christ, with ample doctrine as well.

One who hears the gospel and accepts Jesus as Lord, has salvation as a gift of grace through his or her faith. As they begin their Christian walk, they can be really confused and messed up when it comes to understanding all the doctrinal information. But they can have wrong ideas, really weird ideas, about lots of doctrinal matters and still walk in fellowship with God and other believers.

**Thomas Campbell** was born in County Down, Ireland in 1763. He grew up as a Presbyterian and became a clergyman. But he was distressed by the way all the major denominations had fractured into warring sects. That was true in Ireland and in Scotland, and when he immigrated to Pennsylvania he was shocked to find the same divisions. Christians badly divided over doctrine and how to understand (interpret) it. So he sat down and wrote out his dream of Christian unity and how to achieve it. That was in 1809 and he called the document **"A Declaration and Address."** His Proposition #6 urged caution about turning opinions about doctrinal matters into rules and then to church laws. Here is what he said:

*"That although inferences and deductions from Scripture premises [i.e., facts, SP], when fairly inferred, may be truly called the doctrine of God's holy word, yet **they are not formally binding upon the consciences of Christians farther than they perceive the connection, and evidently see that they are so** [emphasis mine, SP]; for their faith must not stand in the wisdom of men, but in the power and veracity of God. Therefore, no such deductions can be made terms of communion, but do properly belong to the after and progressive edification of the Church. Hence, it is evident that no such deductions or inferential truths ought to have any place in the Church's confession."*

The stark truth is that hard feelings and divisions happen when a man or group of men try to force others to agree with their opinion about a fact of doctrine. So Campbell and many other reformers preferred to think for themselves and recommend that others do the same. They were satisfied with being one in agreement on the facts of the gospel of Jesus Christ. The facts of Christian doctrine lend themselves to a practice of **unity in diversity**, with each reaching his own conclusion. Freedom of speech is vitally important in religious matters, not just in political ones.

Still, doctrine is important to the spiritual growth and maturity of each new believer. More than 3,000 Jews became new Christians on the Day of Pentecost in 33 A.D. Notice in Acts 2 what they did after that:

"41 So that those who gladly received his word were baptized, and the same day there were added unto them about three thousand souls.

"42 And **they continued steadfastly in the apostles' doctrine** (emphasis mine, SP) and fellowship and in breaking of bread and in prayers" (Acts 2:41-41; **Jubilee Bible 2000** – JUB).

John 7 tells us about Jesus going to Jerusalem in the middle of the Jewish "Festival of Shelters." He walked right into the Temple courtyard and began to teach. Some who heard him were amazed at the wise words from one who had never been through rabbinical training. Then we have his reply:

"16 My doctrine is not Mine, but His that sent Me. If any man will do His will, he shall know of the doctrine whether it be from God, or whether I speak from Myself" (John 7:16-17; **21 Century King James Version** – KJ21)

There is that word and concept of doctrine. Other translations, such as the **New International Version**, prefer to translate the Greek **didachē** as "teaching."

So let's pause and recap how "gospel" is so very different from "doctrine." It is hearing the gospel and coming to have faith in Jesus which gets one into the catholic (i.e., universal) church of God, the fellowship of the saved. That is a person's new birth or **induction**.

Then he begins a journey of understanding the many apostolic doctrines which will help him be a stronger, more mature Christian. That last part is his **indoctrination**. They are two distinct processes, with a process of preaching to the lost and the other a process of teaching the saved.

Okay, you knew it was coming.

Time for a test.

Well, sort of.

This little exercise is just to help you get a better feel for the width and depth of Bible doctrine. After all, Christian doctrine and thought deal with such fundamental questions as, "Who is God and what is his nature?" "Why did God love us so much he let his son die on a cross for us?" "Why do good people suffer?" "What must we do to be saved and have remission of our sins and eternal life?" "How can ordinary folks like us serve God?" "God loved us first, but how can we show our love for him?"

Please answer the following questions regarding various Christian doctrines. Just do the best you can.

1. Regarding the millennium, are you amillennial, premillennial or postmillennial... and why?

2. What are the basics of the New Testament doctrine about the role of women in church life and leadership?

3. What are the doctrinal statements regarding the speaking of tongues in Christian worship and in their private lives?

4. Exactly what is the New Testament doctrine regarding a Christian participating in civil government and in the military?

5. Is it doctrinally permissible for Christians to also observe some Jewish holidays, rituals and rules regarding foods, sex, and the ritual circumcision of baby boys?

6. What is the doctrine of "the priesthood of all believers" and contrast it with that of "the perseverance of the saints." Oh, and how is the doctrine of "mutual ministry" supposed to work today?

7. Are some doctrines are more important than others and why?

8. Can you be saved and in good standing with God if you are not on the "right side" of each and every one of the above doctrines and how?

Okay, okay. Don't panic or faint on me.

Doctrinal studies can bring insights and blessings, but one has to keep in mind that even a doctrine (principal or rule) that is clearly stated may be subject to various interpretations (opinions) about how to apply it.

The Bible clearly says getting drunk is a sin. How do we apply that idea? Should we not allow any alcohol to pass our lips, in which we cannot use some mouthwashes and some medicines and some real wine sometimes used in the Lord's Supper. Or should we drink alcohol in strict moderation? That is where the interpretation comes in and personal application of our opinion as to what is right for us.

Again, we may use the example of how we are to follow the instruction of "singing with melodies in our hearts." That is the simple doctrinal fact, the basic principle. Then comes figuring out how we really do that, and right there is where experience, personal preferences, opinions and . . . yes, ignorance . . . can all mingle as we decide. Dare we have a quartet of men sing a song or two in addition to congregational singing? What about a whole choir? What if we don't have a good male singer to lead the congregation, may a talented sister lead? What, if anything, does the New Covenant clearly say about accompanying the singing with a guitar or piano or a whole band? Must our singing always be "*a cappella*? What about chanting as they did in the first century? The instruction to sing is the doctrinal fact and principle, how we fulfill that obligation comes down to opinions. And the plain truth is that honest and holy brothers and sisters may differ dramatically in their opinions of how they want to obey that fact.

It all calls for a healthy measure of kindness, gentleness, patience, and earnest understanding love toward each other.

If you are a new Christian, you need to remember we are all walking under the big umbrella of God's grace. We make mistakes. We have errors in opinions and knowledge. So just cut yourself some slack . . . and enjoy getting to know God's word. Begin by memorizing this statement from W. Carl Ketcherside:

Before you turn the page, I urge you to get a modern translation of the Bible and read with an open mind and heart just three documents in the New Testament. You may go online to places like BibleGateway.com and select a Bible translation from about 30 reliable ones. Read it right there online.

> **Forgiveness is not conditioned upon knowing the Bible by heart, but in knowing Jesus from the heart.**
>
> **— W. Carl Ketcherside**

It will not take that long, maybe an evening or two of your time. It is just that you need to grasp the big picture.

Please read these two accounts of the life of Jesus Christ: **The Gospel of Luke**, by the apostle and physician Luke, and **The Gospel of John** by the apostle John. Then read the **Book of Acts**, also by Dr. Luke. It is an amazing and accurate account of the first gospel sermon and how over 3,000 Jewish men accepted Jesus as their Savior. And then the writer, also the apostle Luke, tells in detail about how that group of a few thousand Christians began to grow as the good news about Jesus was spread throughout the known world. It was all truly a God-thing, and it is an easy read.

So here are the three documents which I recommend you stop and read, one right after the other: **The Gospel of Luke**, **The Gospel of John**, and the **Book of Acts**.

Okay, start reading those books.

Mark and pay close attention to what the lost people of that day did, out of deep faith in Jesus, to have their sins forgiven and to begin a close relationship with God as his children.

After you read those documents, come back here and we will continue.

Right?

Right.

My title for this book is, **Simple Christianity vs Churchianity: The Way Forward is Back to Basics**. It is meant to suggest most modern Christian churches have wandered way off the path of the simple Christianity practiced in the First Century and for a few hundred years afterward. Some have drifted into the dry-bones desert of speculative theology. Others have watered down the powerful and life-changing message of the gospel story of Jesus until it is viewed as a mere ancient myth.

It also means we should each examine anew our traditions. "That's the way we've always done it" just will not cut it today. It means putting the action and adventure back in our journey of faith. It means replacing "Why?" with "Why not?"

It means getting out of our personal comfort zones and getting to know and work with other Christians and other groups which we may have ignored or even demeaned in the past. It means making personal studies of the Bible, forming our own conclusions, standing up for them and allowing the same liberty for other believers.

And underline this: **It means throwing overboard our burdensome denominational baggage and reaffirming the glory of the simple Christian life and of simple Christianity**.

Well, you catch my drift.

I invite you to come along with me for this open and honest look at how we can find or restore the joy of our salvation. We must do a better job of motivating each other to love and good works to the praise of our God. And we must take seriously the clear command of Jesus himself for his disciples – that is you, friend, and that's me -- to practice unity in diversity in order to share the gospel with the whole world.

Hey, let's get started.

# Chapter 2

# Mankind's Need: A Savior

Imagine a spaceship being launched into the skies to meet up with an orbiting space station. Nothing too unusual about that today. Happens frequently. And one thing which allows for such accuracy over hundreds of thousands of miles is the ability of scientists to make course corrections to the spaceship all along the way. If a spaceship strayed off course mid-way there and was not corrected, it would miss docking with the space stations by many thousands of miles.

That vital need for correction happens with people and anything they touch, ranging from spaceships to submarines to political and religious movements. And, like it or not, the truth is that first-century Christians were still imperfect and prone to make mistakes. Likewise, they met in groups (congregations) in Ephesus, Rome, Jerusalem, Athens, Ephesus and elsewhere which were full of errors and needed correction and discipline from time to time.

Every once in a while, someone like a Martin Luther, a John Knox, a John Wesley, or an Alexander Campbell came along and administered an "attitude adjustment" to the Christians of their day. The professional clergy and the sectarian power structures often resisted those efforts. But these men and many other men and women have successful called people to repentance and to a return to the simplicity and clarity of early-day Christian essentials.

While Martin Luther led a "Reformation Movement," Alexander Campbell and Barton W. Stone on the American frontier in the 1800's led a "Restoration Movement" which still continues today. In fact, reformation and/or restoration efforts are ongoing because both individuals and congregations tend over time to veer off course. Preacher, educator, and author Rubel Shelly explained the heart of the "Restoration Movement" this way in 1986:

"The essence of our plea is that people should believe that Jesus is the Son of God and seek salvation by grace through faith in him. We are not promoting ourselves or our opinions on certain important topics. We are seeking to preach and practice the things that are universal and essential to the Christian religion. We plead for all who believe in the atonement of Jesus' blood and who have been baptized in his name (cf. 1 Corinthians 1:13) to stand together as one body in him to proclaim Christ to an unbelieving world. That plea is neither narrow nor bigoted. It is a broad as the great heart of God (Rubel Shelly, **I Just Want to Be a Christian**, Rev. Edition, 1986, p. 23).

Here, then, are other underlying principles which form a foundation for unity within God's family of believers and which encourage us to be patient and understanding with each other when potentially divisive matters arise.

First, though, we need to be reminded of what distinguishes the Christianity found in the New Testament from all other religions.

It all begins with the basic concept that Adam and Eve were originally in a close relationship with God in the garden of Eden (Genesis 1 – 3). God was and is holy and just, with a patient, loving and merciful heart. That is his nature and never changes.

An Old Testament character named Elihu spoke a foundational truth when he proclaimed, "We have seen that God All-Powerful really is all powerful! But he is just and never treats anyone unfairly. 24 That is why people fear and respect him. He shows no respect for those who think they are wise" (Job 37:23-24, ERV).

Then in the New Testament, Paul wrote: "God gave Jesus as a way to forgive people's sins through their faith in him. God can forgive them because the blood sacrifice of Jesus pays for their sins. God gave Jesus to show that he always does what is right and fair. He was right in the past when he was patient and did not punish people for their sins. And in our own time he still does what is right. God worked all this out in a way that allows him to judge people fairly and still make right any person who has faith in Jesus" (Romans 3:25-26, ERV).

So when Adam and Eve rebelled against God and his commands, their sin – being unholy and ungodly – got them booted from the garden. God's sense of justice demanded punishment for their evil behavior. Like it or not, Father Adam and Momma Eve sorta passed on their sin-disposition to their children and all the way down to you and to me.

Here is how Paul in Romans 5:12-14 described the fall into sin by Adam and Eve:

"12 Sin came into the world because of what one man (Adam) did. And with sin came death. So this is why all people must die – because all people sinned. 13 Sin was in the world before the law of Moses. But God does not make people guilty for sin if there is no law. 14 But from the time of Adam to the time of Moses, all people had to die. Adam died because he sinned by not obeying God's command. But even those people that did not sin the way Adam sinned had to die" (ERV).

Then in Romans 5:18-21, Paul contrasts the verdict of physical death brought on all every human being by one guy, Adam, with the overriding verdict of eternal life provided by Jesus Christ by his one sacrificial act on the cross. It is a blessing that comes by grace through faith.

"18 So one sin of Adam, brought the punishment of death to all people. But in the same way, one good thing that Christ did makes all people right with God. And that brings true life for those people. 19 One man (Adam) disobeyed God and many people became sinners. But in the same way, one man (Christ) obeyed God and many people will be made right. 20 The law came to make people have more sin. But when people had more sin, God gave them more of his grace (kindness). 21 Sin once used death to rule us. But God gave people more of his grace so that grace could rule by making people right with him. This brings life forever through Jesus our Lord" (ERV).

Many centuries later, God selected the Israelite people (Hebrews, Jews) as the apple of his eye. And he set about a grand plan to draw them closer to him. So, through Moses (yes, Moses of the 10 Commandments) he made his will and desire for them known. Those were the conditions for them to obey and meet in order to stay in his favor. It was called the Covenant (binding agreement) between God and the Jews.

Unfortunately, the Jewish people soon violated the conditions of the Covenant and fell out of God's favor. This deliberate act of rebellion or sin caused God to punish them. He offered them a "course correction" by which to get back on track and in his favor.

Along the way, they were given a rather personal sign of their relationship with Jehovah God. God directed that all the men of Israel should be circumcised (i.e., have the foreskin of the penis cut off).

Ouch.

And to this day, each newborn Jewish boy child is circumcised in an elaborate ceremony on the 8$^{th}$ day of his life. In time, this "sign" became a badge of honor and ultimately for many, a false sense of security regarding God's favor just because Abraham was their father and they had been circumcised. The problem was pride.

They were also given a professional clergy – Moses and his brother, Aaron – and some of the men in the tribe of Levi. The priests and the people were given exhaustively detailed plans about how and where and when to offer sacrifices to God. Those included sacrifices of the best of their harvest as well as blood offerings from various animals and birds, particularly of bulls, sheep, and goats. Though God told them not to eat blood, it was blood – the life source in the body – which flowed freely in their sacrifices.

Repeatedly, though, they gave only half-hearted attention to the spirt of The Law while performing the rituals like robots. They wound up having more faith in their rituals than they had in God. They counted on their rituals and their acts of merit to put God in their debt. They thought they could win his favor by strictly obeying the letter of the Law, without a heart-felt concern for the spirit of the Law.

Someone has pointed out there are three kinds of bad behavior. First, there is a thing called **"vice."** That is when we do think about or do stupid stuff which is hurtful to our own being. Second, there is a class called **"crime."** That is when we do anything that actually harms another person or a community or society. Third, there is that thing the Bible says is **"sin."** That is when we think or do something against God, directly, or against anything or anyone he loves.

Think about that last item for a minute. There are pockets around the world where people in large numbers are becoming believers in the grace of God and of the saving power of the blood-sacrifice of Jesus. But that is set in the larger context of a world being set on self-destruction while assaulting Christianity on their way out.

Personal sin puts a person on a wide, heavily traveled road to hell. That is not some theory or notion that I created. It is stated as an absolute fact in the Bible, something described in both the Old Testament and the New Testament. Jews in Bible times saw it as something real and awful that was to be avoided, and early Christians believed the same thing. A psalmist asked this rhetorical question, "What man can live on and not see death? Can he deliver his life from the power of Sheol [i.e., hell, a pit of corruption where one is cut off from God - SP]?" (Psalm 89:48).

In the New Testament, our word hell is a translation of the Greek word, ***gehenna***. On the outskirts of Jerusalem, there was a landfill (i.e., garbage dump) conveniently located in the small Valley of Hinnom. It is where officials would unceremoniously dump the bodies of the criminals they had executed. It was a stinking, smoldering mess with small fires flaring up from time to time.

Jesus warned his inner band of disciples to fear God rather than other people. He put it this way in Luke 12:4-7: "4 And I tell you, my friends, do not be afraid of those who kill the body, and after these things do not have anything more to do. 5 But I will show you whom you should fear: fear the one who has authority, after the killing, to throw you into hell! Yes, I tell you, fear this one! 6 Are not five sparrows sold for two pennies? And not one of them is forgotten in the sight of God. 7 But even the hairs of your head are all numbered! Do not be afraid; you are worth more than many sparrows" (**Lexham English Bible** – LEB).

Jesus used the concept of hell as a hammer by which to pound into the minds of religious hypocrites that they were far from God. In Matthew 23:13-15, he said to the Pharisees and the scribes: "13 But woe to you, scribes and Pharisees—hypocrites!—because you shut the kingdom of heaven before people! For you do not enter, nor permit those wanting to go in to enter. 15 Woe to you, scribes and Pharisees—hypocrites!—because you travel around the sea and the dry land to make one convert, and when he becomes one, you make him twice as much a son of hell as you are!" (LEB)

A few verses later, Jesus continued holding hell up as the destination of religious hypocrites. In Matthew 23:29-33, Jesus said: "29 How terrible for you, teachers of the Law and Pharisees! You hypocrites! You make fine tombs for the prophets and decorate the monuments of those who lived good lives; 30 and you claim that if you had lived during the time of your ancestors, you would not have done what they did and killed the prophets. 31 So you actually admit that you are the descendants of those who murdered the prophets! 32 Go on, then, and finish up what your ancestors started!

33 You snakes and children of snakes! How do you expect to escape from being condemned to hell?" (**Good News Translation** – GNT)

In Matthew 25:31-46, Jesus turns the discussion to the final judgment day, that day when he will judge from his throne. And he ends with the threat of eternal punishment for those separated from God and a promise of eternal life to those who have walked with God and obeyed him.

31 "When the Son of Man comes in his glory, and all the angels with him, he will sit on his glorious throne. 32 All the nations will be gathered in his presence, and he will separate them one from another, as a shepherd separates the sheep from the goats. 33 He will put the sheep on his right and the goats on his left. 34 Then the King will say to those on his right, 'Come, you who are blessed by my Father, inherit the kingdom prepared for you from the foundation of the world. 35 For I was hungry and you gave me food to eat. I was thirsty and you gave me something to drink. I was a stranger and you welcomed me. 36 I was lacking clothes and you clothed me. I was sick and you took care of me. I was in prison and you visited me.'

37 "Then the righteous will answer him, 'Lord, when did we see you hungry and feed you, or thirsty and give you a drink? 38 When did we see you a stranger and welcome you, or lacking clothes and clothe you? 39 When did we see you sick or in prison and visit you?'

40 "The King will answer them, 'Amen I tell you: Just as you did it for one of the least of these brothers of mine, you did it for me.'

41 "Then he will say to those on his left, 'Depart from me, you who are cursed, into the eternal fire, which is prepared for the Devil and his angels. 42 For I was hungry and you did not give me food to eat. I was thirsty and you did not give me anything to drink. 43 I was a stranger and you did not welcome me, lacking clothes and you did not clothe me, sick and in prison and you did not take care of me.'

44 "Then they will also answer, 'Lord, when did we see you hungry or thirsty or a stranger or lacking clothes or sick or in prison and did not serve you?'

45 "At that time he will answer them, 'Amen I tell you: Just as you did not do it for one of the least of these, you did not do it for me.' 46 And they will go away to eternal punishment, but the righteous to eternal life" (**Evangelical Heritage Version** – EHV)

No wonder, then, that the apostles later included the doctrine of hell in their teachings. In Philippians 3:17-21, Paul discusses the destruction waiting for hypocrites and, by contrast, the glorious transformation waiting for the faithful:

"17 Brothers, become fellow imitators with me and observe those who walk according to our example. 18 For many are walking in such a way that they are the enemies of the cross of Christ. I have told you of them often and tell you again, even weeping. 19 Their destination is destruction, their god is their appetite, their glory is in their shame, their minds are set on earthly things. 20 But our citizenship is in heaven, from where also we await for our Savior, the Lord Jesus Christ, 21 who will transform our body of humiliation, so that it may be conformed to His glorious body, according to the working of His power even to subdue all things to Himself" (**Modern English Version** – MEV).

Make no mistake about it, a messenger is duty-bound to deliver the entire message entrusted to him by the Master. That means any Christian who is teaching others must teach the whole counsel of God. The challenge there is in getting the right balance. It cannot be all grace and love, but also obedience and judgment.

Now, when I was growing up through my teenage years in the 1950s, I heard more about hell and judgment than I did about grace, love, and heaven. At the age of 16, I walked forward one Sunday morning when the preacher gave the invitation. It was with some fear and a lot of love and anticipation of forgiveness that I confessed Jesus as my Lord and was immersed by **Ralph Downey**.

From what I have read and seen in actual church settings since 1958, fear of God's wrath and punishment is at least a partial factor at work when people respond to the preaching of the gospel. It may be the first emotion often tapped by preachers, but it should never be the major one or the final one.

I first discovered the preaching of New England puritan **Jonathan Edwards** when I was a student at Lipscomb University in Nashville, TN. The man was born in 1703. His father was the preacher for a Puritan-type church in Connecticut. In 1729, after a theological education at Yale, he became the preacher at his late father's prominent congregation in Northampton, MA. And then from 1740-1742, a "Great Awakening" took place across denominations in New England. The stirring was led by two men, George Whitefield (English Methodist) and Gilbert Tennent (Presbyterian), who used very emotional stories and appeals in their respective sermons.

Well, Jonathan Edwards caught the spirit (or maybe the fever). He wrote and delivered in 1741 an emotionally moving sermon titled, **"Sinners in the Hands of an Angry God."** It left the impression in the unsophisticated mind of this raging, angry God which had the unrepentant sinner on a string hanging precariously over a pit filled with the leaping flames of hell. The message was pressed hard: convert or go to hell. A more gospel-focused sermon might have been titled, **"Sinners in the Hands of a Loving God."** The first title was not good news for anybody, but the second title speaks of great news for everybody.

Now, fast-forward to the 1960s and 1970s. A preacher and Bible professor from Arkansas became quite successful in getting large number of people to confess their faith in Jesus and to be baptized. He had a powerful sermon that almost became his trademark. It was titled, **"What Is Hell Like?"** He could preach it so you could smell the smoke from flesh sizzling. That preacher, **Jimmy Allen**, in 2010 (at the age of 79) told an interviewer he had conducted about "1,400 gospel meetings [i.e., revivals – SP] resulting in 40,000 to 50,000 responses and at least 10,000 baptisms."

These examples of these two men, Edwards and Allen, should be sufficient to show that sometimes preachers can get their preaching out of balance. The vast majority of preaching to unbelievers should center directly on the love of God, the sacrifice of Jesus, the leading and comforting of the Holy Spirit, and the promised that is sealed and guaranteed that all people of faith from all ages will spend eternity in heaven.

You see, fear of hell and the wrath of God is certainly part of what is going through a non-Christian's mind as he or she decided whether to accept the free grace of God. It may even be the dominate emotion at the moment, with love pushed toward the back of the person's mind.

There is a king-sized problem with fear as a motivator. It is a temporary impulse that won't get a person very far down the road toward eternal life. Someone wiser than me has said that you cannot get to heaven by just running from hell. You might get a short distance, but then fear fades away as love becomes the dominant driver of your life. The aged apostle John said it this way in 1 John 4:7-21:

"7 Dear friends, we must love each other because love comes from God. Everyone who loves has been born from God and knows God. 8 The person who doesn't love doesn't know God, because God is love. 9 God has shown us his love by sending his only Son into the world so that we could have life through him. 10 This is love: not that we have loved God, but that he loved us and sent his Son to be the payment for our sins. 11 Dear friends, if this is the way God loved us, we must also love each other. 12 No one has ever seen God. If we love each other, God lives in us, and his love is perfected in us. 13 We know that we live in him and he lives in us because he has given us his Spirit.

"14 We have seen and testify to the fact that the Father sent his Son as the Savior of the world. 15 God lives in those who declare that Yeshua is the Son of God, and they live in God. 16 We have known and believed that God loves us. God is love. Those who live in God's love live in God, and God lives in them.

**17 God's love has reached its goal in us. So we look ahead with confidence to the day of judgment. While we are in this world, we are exactly like him with regard to love. 18 No fear exists where his love is. Rather, perfect love gets rid of fear, because fear involves punishment. The person who lives in fear doesn't have perfect love.** [Emphasis mine – SP]

19 We love because God loved us first. 20 Whoever says, "I love God," but hates another believer is a liar. People who don't love other believers, whom they have seen, can't love God, whom they have not seen. 21 Christ has given us this commandment: The person who loves God must also love other believers" (**Names of God Bible** – NOG).

Okay, let's go back to the topic of sin.

It was the great Presbyterian (Church of Scotland) theologian, professor and author William Barclay who pointed out the really bad part of sin. He said that when a person sins, he not only breaks God's stated Law but he breaks God's heart. It is much like in our families when a child disobeys the parents, they are offended by the transgression but their hearts are broken by the child's spirit of rebellion. That concept certainly applied to all people who have ever lived, to everyone now living and to all who may come after us.

Historian Jon Meacham was the official biographer of Barbara Bush and, later, of her husband, former president George Henry Walker Bush. During his research on President Bush's bio, Jon Meacham spent a lot of time with the aging past president at his home on the coast of Maine. One day, he was interviewing the old political warrior about his life as a young man and father. He asked about their little daughter, Robin, who died from leukemia at the age of three on Oct. 11, 1953. Bush stopped in the middle of his reply and began to cry, uncontrollably. Sobbing loudly with tears running down his cheeks.

A staff person heard the wails, rushed in, and demanded to know why Mecham had so upset the president. Bush regained his composure and told the aide, "Jon is only doing his job. You can't really say you know a man until you know what breaks his heart." The death of that beautiful child had broken the hearts of George and Barbara.

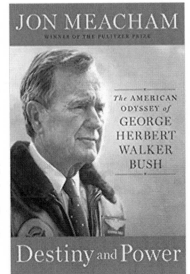

I have to tell you something very personal. I have told that story in print a couple of times before, and I have verbally shared it with a few others. I have yet to be able to write about it or talk about it without choking up and tears running down my own cheeks . . . like they are right now.

Just imagine the grief God experiences when his own children are hurting or are disobeying him. It is also a personal thing with him.

The very personal question for you is this: Are you blessing God's heart by loving him back . . . or are you, by your distrust and disobedience, breaking God's heart?

# Chapter 3

# Progressive Revelation:
# Minimal Light for the Masses

**AN EXPLANATION:**

*I pause here to explain why there are so many scriptures quoted in my book. My goal is to make sure you understand the final authority in this discussion is the Word of God. I have no interest in insisting that my views must also be your views. Therefore, I simply invite you to read the Word itself and then after meditation and prayer, see whether you reach similar conclusions and observations as mine. If that doesn't happen, I might be mistaken. Or you might be mistaken. Or . . . both of us may be mistaken. Further study may be required. Just please do not skip the extended passages of scriptures. Thanks.*

It is vital for us to really understand how much God loved his created beings . . . and still does today. We are going to take important steps in that direction right now. For we are entering an area of vital principles of how to establish a strong bond with God and with every one of his children.

**One foundational truth of scripture is this: In every age, God has provided some amount and kind of light to virtually every person. And God, who always tempers justice with love, never holds a person responsible for what he had no way of knowing. He establishes his requirements according to mankind's condition at the time. There have been four distinct stages of progressive revelation.**

**In each stage, God has always created agreements (called "covenants" in the Bible) between himself and his people. God, being God, set the terms and the second party agreed to them. Whenever God changed the agreement, it was not because he was capricious but to be just in the light of mankind's changing world and condition.**

Underline that entire statement. Think about what it says about the nature of God, his sense of justice and his sense of mercy. I was way past 30 years of age before I stumbled across that concept. It changed the way I look at people and how I relate to them, the way I read and interpret the Bible, and the way I view the very nature of God.

For example, take an illiterate family in 3000 BC living deep in a jungle on the continent of Africa. And say the only light they had available to them was that of nature itself. Our loving and just God would not punish them because they did not obey the 10 Commandments given to Jews hundreds of years after this primitive African family had already died. God would not punish them because they did not believe in Jesus, did not turn away from their sins and submit to Christian baptism. That was not possible for them, so no responsibility, other than the dim light of nature pointing them toward the Creator.

That also holds true for a person who was born and then died before being old enough to learn God's plan for his life, and the same applies to that person who is mentally challenged and unable to comprehend God in nature, much less the virtues of faith and obedience.

In other words, **our loving God will always act fairly in judging people on how they responded to the amount of light or knowledge available to them**. It is not our job to second-guess how he judges any person, since we never know all of the facts and circumstances. We just believe God is loving, and he will always be just and fair.

> ## Our loving God will always act fairly in judging people on how they respond to the amount of light or knowledge available to them. God is loving, and he will always be just and fair.
>
> ## -- Stan Paregien Sr.

Graphic created by Stan Paregien Sr on Dec 14, 2020

In 1:9, John said "The true Light was coming into the world. This is the true Light that gives light to all people." He was talking about the Son of God, Jesus as Christ, and Jesus as Lord. Jesus was the real deal, the authentic light, and genuine Word of God. And as one comes to believe in him, Jesus reveals even more light or truth. And the nature of that light or relationship as it evolved through different cultures.

Through the ages, God has revealed himself in any given time in at least one of four ways. Perhaps we can understand this best if we think of the process our teachers in high school used to help us grasp, say, algebra. They did not try to tell us every concept and formula the first hour of class. They started with the simple and worked up to the most complex. That is not a perfect comparison, but maybe it makes the process which follows a bit easier to understand.

Here, then, are the four ways in which God has revealed his nature to mankind. You will find it helpful to read part 1 through two or three times before moving on to part 2. Repeat that process for each of the 4 truths about God's revelation of himself.

1. God reveals a very tiny part of himself by what people see in nature itself.

2. God reveals just a bit more of himself by what people can see in the behavior of others and of themselves.

3. God revealed many previously unknown things about himself and about his will through Moses and the Jewish poets and prophets. Their words were collected in what we call the "Old Testament" part of our Bible. The message was specifically for the nation of Israel.

4. God made the final revelation of himself through the life and teachings of Jesus and other selected people from about 5 B.C. to 100 A.D. Those concepts were collected into the documents that make up the "New Testament" section of our Bible.

Alright, now let's look at item Number One.

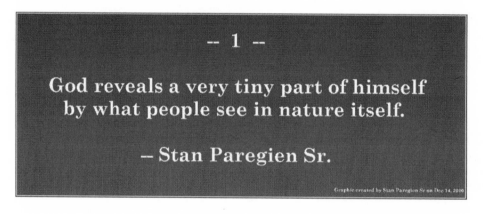

-- 1 --

**God reveals a very tiny part of himself by what people see in nature itself.**

**— Stan Paregien Sr.**

Graphic created by Stan Paregien Sr on Dec 14, 2020

The heavens declare the glory of God, and the skies announce what his hands
have made. — Psalm 19:1  (New Century Version)

The author of Psalm 19 said, "The heavens speak about God's glory. The skies tell
about the good things his hands have made. Each new days tells more of the story. And
each night reveals more and more about God's power. You can't really hear any
speech or words. They don't make any sound we can hear. But their 'voice' goes
throughout the world. Their 'words' go to the ends of the earth. The sky is like a home
for the sun. The sun comes out like a happy bridegroom from his bedroom. The sun
begins its path across the sky like an athlete eager to run his race. The sun starts at one
end of the sky, and it runs all the way to the other end. Nothing can hide from its heat.
The Lord's teachings are like that" (Psalm 19:1-6).

The truth is, most people reject even this extremely basic evidence of God's existence and of his providing a habitat for his human beings. That is what the apostle Paul spoke of in Romans 1:17-32:

"17 The Good News shows how God makes people right with himself. ***God's way of making people right begins and ends with faith [Emphasis mine, SP].*** Like the Scripture says, 'The person that is right with God by faith will live forever' [quote from Habakkuk 2:4 – SP]

"18 God's anger is shown from heaven. God is angry with all evil and wrong things that people do against God. They have the truth, but by their evil lives they hid the truth. 19 God shows his anger, because everything that is known about God has been made clear to them. Yes, God has clearly shown people everything that is known about him. (20) There are things about God that people cannot see – his eternal power and all the things that make him God. But since the beginning of the world those things have been easy for people to understand. Those things are made clear in the things that God has made. So people have no excuse for the bad things they do. 21 People knew God. But they did not give glory to God and they did not thank him. People's thinking became useless. Their foolish minds were filled with darkness (sin). 22 People said they were wise, and they became fools. 23 They gave up the glory of God who lives forever. People traded that glory for the worship of idols made to look like earthly people. People traded God's glory for things that look like birds, animals, and snakes.

"24 People were full of sin, wanting only to do evil things. So God left them and let them go their sinful way. And so they became full of sexual sins, using their bodies wrongly with each other. 25 Those people traded the truth of God for a lie. Those people worshiped and served things that were made. But people did not worship and serve the God who made those things. God should be praised forever. Amen.

"26 Because people did those things, God left them and let them do the shameful things they wanted to do. Women stopped having natural sex with men. They started having sex with other women. 27 In the same way, men stopped having natural sex with women. The men began wanting each other all the time. Men did shameful things with other men. And in their bodies they received the punishment for those wrong things they did.

"28 People did not think it was important to have a true knowledge of God. So God left them and allowed those people to have their own worthless thinking. And so those people do the things that they should not do. 29 Those people are filled with every kind of sin, evil, selfishness, and hatred. Those people are full of jealousy, murder, fighting, lying, and thinking the worst things about each other. Those people gossip 30 and say evil things about each other. Those people hate God. They are rude and conceited and boast about themselves. Those people invent ways of doing evil. They don't obey their parents, 31 they are foolish, they don't keep their promises, and they show no kindness or mercy to other people. 32 Those people know God's law. They know that God's law says that people that live like this should die. But they continue to do these things. And they also feel that people who do these things are doing right."

Paul's point is that one can only glean a small amount of understanding about God from appreciating the moon, stars, lakes, mountains, birds, and animals he has created. The problem kicks in when nature lovers, let's call them, reject that small about of understanding or light revealed to them. Paul explained it this way in Romans 2:12-16:

"12 People that have the law [i.e., Law of Moses – SP] and people that have never heard of the law are all the same when they sin. People that don't have the law and are sinners will be lost. And, in the same way, people that have the law and are sinners will be judged by the law. 13 Hearing the law does not make people right with God. The law makes people right with God only if those people always obey everything the law says. 14 (The non-Jews don't have the law. But when they freely do things that the law commands without even knowing the law, then they are the law for themselves. This is true even though they don't have the law. 15 They show that in their hearts they know what is right and wrong the same as the law commands. And those people also show this by the way they feel about right and wrong. Sometimes their thoughts tell them that they did wrong, and this makes them guilty. And sometimes their thoughts tell them that they did right, and this makes them not guilty.) 16 All these things will happen on the day when God will judge the secret things inside of people. The Good News that I tell people says that God will judge people through Christ Jesus" (ERV).

Finally, the apostle Paul in Romans 5:12-13 neatly says in a few words what I have tried to convey in many:

"12 Sin came into the world because of what one man (Adam) did. And with sin came death. So this is why all people must die – because all people sinned. 13 Sin was in the world before the law of Moses. But God does not make people guilty for sin if there is no law" (ERV).

Whew, time to take a deep breath and reflect on what you just read.

To summarize Paul's thoughts, he is saying this about that class of people – back in the early years of human life and even to some people today – whose only insight into a Higher Being comes from looking at his creation. Paul states most of those people do not draw closer to God but, instead, reject that light and drift farther away. In time, that drifting became a downward spiral until they splashed down in a moral and ethical cesspool.

God, through Christ, will judge them by their response to the candlelight they had, not by the brilliant spotlight (Law of Moses; teaches of Jesus) other people have had but to which they had no access. ***Our loving God will always do what is right and just***. That is what makes him God, not us.

Now, let's review for just a minute where humanity was in the earliest years of its creation and procreation. The first man and woman, Adam and Eve, had three sons: Cain, Abel, and sometime later, Seth (later, the couple would have more children). Cain resented his brother Abel, and he finally killed him and went away to start his own lineage of people. When Seth was born, he grew up and he fathered many sons and daughters.

By the time Seth's grandson, Noah, was born, the people were wallowing in wickedness of all kinds. So Jehovah God decided to wipe them from the earth, except for Noah and his family because Noah "found favor with the Lord" (Genesis 6:8). He "was a righteous man, blameless among his contemporaries; Noah walked with God"(Genesis 6:9; **Holman Christian Study Bible** – HCSB).

At the time, Noah and his wife had three sons and three daughters-in-law. God gave them the explicit blueprints for the building of an ark that would survive a world-wide flood for a year's time. And it had to be large enough to house and feed a great number of paired-creatures (animals, birds, reptiles, etc.).

[NOTE: My wife and I made a special trip to see **"Ark Encounter"** at Williamstown, Kentucky in about 2018. The Ark, built as closely as possible to the original specifications, is 510 long, 85 feet wide and 51 feet high. It is far bigger than you can imagine, and it will take you far more time to see it all than you expect. Plan on staying in the area overnight and pacing yourself to enhance the experience. The restaurant adjacent to the Ark accommodates over 1,500 people, easily making it one of the largest eateries in the world. You may not agree with many of the dates on the displays, but ignore that and catch the essence of the place. See their web site at **arkencounter.com** .]

After the flood covered the earth and receded, Noah and his family and all the creatures left the ark. It was then that God made his very first recorded agreement with mankind. It was with Noah and his sons, plus all the creatures that had be on ark. Yep, that is right. Here is a summary from Genesis 9:8-17:

## 1st Covenant - God with Noah

"8 Then God spoke to Noah and to his sons with him, saying: 9 'And as for Me, behold, I establish My covenant with you and with your descendants after you, 10 and with every living creature that is with you: the birds, the cattle, and every beast of the earth with you, of all that go out of the ark, every beast of the earth. 11 **Thus I establish My covenant with you: Never again shall all flesh be cut off by the waters of the flood; never again shall there be a flood to destroy the earth.'** [emphasis mine, SP]

"12 And God said: 'This is the sign of the covenant which I make between Me and you, and every living creature that is with you, for perpetual generations: 13 I set My rainbow in the cloud, and it shall be for the sign of the covenant between Me and the earth. 14 It shall be, when I bring a cloud over the earth, that the rainbow shall be seen in the cloud; 15 and I will remember My covenant which is between Me and you and every living creature of all flesh; the waters shall never again become a flood to destroy all flesh. 16 **The rainbow shall be in the cloud, and I will look on it to remember the everlasting covenant between God and every living creature of all flesh that is on the earth.'** [emphasis mine, SP] 17 And God said to Noah, 'This is the sign of the covenant which I have established between Me and all flesh that is on the earth' (**New King James Version** – NKJV).

Each time Noah and his descendants saw a rainbow in the sky, they could rejoice and praise God that they would never see another world-wide flood like that one. And they could be encouraged by the absolute faithfulness of God that he would keep his part of the agreement.

Unfortunately, one of Noah's grandsons through Ham – a good sportsman named Nimrod – led a resistance movement against God's plan to disperse the people. His group set about to build a huge tower in their effort to maintain one language. But God defeated them by inflicting many dialects upon them, and that was the end of what we know as the "Tower of Babel."

God certainly recognized that the majority of the people were abandoning the idea of "one true God" (**monotheism**) and were into idolatry and superstitions, with each nation having one or more false gods. Jehovah thus decided to make a covenant with only one nation and to build that nation from scratch.

So he chose a man named Abram to become the father of this still non-existent nation. From a human standpoint, that choice seems odd since both Abram's father and grandfather worshiped idols and false gods. But Abram led a caravan all the way to Canaan (present-day Palestine). That was no small chore. The principals included Abram and his wife as well as his brother Lot and his wife, plus all their children, servants, and flocks. When Abram and Lot had a falling out, Lot took his entourage over to the rag-tag town of Sodom with the nearby rich grasses and trees of Jordan.

Then one night, when Abram was old and wondering how God would make a great nation out of him, God led him outdoors for an object lesson. He told Abram to try counting the sky full of stars and told him "Your offspring will be that numerous." And we are told, "**Abram believed the Lord, and he credited it to him as righteousness** [Emphasis mine, SP]." In other words, Abram's rock-solid faith allowed God to make a judicial declaration (or an accounting calculation) that Abram was righteous in God's sight. God and Abram were right in their relationship, so God showed his grace (unmerited, unearned favor) by giving most of the land of Canaan to Abram.

## 2<sup>nd</sup> Covenant - God with Abram

In Genesis 12:1-3, we have the first hint of a national covenant between God and a nation which was still only in his mind and plans. He said to Abram, "1 Get out of your country and away from your relatives and from your father's house and go to the land that I will show you. 2 I will bless those who bless you, and I will curse anyone who dishonors you. All of the families of the earth will be blessed in you" (**Evangelical Heritage Version** – EHV).

The two parts of the Covenant are explained in detail in Genesis 17:1-14. God told Abram about his own part, the first part: "1-2 When Abram was ninety-nine years old, God showed up and said to him, 'I am The Strong God, live entirely before me, live to the hilt! I'll make a covenant between us and I'll give you a huge family.'

"3-8 Overwhelmed, Abram fell flat on his face.

Part 1 – God will create from Abram a Nation

"Then God said to him, 'This is my covenant with you: You'll be the father of many nations. Your name will no longer be Abram, but Abraham, meaning that 'I'm making you the father of many nations.' I'll make you a father of fathers — I'll make nations from you, kings will issue from you. I'm establishing my covenant between me and you, a covenant that includes your descendants, a covenant that goes on and on and on, a covenant that commits me to be your God and the God of your descendants. And I'm giving you and your descendants this land where you're now just camping, this whole country of Canaan, to own forever. And I'll be their God.'

Part 2 – All of Abram's male descendants must be circumcised

"9-14 God continued to Abraham, 'And you: You will honor my covenant, you and your descendants, generation after generation. This is the covenant that you are to honor, the covenant that pulls in all your descendants: Circumcise every male. Circumcise by cutting off the foreskin of the penis; it will be the sign of the covenant between us. Every male baby will be circumcised when he is eight days old, generation after generation—this includes house-born slaves and slaves bought from outsiders who are not blood kin. Make sure you circumcise both your own children and anyone brought in from the outside. That way my covenant will be cut into your body, a permanent mark of my permanent covenant. An uncircumcised male, one who has not had the foreskin of his penis cut off, will be cut off from his people—he has broken my covenant' (**The Message** – MSG)."

It was during this announcement that Abram's name ("father is exalted") became Abraham ("father of multitudes") and his wife Sarai's name became Sarah ("princess").

> # -- 2 --
>
> ## God reveals just a bit more of himself by what people can see in the behavior of others and of themslves.
>
> ## -- Stan Paregien Sr.
>
> Graphic created by S Paregien Sr on Dec 14, 2020

Further on in Psalm 19, the writer said, "The Lord's teachings warn his servant. Good things come from obeying them. Lord, no person can see all of his own mistakes. So don't let me do secret sins. Don't let me do the sins I want to do. Don't let those sins rule me. If you help me, then I can be pure and free from my sins. I hope my thoughts please you. Lord, you are my Rock, you are the One who saves me"(Psalm 19:11-14).

Atheists and evolutionists are fond of saying that we humans have no intrinsic value. We are the product of a mindless, soupy, spinning environment that randomly combined one tiny cell with another until we became a simple amoeba, then a monkey, and then a monkey's uncle.

An unknown writer penned these lines: "The belief that there is nothing, and nothing happened to nothing. And then nothing magically exploded for no reason, creating everything. And then a bunch of everything magically rearranged itself for no reason whatsoever into self-replicating bits which then turned into dinosaurs and monkey-men. And then the proponents of atheistic evolution actually dare to mock the logic and proof of Christian beliefs. That is amazingly inconsistent."

Those folks often follow Charles Darwin's theory of evolution and the principle of "survival of the fittest." The more honest ones argue for total individuality, "each person for himself or herself." Those who win the genetic lottery and become "the fittest" of society should just enjoy their good fortune while the "losers" fade into oblivion. High-class amoebas have no need for ethics or mercy. In fact, they say, the way to further advance the evolutionary process is to kill or euthanize the old, the unwanted young, and those with mental or physical handicaps.

Hmmm. I wonder, would that include you or someone you dearly love, like a grandchild or your precious grandmother?

Yikes. That is a pretty ugly picture, isn't it?

Yet it has been a constant, often unclearly stated, practice around the world for centuries. In the old Roman society, if a couple did not want a newborn baby, they just put the child out in a field to die. During the 1930s and 1940s, the world was shocked when the Nazi leaders took over Germany and most of Europe. That was only the prelude. Soon the Nazi soldiers carried out their philosophy by torturing and killing large numbers of Jewish men, women, and children. Their plan was to establish themselves as the master race and eliminate everyone else. And then, more recently, we had the genocide war in Rwanda operating with the same guidelines.

Okay, enough of that.

Here are two little essays I had put in my file cabinet years ago. They had appeared in the February, 2014 newsletter published by my friend and half-cousin-in-law, Victor Knowles. There is, first, "An Atheist's View on Life," and then "A Christian's View on Life."

### An Atheist's View on Life
Author Unknown

I will live my life according to these beliefs
God does not exist
It is foolish to think
That there is a God with a cosmic plan
That an all-powerful God brings redemption and healing
to the pain and suffering in the world
Is a comforting thought, however.
It
Is only wishful thinking
People can do as they please without eternal consequences
The idea that
I am deserving of Hell
Because of sin
Is a lie meant to make me a slave to those in power
"The more you have, the happier you will be."

Our existence has no grand meaning or purpose
In a world without God
There is freedom to be who I want to be
But with God
Everything is fine
It is ridiculous to think
I am lost and in need of saving

Then we have the opposite view. It is actually the atheist essay read backwards or, to be exact, from bottom to top. Kinda clever, actually. But some readers may struggle with doing that, so I have done it for you below.


## A Christian's View on Life
Author Unknown

I am lost and in need of saving
It is ridiculous to think
Everything is fine
But with God
There is freedom to be who I want to be
In a world without God
Our existence has no grand meaning or purpose
"The more you have, the happier you will be."
Is a lie meant to make me a slave to those in power
Because of sin
I am deserving of Hell
The idea that
People can do as they please without eternal consequences
Is only wishful thinking
It
Is a comforting thought, however.
That an all-powerful God brings redemption and healing
to the pain and suffering in the world
That there is a God with a cosmic plan
It is foolish to think
God does not exist
I will live my life according to these beliefs

Wow, the person who worked out that comparison must be walking around with a tangled tongue and crossed eyes. But it certainly contrasts the mindset of the non-believer with a believer. If the atheist is right, and there is nothing to this God thing, what difference does that mean? Not a whole lot. But . . . if the Christian is right, and there is a God and a savior named Jesus and a comforter called the Holy Spirit, then the unbeliever misses the joyful life of love and service and faces judgement with no hope.

Let's say that you do believe in "super individualism," because you accept the idea we have no ethical duty to anyone besides self. But one winter day, you see a child fall off a bridge and into an icy river. You stand there as a stranger sees the situation, jumps into the water, and saves the child. Here is the big question: Was he stupid or was he courageous? Why would one amoeba risk its existence to save another competing amoeba? What would cause that unselfish, other-centered action?

Real life: Firefighters in Connecticut rescuing three boys
from the center of an icy pond in 2015. (The Day
Publishing Co. in New London, CT. Fair Use Domain)

How do you explain the actions of doctors and nurses who put their own lives at risk to save people from a disease? Why in the world would a man or woman in a blue uniform rush in where four armed thugs were raping and beating a young mother? Why should authorities spend any time rescuing young boys and girls from horrible working conditions or even from child sexual slavery? Why do soldiers volunteer for duty in the face of almost certain death? When terrorists flew passenger jets into the Twin Towers in New York City on September 11, 2001, why did hundreds of police, firemen, and medics ignore the obviously high danger to themselves and rush into the burning buildings?

Why? Why? Why?

Where did all this good-heartedness come from?

Well, it makes more sense to believe that we humans have an innate sense of goodness and a concern for others that cannot be explained by science. Have you considered the possibility that a Creator, God, installed a capacity for decency into each of us?

March 1, 2020, the world as most of us knew it disappeared before our very eyes. The CoronaVirus (COVID-19 19) hatched out and quickly spread around the world. It brought the economies of almost all nations to their knees.

Early on Thursday, July 2, 2020, I turned on my home computer. I was bracing myself against another day of depressing statistics and horror stories about the CoronaVirus and about the terribly depressed economy.

However, to my delight, parent company Microsoft had set up an entire front page of "Good News" on the MSN newsfeed via my Edge browser. It featured dozens of stories and photos of ordinary people doing extraordinary things for those who were in some kind of need. It was wonderful, fabulous, uplifting, and amazing. Here is that link: **msn.com/en-us/news/good-news?ocid=ems.msn.goodnews2020**

These were generous, good-hearted people of every age and color taking the time to help/bless a neighbor, a friend, a policeman, a janitor, a teacher, a nurse, or a soldier. Mostly, they did something that inspired, befriended, and assisted absolute strangers.

**Try Your Own Experiment**.

No one has to know you are doing it. Go about your regular activities for one week, just seven days. During that time, write down in a simple journal or computer file every single time you see someone do something "good" for someone else. Number and briefly describe each act. I am confident you will be amazed and sensitized to the great amount of good that we do for each other every single day.

Your list might include a woman taxi driver who stops to show a teenage driver how to change the flat tire on his father's car. An old man sits on a park bench and simply tips his hat to the other old people who know it is a greeting and a sign of respect. A little girl picks flowers from her mother's garden to share with a legless young soldier near the entrance to his apartment. A new retiree delivers free meals for the homeless. A long-retired U.S. President still teaches his Sunday School. A Black college professor needs a kidney transplant and after the word is spread, a Hispanic truck driver finds out he is a match and donates to this man he does not even know. The list goes on and on.

Then the lightbulb in your head (i.e., your brain) begins to flicker with activity. Yes, maybe there is a God. Even better yet, maybe there is a God who has installed a caring heart like that beating in the hearts of most humans.

Wow.

So far, we have seen where people through every age right up to today have had an opportunity to know something basic about God through observing nature around them.

In addition, they have had the opportunity to learn something about God by observing an element of decency and goodness in most everyone. They had these two avenues of at least acknowledging the existence of God and thanking him for his blessings. Again, the judgement is directly in proportion to what they did with whatever light they had. **God's judgement is always just, right, and according to the truth a person received and how the person responded to it.**

Please understand this: **There is a day of Judgement coming**. Those who have loved and walked with God will be saved and rewarded, but those who have actually rejected God will be condemned and separated from God forever. Do not take my word. Study the scriptures.

For example, the apostle Paul in Acts 17 made a visit to the bustling city of Athens, Greece. It was a great commercial center. It features the best in sports, music, literature, philosophy, and education. And it was a city of statues to this god, that god and even one inscribed "To the Unknown God." He was able to speak before a large group of prominent leaders and judges. Here in Acts 17:30-31, Paul told them about a coming judgement:

"30 In the past, people did not understand God, but God ignored this. But now, God tells every person in the world to change his heart and life. 31 God has decided a day when he will judge all the people in the world. He will be fair. He will use a man (Jesus) to do this. God chose this man long ago. And God has proved this to every person; God proved it by raising that man from death!"

In John 5:22-30, Jesus said: "22 The Father judges no one. But the Father has given the Son power to do all the judging. 23 God did this so that all people will respect the Son the same as they respect the Father. If a person does not respect the Son, then that person does not respect the Father. The Father is the One who sent the Son.

"24 I tell you the truth. If a person hears what I say and believes in the One who sent me, that person has life forever. That person will not be judged guilty. He has already left death and has entered into life. 25 I tell you the truth. An important time is coming. That time is already here. People that are dead in sin will hear the voice of the Son of God. And the people that accept the things they hear from the Son will have life forever. 26 Life comes from the Father (God) himself. So the Father has also allowed the Son (Jesus) to give life. 27 And the Father has given the Son the power to judge all people. Why? Because that Son is the Son of Man [i.e., the Messiah; see Daniel 7:13-14 – SP]. 28 Don't be surprised at this. A time is coming when all people that are dead and in their graves will hear his voice. 29 Then they will come out of their graves. The people that did good in life will rise and have life forever. But the people that did evil will rise to be judged guilty."

Alright, there is going to be a judgement. And here is how that will work.

On the coming day of Judgement, the Bible teaches that the people with these two opportunities to know and acknowledge and thank God will be judged by how they reacted to that amount of light – the only light they had. God's judgement is certainly just, right, and according to truth.

All that is well and good. The fact is, though, there is only so much of himself that God allows to be revealed through nature or by studying the behavior of others and of ourselves.

# Chapter 4

# Progressive Revelation:
# God as Revealed to the Jews

That brings us to the third step of God's progressive revelation of himself and his will. This was a major step forward and in it God actually spoke the truth about himself and his will through selected people and to selected people. In this case, we are talking about the Jewish people, also known as Israelites and the Nation of Israel.

> **-- 3 --**
>
> *God continued his progressive revelation about himself through Moses and the Jewish poets and prophets. Their words were collected in what we call the "Old Testament" part of our Bible. The message was specifically for the nation of Israel.*
>
> Graphic created by Stan Paregien on Dec 15, 2020

In Hebrews1:1, the writer brings up the ancient heritage of the Jews. He wrote, "Long ago God spoke many times and in many ways to our ancestors through the prophets" (**New Living Translation** – NLT).

Again in Psalm 19, the writer honors the power of God's living word:

"The Lord's teachings are perfect. They give strength to God's people. The Lord's Agreement can be trusted. It helps foolish people become wise. The Lord's laws are right. They make people happy. The Lord's commands are good. They show people the right way to live. Worshiping the Lord is like a light that will shine bright forever. The Lord's judgments are good and fair. They are completely right. The Lord's teachings are worth more than the best gold. They are sweeter than the best honey that comes straight from the honeycomb" (Psalm 19:7-10).

How wonderful it would be if friends could more often just get together and talk about all the interests and concerns we have in common.

However, we are a distracted bunch of folks, aren't we?

We have our wide loop of acquaintances, distant relatives, and long-distance friends. We also have our more intimate circle of close friends and relatives. Add to that mix our careers, our neighborhood matters, our political interests, our health issues, the economic situation for not only us but for so many we love, our religious interests and activities – or a virtual absence thereof, and a vast range of other things which elbow for our attention.

So let me ask you this, seriously: When was the last time you sat down with someone outside your household and had a heart-to-heart discussion about how important a spiritual faith is . . . or maybe is not . . . to you?

For many of us, that kind of interaction has been a rare experience. And even when it has happened, you may have walked away with a really bad taste in your mouth and no desire to try it, again.

I understand that.

So all I am asking here is for those readers who are religious Jews or who strongly identify with the historic Jewish culture to take a few minutes to read and consider the following statements in this chapter. There is no 100-item test at the end. There is no pressure at all, certainly not from little ol' me. At the end of this book, I hope we remain friends and open to discussion of this and most any subject.

One other note: We have taken the extra time necessary to cite the various places in the Old Testament from which Paul often quotes. Those are respected texts from the original Jewish documents; that is why Paul quotes them. So, just for your personal comfort and confirmation, turn to your own Bible and read. Each time you see here a **"Quoted from . . ."** citation. That will be your friendly cue to look it up.

Okay, then, let's start.

As part of this transformation to a Nation, Abraham's nomadic descendants would have to be molded into city dwellers who would submit to a central power. And prophets would tell them of the coming of the great Messiah (Jesus) one day. As it turned out, they would serve a 400 year internship as slaves in perhaps the most powerful and enlightened nation of the period, the nation of Egypt. There they were often reminded of the existence of the one true God (Exodus 12:12). And their numbers would grow from only about 70 people to a hearty group of nearly two million.

Moses led the enthusiastic, but rebellious, children of Abraham out of Egypt. Because of their various sins and lack of faith in God, the escapees had to wander in the desert for 40 years. Most of the original group died before reaching the promised land. But it was there in the desert that God established a mighty Covenant with the Nation, not with any individuals.

## 3rd Covenant – With a Nation

As usual, God revealed himself to the extent the religious and cultural environment of the time could absorb. It was in keeping with his plan to develop a strong nation that would promote the concept of "one true God" (monotheism; Deuteronomy 4:34). And through that nation's spokespeople and prophets God would instill hope for the coming of a Messiah, that Messiah being the Son of God, Jesus.

The first step with these wanderers was to established of what God expected of them and how they ought to treat their fellow sojourners and outsiders. This Nation of Israel was to be a theocracy, a God-led government and people. God even sent word though Moses, "Now if you will carefully listen to me and keep my covenant, **you will be my own possession out of all the peoples, although the whole earth is mine, and you will be my kingdom of priests and my holy nation** [emphasis mine, SP] " (Exodus 19:5-6; **Holman Christian Study Bible** – HCSB).

It was deep in the wilderness, at the base of Mount Sinai, that God's covenant with the nation would be revealed. This was in about 1446 B.C. Much later, the leaders of the nation of Israel believed they were far superior to non-Jews because Moses himself had given them special directions from God. All this came to be known as the Mosaic Law (or Law of Moses; or The Talmud). Their natural pride in being "special" or "the apple of God's eye" slowly crossed over the line and became sinful presumption and arrogance. That is seen in this prayer many Jewish men offered, "God, I thank you I am not a heathen, that I am not a dog, that I am not a Gentle (i.e., non-Jew – SP), and that I am not a woman."

Well, Moses came down from Mt. Sinai with the ten commandments on two clay tablets. NOTE: These were not called "The 10 Suggestions." These rules of living were right from the heart of God. In the original Hebrew, the ten rules start with emphatic warnings as from one of stature to a general crowd and the sense is, "**Don't ever** . . . worship any other gods except me" and "**Don't ever** make any idols."

He loved them enough to put up "guard rails" to help them behave how he wanted them to do. These rules would protect them and make life happier and more orderly. This was the foundation or starting point of what would eventually include hundreds of laws. The aim was to lead and correct the people as they sought to love and obey God.

The basic motivation of the Jewish people for obeying these rules was to show their appreciation to their loving God for delivering them from slavery in Egyptian and for their survival from the wandering in the desert on the way to the Promised Land.

### The Ten Commandments
(Exodus 20:1-17, Simplified)

1. You must not worship any other gods except me.
2. You must not make any idols (statues of false gods).
3. You must not use the name of the Lord your God in a wrong way.
4. You must remember to keep the Sabbath (Saturday) a special day of rest.
5. You must honor your father and your mother.
6. You must not murder anyone.
7. You must not do the sin of adultery (sexual sin outside of marriage).
8. You must not steal anything.
9. You must not tell lies about other people.
10. You must not want to take your neighbor's house, wife or anything that belongs to him.

Interestingly, the Ten Commandments have had an enduring influence of basic morality and ethics on not only the Jewish community but on Christians as well. The rules themselves provide a balance of how to please God and how to get along with other humans. The first four commandments deal with living so as to please a holy God. The next six commandments show individuals how to get along with other people.

God's main method for teaching others about his Covenant with Israel was by fathers ("the patriarchs" in that society") teaching their children (Deuteronomy 6:6-7). This certainly suggests that whatever was covered was simple enough for men who were ordinary carpenters, herdsmen, fishermen, and storekeepers to fully grasp and easy enough for their children to fully understand. That seems to rule out a line-by-line study of the Pentateuch in favor of just the Ten Commandments, selected passages, singing chants, and the father telling stories about Abraham and others.

There were no organized evangelistic efforts to convert non-Israelites. If such a family presented themselves, they first had to have all men and male children circumcised. After that, there did not seem to be any special treatment. Certainly, there was not a "New Members Class & What You Need to Know" sort of thing.

**"The Pentateuch"** referred to the first five books of the Jewish Bible: Genesis, Exodus, Leviticus, Numbers and Deuteronomy. Here were more religious laws, community laws and ceremonial rituals and regulations, all designed to help Israel walk with God. Modern Jews sometimes refer to the **Pentateuch** as "the Written Law." And today they often use the word "**Torah**" (i.e., the Oral Law) to include the Pentateuch and all of the other rabbinical teachings and rules.

Moses, who was personally instructed by God, was clear in stating what God expected of them. What Moses said to them is recorded in Deuteronomy 6:3-6:

"3 People of Israel, listen carefully and obey these laws. Then everything will be fine with you. You will have many children, and you will get the land filled with many good things – just like the Lord, the God of your ancestors, promised.

"4 Listen, people of Israel! The Lord is our God. The Lord is one! 5 You must love the Lord your God with all your heart, with all your soul, and with all your strength. 6 Always remember these commands that I give you today."

However, it did not work out that way.

In time, most of the Jews considered "the traditions of the elders" and "the teachings of the rabbis" as an extension of the law. And that evolved into a legalistic mindset. They got the mistaken idea that by diligently keeping the rules one could earn his salvation. One's effort and perfect performance would mean God was duty-bound to be pleased. Never mind whether you even liked God, much less loved him. Keep the rules and you win the game. Period.

Hmmmm.

For those of us in the body of Christ, the Christian community, this soulless salvation based on accounting principles sounds uncomfortable familiar. You see, it is a fact of group psychology and social organization that people often start off with great religious or spiritual fervor and then deceive themselves into believing they can save themselves by their glittering performances of piety. Some people call that "pulling yourself up by your own bootstraps."

Phooey on that wacky idea.

Law-keeping did not work for Adam and Eve. It did not work for Abraham. It did not work for the nation of Israel. And it will not work for today's Christians, either. We are neither good enough, bright enough or strong enough to get through the gates of Heaven on our own merits.

Well, by God's design, nobody could keep the Law of Moses perfectly. The purpose behind it all was to convict their hearts of their sinful nature. It was to teach them they could not save themselves by rule-keeping, neither by the Law of Moses nor by any other salvation-by-law-keeping plan.

What follows is largely from the pen of the apostle Paul. He was born into an orthodox Jewish family, was educated in Jewish institutions, affiliated himself with the party of the Pharisees, and adopted as his favorite sport the persecution and extermination of all Christian Jews. There came that day, though, in 35 A.D. when he became a disciple of a Jewish man named Jesus and an advocate for the Christian way of life.

Why would any orthodox Jew do such a thing? Here are some answers from his own mouth. Please, I beg you, read them carefully and objectively. Then decide for yourself if you hear the ring of truth.

## Romans 2:17-24 – Jews break the Law

" 17 What about you? You say you are a Jew. You trust in the law and boast that you are close to God. 18 You know what God wants you to do. And you know the things that are important because you have learned the law. 19 You think you are a guide for people that don't know the right way. You think you are a light for people that are in darkness (sin). 20 You think you can show foolish people what is right. And you think you are a teacher for people that still need to learn. You have the law and so you think that you know everything and have all truth. 21 You teach other people. So why don't you teach yourself? You tell people not to steal. But you yourselves steal. 22 You say that people must not do the sin of adultery. But you yourselves are guilty of that sin. You hate idols. But you steal from temples. 23 You boast about God's law. But you bring shame to God by breaking his law. 24 It is written in the Scriptures: 'The non-Jews say bad things about God because of you Jews'" (quote from Isaiah 52:5 – SP).

That is a tough lesson, a real smack in the face and a forced look at reality. They were law-breakers on such a scale to even cause non-Jews to abhor their God.

## Romans 2:25-29 – Jews got circumcision all wrong

[NOTE: Circumcision is a ritual in which a rabbi cuts the foreskin off of the penis of the Jewish boy. It is done 8 days after birth. It was established as a remembrance that God had made a covenant or agreement with Abraham in Genesis 17:9-14. – SP]

"25 If you follow the law, then your circumcision has meaning. But if you break the law, then it is like you were never circumcised. 26 The non-Jews are not circumcised. But if they do what the law says, then it is like they were circumcised. 27 You Jews have the written law and circumcision, but you break the law. So the people that are not circumcised in their bodies, but still obey the law, will show that you people are guilty.

"28 A person is not a true Jew if he is only a Jew in his physical body. True circumcision is not only on the outside of the body. 29 A person is a true Jew only if he is a Jew inside. True circumcision is done in the heart. It is done by the Spirit, not by the written law. And a person that is circumcised in the heart by the Spirit gets praise from God, not from people."

## Romans 3:1-8 -- Jews were given God's teachings

"1 So, do Jews have anything that other people don't have? Is there anything special about being circumcised? Yes, the Jews have many special things. The most important is this: God trusted the Jews with his teachings. 3 It is true that some Jews were not faithful to God. But will that stop God from doing what he promised? 4 No! God will continue to be true even when every person is false. Like the Scriptures say: 'You will be proved right in your words, and you will win when you are being judged' (Psalm 51:4)

"5 When we do wrong, that shows more clearly that God is right. So can we say that God does wrong when he punishes us? (I am using an idea that some people might have.) 6 No! If God could not punish us, then God could not judge the world.

"7 A person might say, 'When I lie, it really gives God glory, because my lie shows God's truth. So why am I judged a sinner?' 8 It would be the same to say, 'We should do evil so that good will come.' Many people criticize us and say that we teach those things. People that say those things are wrong, and they should be condemned."

## Romans 3:9-20 -- Jews & non-Jews: all are guilty

"9 So are we Jews better than other people? No! We have already said that Jews and non-News are the same. They are all guilty of sin. 10 Like the Scriptures say:

11 – 'There is no person without sin. None!
'There is no person that understands.
'There is no person that really wants to be with God.
'12 – All people have turned away,
'and all people have become worthless.
'There is no person that does good. None!'
Psalm 14:1-3

13 – 'People's mouths are like open graves;
'they use their tongues for telling lies.'
'The things they say are like the poison
'of snakes'; Psalm 140:3
14 – 'their mouths are full of cursing and bitterness.'
Psalm 10:7

15 – 'People are always ready to hurt and kill;
16 – 'everywhere they go they cause ruin and sadness.
17 – 'People don't know the way of peace.'
Isaiah 59:7-8
18 – 'They have no fear or respect for God.'
Psalm 36:1

"19 These things the law says are for the people that are under the law. This stops all Jewish people from making excuses and brings the whole world (Jews and non-Jews) under God's judgment. 20 Why? Because no person can be made right with God by following the law. The law only shows us our sin."

Periodically, the prophets of Israel gave them a glimpse of better times to come. They told of how God's appointed "Messiah" would someday come and set things right. Many of them not only believed that message but believed it so much many couples prayed they would be blessed by being the actual parents of that coming Messiah. It became a focal point of their thoughts, with different interpretations of what this Messiah would be like and how he would exert his power.

Still, there was always this dark cloud over their heads because they kept on sinning. And God, in keeping with his holy sense of justice, kept on punishing them until they changed their ways (repented) and started trying to obey the conditions of the Law. It seemed to be a never ending cycle, except there was a glimmer of hope the coming Messiah would rescue them.

However, Jesus frankly and honestly rebuked the hypocrisy of religious Jews. They praised the Law of Moses. They studied it in the temple and in the synagogues. They even attached to their robes pieces of parchment containing verses from the Old Testament. They placed larger pieces in little boxes tied to their heads. But they did not love the God of those words and, therefore, had little motivation to obey him.

In John 5:38-40, it is recorded that Jesus said to them: "The Father's teaching does not live in you. Why? Because you don't believe in the One the Father sent. 39 You carefully study the Scriptures. You think those Scriptures give your life forever. Those same Scriptures tell about me! 40 But you refuse to come to me to have that life you want" (ERV).

In John 5:30-47, Jesus takes the Jews of his day – his own countrymen – to task for paying more attention to what John the Baptist was saying about him than what his own deeds and miracles said about him and testified to him.

Jesus leveled his most damning criticism toward the Jewish leaders, not toward the ordinary people. And his sharpest barbs were toward a group of Biblical scholars called "Pharisees." They were arrogant in their claims of obeying the Law of Moses perfectly and being holy in observing every ritual. They were the keepers of orthodox Judaism and Jewish culture. These Pharisees despised non-Jews. They also hated their kinsmen, the Sadducees, because this latter group did not believe in a resurrection and they had absorbed a lot of Greek culture and philosophy just like a sponge. The Pharisees considered themselves to be the most holy of all holy people in Israel.

Jesus did not share that view. He often spoke of how bad off such people would be on Judgement Day. In Matthew 23:13, Jesus said: "13 It will be bad for you teachers of the law and Pharisees. You are hypocrites. You close the way for people to enter the kingdom of heaven. You yourselves don't enter, and you stop the people that are trying to enter" (ERV).

In Matthew 23:15, Jesus said: "15 It will be bad for you teachers of the law and Pharisees. You are hypocrites. You travel across the seas and across different countries to find one person that will follow your ways. When you find that person, you make him worse than you are. And you are so bad that you belong in hell!" (ERV)

In Matthew 23:23, Jesus said: "23 It will be bad for you teachers of the law and Pharisees. You are hypocrites. You give God one tenth of everything you own – even your mint, dill, and cumin. But **you don't obey the really important teachings of the law – being fair, showing mercy, and being honest** [emphasis mine, SP]. These are the things you should do. And you should also continue to do these other thing. 24 You guide the people, but you are blind! Think about a person picking a little fly out of his drink and then swallowing a camel! You are like that" (ERV).

Nothing is said in this context about the response of the Pharisees. One has to think as they walked away these men felt like they had been beaten about the head and shoulders with a verbal hammer.

*A Basic Rule for Understanding the Bible*

**All Bible verses are equally inspired of God, but some are far more important than others.**
**-- Stan Paregien Sr.**

Graphic by Stan Paregien Sr on Dec 15, 2020

This verse in **Matthew 23:23** needs some special attention before we move on. There Jesus presents a concept that some people still do not get today. That simple idea is this: **Some Bible verses and ideas are far more important than others.** Or to put it another way, not all Bible verses were created equal and, therefore, some verses have more weight and importance than others. Jesus said it, so we better take time to understand it and believe it.

Keep in mind the situation of the Jews at this time. They were saddled with not only the 10 Commandments, but hundreds of other rules found in the first five books of the Old Testament (the Pentateuch). And . . . then there were the hundreds of rules created over time by rabbinical interpretations of the Law and by cultural traditions ("The Torah").

In fact, by the time of Jesus, the rabbinical theologians had formulated a complicated system of holiness containing 613 religious laws. Yes, 613 of them. They further organized this maze of regulations into 248 prescriptions (things which must be done) and 365 prohibitions (things which must not be done). Then things got really confusing when they divided the 613 into actually binding commands and commands in which they might cut a person a little slack. Still not satisfied, they sat around arguing about how to rank the laws within the two major divisions.

Hey, and you thought the Ten Commandments were complicated. In the end, of course, it was impossible to perfectly keep all 613 of these laws and ritual rules.

So Jesus, in Matthew 23:23, tells them they better take care of the weightier, more important commands and worry about the others later. Nowhere does this principle shine more brightly than in Matthew 22:34-40. A certain Pharisee, known as a living authority on the Law of Moses, came up with a trick question for Jesus. The man's aim was to discredit and shut up this pup from Nazareth. And the question was a hot button topic in rabbinical circles of the day, with some advocating for this verse or that verse.

Jesus shocked this Jewish scholar all the way down to his sandals by authoritatively affirming that the **Shema** (Deuteronomy 6:5) was the greatest commandment and then going far beyond that to argue that the second-greatest command was that found in Leviticus 19:18. Here is how the conversation flowed in Matthew 22:37-40:

**"37 'You must love the Lord your God. You must love him with all your heart, all your soul, and all your mind.' 38 This is the first and most important command. 39 And the second command is like the first: 'You must love other people the same as you love yourself.' 40 All of the law and the writings of the prophets take their meaning from these two commands'** [emphasis mine, SP]" (ERV).

Not only could Jesus turn water into wine, but he could also reduce the entire rabbinical scheme of 613 rules to just two very similar ones. He replaced a confusing, complex system of law-keeping with a simple rule of life: let your heart overflow with love for God and for all other people.

Absolutely amazing, don't you think?

## Romans 7:5-13 – A Pharisee's personal struggle with law-keeping

Paul's original name was "Saul," perhaps named after Jewish leader King Saul. He was born into a Jewish family in Tarsus, a Roman-controlled inland city in what today is the country of Turkey. Therefore, **Paulos** (his Roman name) was a natural-born Roman citizen and had the benefits thereof. As a Jew, he observed all of their holy days and probably was enrolled early on in a day school provided by the nearest Jewish synagogue. He, like the other students, worked hard to learn to read and write the Hebrew language – though in their homes, most local people of the day spoke Aramaic. Later, he became proficient in the Greek language as well. It was customary for each Jewish boy to learn a useful trade. His choice was tentmaking, a skill he often used to support himself (Acts 18:3).

Then, somewhere between the ages of 13 and 18, Paul moved to the bustling city of Jerusalem. He went there specifically to study under one of the most highly respected Jewish teachers of the day, Rabbi Gamaliel (Acts 22:3; Galatians 1:14; Philippians 3:5). He affiliated himself with the Pharisees, a Jewish sect known for zealously protecting orthodox laws and traditions. He was so dedicated that he persecuted the people who were members of what the Pharisees first thought of as quirky, unorthodox sect of Jews – those known as Christians (Acts 8:1-3; 9:1-2; 26:9-14; Galatians 1:13; Philippians 3:6). He thus became a Pharisee who was a veteran warrior against Jewish unorthodoxy and non-Jews in general. He even carried credentials from the Sanhedrin authorizing him to arrest Jews suspected of unorthodoxy. This guy was a religious thug, a man to be feared.

Lightning struck, so to speak, in about 35 A.D. Paul had started down to Damascus to arrest some Jewish Christians. Before he got there, a blinding light sent him to his knees. He heard the voice of Jesus directing him to go learn more from Ananias. That man had the pleasure of telling Paul the real facts about Jesus – the gospel account. Then and there, Paul confessed Jesus as Lord. And as people always did back then, immediately he was baptized in water as a sign or testimonial symbol of his new life in Christ that was accomplished by his faith-experience (Acts 9:3-19; 22:6-21; 26:13-23).

What a dramatic change. The Pharisee enforcer became a Christian persuader. The Mosaic law-keeper became a proclaimer of salvation by grace through faith, apart from any do-it-yourself meritorious acts. Oh, I do not want to forget, the persecutor instantly became the persecuted. Where once he persecuted to the death members of the Christian sect, now he considered it an honor when he himself was scorned, threatened, beaten, and maligned in the service of his King, Jesus.

I pause here to explain – but not to apologize – for the length of this chapter. There was a need to make all of us keenly aware of the baggage Paul brought to his Christian ministry. He was circumcised at 8 days of age, and celebrated the achievement of manhood in a Bar mitzvah ceremony at age 13. This intelligent, educated Jewish man knew the Torah inside and out. He loved the scriptures and his own Jewish heritage.

However, Paul he also knew that it was all too easy to forget about loving God and others, while sinking into the quicksand of "religion by law-keeping." That was never successful. If a Jewish person were honest with himself, he would admit he repeatedly failed to keep the law perfectly. It could only lead to a burdensome, frustrating, self-defeating, and depressing round of failures. It put one's sins front and center, ever on the brain. It branded, "Sinner" on his forehead and in his mind.

Now that you know more of Paul's spiritual resume, please read his insightful words in Romans 7:5-13 about his own struggle with **legalism**:

"5 In the past, we were ruled by our sinful selves. The law [of Moses – SP] made us want to do sinful things. And those sinful things we wanted to do controlled our bodies, so that the things we did were only bringing us spiritual death. 6 In the past, the law held us like prisoners. But our old selves died and we were made free from the law. **So now we serve God in a new way, not in the old way with the written rules. Now we serve God in the new way with the Spirit [Emphasis mine, SP].**

"7 You might think that I am saying that sin and the law are the same thing. That is not true. But the law was the only way I could learn what sin means. I would never have known what it means to want something wrong. But the law said, 'You must not want things that belong to other people. 8 And sin found a way to use that command and make me want every kind of wrong thing. So sin came to me because of that command. But without the law, sin has no power. 9 I was alive without the law before I knew the law. But when the law's command came to me, then sin began to live. 10 And I died spiritually because of sin. The command was meant to bring life, but for me that command brought death. 11 Sin found a way to fool me by using the command. Sin used the command to make me die spiritually.

"12 So the law is holy, and the command is holy and right and good. 13 Does this mean that something that is good brought death to me? No! But sin used something that is good to bring death to me. This happened so that I could see what sin is really like. It happened to show that sin is something unbelievably bad. And the command was used to show this" (ERV).

## Romans 9:1-32 – Paul's desire for his Jewish family

"1 I am in Christ and I am telling you the truth. I am not lying. And my conscience, ruled by the Holy Spirit, agrees that what I say now is true. 2 I have great sorrow and always feel much sadness 3 for my own people. They are my brothers and sisters, my earthly family. I wish I could help them. I would even have a curse on me and cut myself off from Christ if that would help them. 4 They are the people of Israel, God's chosen children. They have the glory of God and the agreements he made between himself and his people. God gave them the Law of Moses, the Temple worship, and his promises. 5 They are the descendants of our great fathers, and they are the earthly family of the Messiah, who is God over all things. Praise him forever! Amen.

"6 I don't mean that God failed to keep his promise to the Jewish people. But only some of the people of Israel are really God's people. 7 And only some of Abraham's descendants are true children of Abraham. This is what God said to Abraham: 'Your true descendants will be those who come through Isaac' [Quote from Genesis 21:12 – SP]. 8 This means that not all of Abraham's descendants are God's true children. Abraham's true children are those who become God's children because of the promise he made to Abraham. 9 Here is what God said in that promise: 'About this time next year I will come back, and Sarah will have a son' [Quote from Genesis 18:10,14 – SP].

"10 And that is not all. Rebecca also had sons, and they had the same father. He is our father Isaac. 11-12 But before the two sons were born, God told Rebecca, 'The older son will serve the younger' [Quote from Genesis 25:23 – SP]. This was before the boys had done anything good or bad. God said this before they were born so that the boy he wanted would be chosen because of God's own plan. He was chosen because he was the one God wanted to call, not because of anything the boys did. 13 As the Scriptures say, "I loved Jacob, but I hated Esau." [Quote from Malachi 12:3 – SP]

"14 So what does this mean? That God is not fair? We cannot say that. 15 God said to Moses, "I will show mercy to anyone I want to show mercy to. I will show pity to anyone I choose' [Quote from Exodus 33:19 – SP. 16 So God will choose anyone he decides to show mercy to, and his choice does not depend on what people want or try to do. 17 In the Scriptures God says to Pharaoh: 'I made you king so that you could do this for me. I wanted to show my power through you. I wanted my name to be announced throughout the world.' [Quote from Exodus 9:16 - SP]. 18 So God shows mercy to those he wants to show mercy to and makes stubborn those he wants to make stubborn.

"19 So one of you will ask me, "If God controls what we do, why does he blame us for our sins?" 20 Don't ask that. You are only human and have no right to question God. A clay jar does not question the one who made it. It does not say, 'Why did you make me like this?' 21 The one who makes the jar can make anything he wants. He uses the same clay to make different things. He might make one thing for special purposes and another for daily use.

"22 It is the same way with what God has done. He wanted to show his anger and to let people see his power. But he patiently endured those he was angry with—people who were ready to be destroyed. 23 He waited with patience so that he could make known the riches of his glory to the people he has chosen to receive his mercy. God has already prepared them to share his glory. 24 We are those people, the ones God chose not only from the Jews but also from those who are not Jews. 25 As the Scriptures say in the book of Hosea,

'The people who are not mine—
I will say they are my people.
And the people I did not love—
I will say they are the people I love.'
[Quoted from Hosea 2:23 – SP]

26 And,
'Where God said in the past,
'You are not my people'—
there they will be called children
of the living God.
[Quoted from Hosea 1:10 – SP]

27 And Isaiah cries out about Israel:

'There are so many people of Israel,
they are like the grains of sand by the sea.
But only a few of them will be saved.
28 Yes, the Lord will quickly finish
judging the people on the earth."
[Quoted from Isaiah 10:22-23]

29 It is just as Isaiah said:

'The Lord All-Powerful
allowed some of our people to live.
If he had not done that,
we would now be like Sodom,
and we would be like Gomorrah.'
[Quoted from Isaiah 1:9 – SP]

"30 So what does all this mean? It means that people who are not Jews were made right with God because of their faith, even though they were not trying to make themselves right. 31 And the people of Israel, who tried to make themselves right with God by following the law, did not succeed. 32 They failed because they tried to make themselves right by the things they did. They did not trust in God to make them right. They fell over the stone that makes people fall. 33 The Scriptures talk about that stone:

'Look, I put in Zion a stone that will make people stumble.
It is a rock that will make people fall.
But anyone who trusts in him
will never be disappointed.'
[Quoted from Isaiah 8:4; 28:16 – SP]

## Romans 10:1-21 - Paul wanted Israel to be saved

"1 Brothers and sisters, what I want most is for all the people of Israel to be saved. That is my prayer to God. 2 I can say this about them: They really try hard to follow God, but they don't know the right way. 3 They did not know the way that God makes people right with him. And they tried to make themselves right in their own way. So they did not accept God's way of making people right. 4 **Christ ended the law so that everyone who believes in him is made right with God** [emphasis mine, SP].

"5 Moses writes about being made right by following the law. He says, 'The person who obeys these laws is the one who will have life through them' [Quote from Leviticus 18:5 – SP]. 6 But this is what the Scriptures say about being made right through faith: "Don't say to yourself, 'Who will go up into heaven?'" (This means "Who will go up to heaven to get Christ and bring him down to earth?") 7 "And don't say, 'Who will go down into the world below?'" (This means "Who will go down to get Christ and bring him up from death?")

"8 This is what the Scripture says: 'God's teaching is near you; it is in your mouth and in your heart' [Quote from Deuteronomy 30:12-14 – SP]. **It is the teaching of faith that we tell people. 9** ***If you openly say, "Jesus is Lord" and believe in your heart that God raised him from death, you will be saved.*** **10 Yes, we believe in Jesus deep in our hearts, and so we are made right with God. And we openly say that we believe in him, and so we are saved** [emphasis mine, SP].

"11 Yes, the Scriptures say, 'Anyone who trusts in him will never be disappointed' [Quote from Isaiah 28:16 – SP]. 12 It says this because there is no difference between those who are Jews and those who are not. The same Lord is the Lord of all people. And he richly blesses everyone who looks to him for help. 13 Yes, 'everyone who trusts in the Lord will be saved' [Quote from Joel 2:32 – SP]."

"14 But before people can pray to the Lord for help, they must believe in him. And before they can believe in the Lord, they must hear about him. And for anyone to hear about the Lord, someone must tell them. 15 And before anyone can go and tell them, they must be sent. As the Scriptures say, 'How wonderful it is to see someone coming to tell good news!' [Quote from Isa. 52:7 – SP]"

"16 But not all the people accepted that good news. Isaiah said, 'Lord, who believed what we told them?' [Quote from Isaiah 53:1." 17 So faith comes from hearing the Good News. And people hear the Good News when someone tells them about Christ.

"18 But I ask, "Did those people not hear the Good News?" Yes, they heard—as the Scriptures say,

'Their voices went out all around the world.
Their words went everywhere in the world.'
[Quote from Psalm 19:4 – SP]

"19 Again I ask, "Did the people of Israel not understand?"
Yes, they did understand. First, Moses says this for God:

'I will use those who are not really a nation to make you jealous.
I will use a nation that does not understand to make you angry.'
[Quote from Deuteronomy 32:21 – SP]

"20 Then Isaiah is bold enough to say this for God:

'The people who were not looking for me—
they are the ones who found me.
I made myself known to those who did not ask for me.'
[Quote from Isaiah 65:1 – SP]

"21 But about the people of Israel God says,

'All day long I stood ready to accept those people,
but they are stubborn and refuse to obey me.'
[Quote from Isaiah 65:2 – SP]

## Romans 11:1-32 – Paul's Hope for Israel's Future

"1 So I ask, 'Did God force his people to leave him?' Of course not. I myself am an Israelite. I am from the family of Abraham, from the tribe of Benjamin. 2 God chose the Israelites to be his people before they were born. And he did not force them to leave. Surely you know what the Scriptures say about Elijah. The Scriptures tell about Elijah praying to God against the people of Israel. He said, 3 'Lord, they have killed your prophets and destroyed your altars. I am the only prophet still living, and they are trying to kill me now' [Quote from 1 Kings 19:10, 14 - SP] 4 But what answer did God give to Elijah? God said, 'I have kept for myself seven thousand men who have never given worship to Baal' [Quote from 1 Kings 19:18 – SP].

"5 It is the same now. **God has chosen a few people by his grace. 6 And if he chose them by grace, then it is not what they have done that made them his people** [emphasis mine, SP]. If they could be made his people by what they did, his gift of grace would not really be a gift.

"7 So this is what has happened: The people of Israel wanted God's blessing, but they did not all get it. The people he chose did get his blessing, but the others became hard and refused to listen to him. 8 As the Scriptures say,

'God caused the people to fall asleep.'
'God closed their eyes so that they could not see,
and he closed their ears so that they could not hear.
This continues until now.'
"9 And David says,

'Let those people be caught and trapped at their own feasts.
Let them fall and be punished.
10 Let their eyes be closed so that they cannot see.
And let them be troubled forever.'

"11 So I ask: When the Jews fell, did that fall destroy them? No! But their mistake brought salvation to those who are not Jews. The purpose of this was to make the Jews jealous. 12 Their mistake brought rich blessings to the world. And what they lost brought rich blessings to the non-Jewish people. So surely the world will get much richer blessings when enough Jews become the kind of people God wants.

"13 Now I am speaking to you people who are not Jews. I am an apostle to the non-Jewish people. So while I have that work, I will do the best I can. 14 I hope I can make my own people jealous. That way, maybe I can help some of them to be saved. 15 God turned away from the Jews. When that happened, he became friends with the other people in the world. So when he accepts the Jews, it will be like bringing people to life after death. 16 If the first piece of bread is offered to God, then the whole loaf is made holy. If the roots of a tree are holy, the tree's branches are holy too.

"17 It is as if some of the branches from an olive tree have been broken off, and the branch of a wild olive tree has been joined to that first tree. If you are not a Jew, you are the same as that wild branch, and you now share the strength and life of the first tree. 18 But don't act as if you are better than those branches that were broken off. You have no reason to be proud of yourself, because you don't give life to the root. The root gives life to you. 19 You might say, 'Branches were broken off so that I could be joined to their tree.' 20 That is true. But those branches were broken off because they did not believe. And you continue to be part of the tree only because you believe. Don't be proud, but be afraid. 21 If God did not let the natural branches of that tree stay, he will not let you stay if you stop believing.

"22 So you see that God is kind, but he can also be very strict. He punishes those who stop following him. But he is kind to you, if you continue trusting in his kindness. If you don't continue depending on him, you will be cut off from the tree. 23 **And if the Jews will believe in God again, he will accept them back. He is able to put them back where they were** [emphasis mine, SP]. 24 It is not natural for a wild branch to become part of a good tree. But you non-Jewish people are like a branch cut from a wild olive tree. And you were joined to a good olive tree. But those Jews are like a branch that grew from the good tree. So surely they can be joined to their own tree again.

"25 I want you to understand this secret truth, brothers and sisters. This truth will help you understand that you don't know everything. The truth is this: Part of Israel has been made stubborn, but that will change when enough non-Jewish people have come to God. 26 And that is how all Israel will be saved. The Scriptures say,

"The Savior will come from Zion;
he will take away all evil from the family of Jacob.
27 And I will make this agreement with those people
when I take away their sins."

"28 The Jews refuse to accept the Good News, so they are God's enemies. This has happened to help you who are not Jews. But they are still God's chosen people, and he loves them because of the promises he made to their ancestors. 29 God never changes his mind about the people he calls. He never decides to take back the blessings he has given them. 30 At one time you refused to obey God. But now you have received mercy, because the Jews refused to obey. 31 And now they are the ones who refuse to obey, because God showed mercy to you. But this happened so that they can also receive mercy from him. 32 All people have refused to obey God. And he has put them all together as people who don't obey him so that he can show mercy to everyone.

"33 Yes, God's riches are very great! His wisdom and knowledge have no end! No one can explain what God decides. No one can understand his ways. 34 As the Scriptures say,

"Who can know what is on the Lord's mind?
Who is able to give him advice?"
35 "Who has ever given God anything?
God owes nothing to anyone."

"36 Yes, God made all things. And everything continues through him and for him.
To God be the glory forever! Amen."

The Jews in the above account are symbolically described as "natural branches" on God's tree of life. That tree really stands for the Messiah, Jesus the Christ. They had Moses and the Law and the prophets as the "roots" of their spiritual heritage. All the advantages were theirs. But most of them sinned and rebelled and lost that advantage

71

for a time. Their branch was broken off, signifying separation from fellowship with God.

During that time, God chose used his sovereign power to graft a "wild branch" – the non-Jews ("Gentiles") – into his tree. For these precious believers, their path to Christ was different. They did not live the Jewish culture. Most never set foot into a synagogue or the Temple. They certainly never studied the Law under any of the leading rabbi's. In other words, these non-Jews – including most of us reading these words – did not find Jesus Christ by being "baptized" into Moses or the Law.

In the first few sentences of The Gospel of John, the apostle John described how the Son of God became human and walked among men. He also mentions the basis of the relationship between Jesus and his disciples. **They were accepted by him on the basis of their faith in him as the Messiah**. Here is his statement in John 1:10-17:

> "10 He was in the world,
> and the world was created through Him,
> yet the world did not recognize Him.
> 11 He came to His own, and His own people
> did not receive Him.
> 12 But ***to all who did receive Him,***
> ***He gave them the right to be children of God,***
> ***to those who believe in His name,*** [emphasis mine – SP]
> 13 who were born, not of blood, or of the will of the flesh,
> or of the will of man, but of God.
> "14 The Word became flesh and took up residence among us.
> We observed His glory, the glory as the One and Only Son
> from the Father, full of grace and truth.
> 15 (John testified concerning Him and exclaimed,
> 'This was the One of whom I said,
> 'The One coming after me has surpassed me,
> because He existed before me.')
> 16 Indeed, **we have all received grace after grace**
> **from His fullness, 17 for the law was given**
> **through Moses, grace and truth came**
> **through Jesus Christ** [emphasis mine, SP]."
> (**The Holman Christian Study Bible**)

You see, friends, the Jewish people in the first century were trapped in that **performance-based** brand of religion. They knew they were sinking in deep doo-doo. So they longed for the appearance of the Messiah their prophets had said would take over and make things right. That Messiah would come in due time. And he would shake-up the world with his good news.

The late William Barclay (1907-1978) in his excellent commentary, **The Letter to the Hebrews**, describes the dilemma of the Jews and the solution for it in this words:

"What men needed was a **perfect priest** and a **perfect sacrifice**, someone who was such that he could bring to God a sacrifice which once and for all opened the way of access to him. That, said the writer to the Hebrews, is exactly what Christ did. He is the perfect priest because he is at once perfectly man and perfectly God. In his manhood he can take man to God in his Godhead he can take God to man. He has no sin. The perfect sacrifice he brings is the sacrifice of himself, a sacrifice so perfect that it never needs to be made again. To the Jew the writer to the Hebrews said: 'All your lives you have been looking for the perfect priest who can bring the perfect sacrifice and give you access to God. You have him in Jesus Christ and in him alone.'

"To the Greek the writer to the Hebrews said: 'You are looking for the way from the shadows to reality; you will find it in Jesus Christ.' To the Jew the writer to the Hebrews said: 'You are looking for that perfect sacrifice which will open the way to God which your sins have closed; you will find it in Jesus Christ.' Jesus was the one person who gave access to reality and access to God. That is the key thought of this letter" (pp. 4-5; Fair Use Domain).

# Chapter 5

## Progressive Revelation:
## God as Revealed by Jesus

**-- 4 --**

*God made the final revelation of himself through the life and teachings of Jesus and other selected people from about 5 B.C. to 100 A.D. Those concepts were collected into the documents that make up the "New Testament" section of our Bible.*

Graphic created by Stan Puregien Sr on Dec 15, 2020

This message was directed first to the nation of Israel. When most rejected it, God also made it available to everyone else. And it is still offered as a free gift to all who chose to understand, even to you and to me.

The writer of the book of Hebrews testified that it is Jesus, alone, who "expresses the very character of God":

"1 Long ago God spoke many times and in many ways to our ancestors through the prophets. 2 And now in these final days, he has spoken to us through his Son. God promised everything to the Son as an inheritance, and through the Son he created the universe. 3 The Son radiates God's own glory and expresses the very character of God, and he sustains everything by the mighty power of his command. When he had cleansed us from our sins, he sat down in the place of honor at the right hand of the majestic God in heaven" (Hebrews 1:1-3. **New Living Translation** – NLT).

In about 4 B.C., the Messiah finally came to the people of Israel. A child was born to a young woman named Mary who was living temporarily in Bethlehem. They called him Jesus and he was reared in the village of Nazareth. When God's timing was right, John the Baptist (a cousin to Jesus), went about the countryside telling everyone who would listen that the longed-for Messiah was coming soon. In addition, he rebuked people for their sins and called upon them to change their ways and be baptized.

One day, near the end of the life of John the Baptist, Jesus showed up among the crowd on the banks of the Jordan River. That very day Jesus humbly submitted to being baptized by John. And the voice of Jehovah God boomed out from heaven his pleasure in the Son of God. His baptism was a spiritual anointment and certification by God that he was the longed-for Messiah. It also served as an announcement of his public ministry that would last about three years.

**NOTE**: Please understand that the baptism of Jesus was totally different than Christian baptism which began being practiced about three years later. His baptism was even different from what John the Baptist performed on many people. **In the case of the baptism of Jesus, it was vitally different because neither repentance nor forgiveness of sins was a part of it**. After all, Jesus had never sinned and never would. Therefore, he had nothing to repent of nor any sin to be forgiven.

When Jesus was about 30 years of age, he began a life as a wandering teacher and preacher. His bold message was shocking to most listeners for he told them he was the Messiah (or Christ), the Savior of Israel of which the prophets spoke and for which the Jews still longed to see. It soon became apparent, because of the miracles he performed, this was no ordinary man.

Eventually, after about three years, the Jewish clerics, and authorities tired of his exposing their hypocrisy and corruption. Their own temple guards arrested Jesus in the middle of the night. They beat him unmercifully and used whips with bits of bone embedded in the lashes to make hamburger meat of his back. Then they handed him over to the Roman government for them to actually execute him. They falsely charged he was claiming to be God in the flesh, a claim which infuriated the Jewish leaders and which they knew would not sit well with the Romans. After all, it was their own ruler in Rome, Italy who claimed to be a god.

The Romans nailed Jesus to a cross and taunted him while he was slowly dying. Then a Roman soldier jammed his spear into his side, spilling the blood of Jesus down his dead body and onto the ground.

On the third day after his death, early on a Sunday morning, Jehovah God raised his Son from the dead. And he removed the heavy stone covering the entrance to the tomb. Jesus left the cave-like tomb and went on his way.

Shortly after his resurrection, two female disciples of Jesus walked up to the tomb. From a distance, they starred in shock that the stone door had been moved aside. Mary approached the tomb first. And as she got close angels appeared gave her the wonderful news that he was not there, that Jesus had been raised from the dead and had walked away from his grave.

Later, Jesus appeared to his inner core of followers. He showed them the spike punctures in his hands and feet. And he went to a house and had a meal with them. He carefully explained that he was leaving them to return to his father in heaven. He gave them instructions to stay in Jerusalem until they were given "power from on high." They had no clue exactly what that meant. But they clearly understood the command to stay in Jerusalem until something very unusual happened to them. And they took him at his word and obeyed him.

A few days later, early in the evening, some 120 of the disciples of Christ were gathered together in a house in Jerusalem. That included the apostles (minus Judas Iscariot; but with his replacement, Matthias) and probably their wives.

These devout followers of Christ received their notice to sit up and pay attention. Jesus had commanded them to stay in Jerusalem until they received power from heaven. That happened in a dramatic way which would be recognized by all:

"Suddenly a sound like that of a violent rushing wind came from heaven, and it filled the whole house where they were staying. They saw tongues like flames of fire that separated and rested on each one of them. Then they were all filled with the Holy Spirit and began to speak in different tongues, as the Spirit enabled them" (Acts 2:2-4; **Holman Christian Study Bible** - HCSB).

This was not a case of that wind-like event softly sounding like a barely noticeable morning breeze drifting from the mountains over to the Mediterranean Sea. No, it was sounded something like thirty Roman chariots rushing down their cobblestone street or something like a powerful thunderstorm. It sounded more like a powerful, sweeping wind sure to make a person have a bad hair day if they were out in it. But they were not out in it; no, it came to them. Whatever it was, it filled the entire house.

In addition to a unique sound, there was a unique sight. The 120 disciples gathered there saw with their own eyes saw something like a bundle of dancing, flicking tongues of fire. That one mass of flame in one instant fractured into 120 different flame-looking items and rested on each and every person.

It was a special presence of the Holy Spirit displayed in two human senses, sound and sight. Of course, God himself had assumed the vision of flames on several occasions (Genesis 15:17; Exodus 3:2-6; 13:21-22; 19:18; 40:28; and Matthew 3:11; and Luke 3:16).

This "filling" of the Spirit may happen for a particular Christian on just one occasion or on many occasions, usually after that person's testimonial baptism (see Acts 4:8, 31; 6:3, 5; 7:55; 9:17; 13:9, 52).

This Spirit-given ability to speak with other tongues is a seldom-bestowed gift. This does not appear to be **glossolalia** (speaking in totally unintelligible syllables), as sometimes seen in the speech of people with mental health issues such as schizophrenia. The evidence points to this being a case of the Spirit enabling these Christians to each speak one or more of the standard, known and living foreign languages being spoken by the visitors from other countries to the Pentecost celebration. This explanation fits the purpose of the gift, which was to enable all of the Pentecost crowd to hear the testimony of the apostles.

The next morning, they awoke early on the feast day for the Day of Pentecost (also called the Festival of Weeks). This holy feast day came on the heels of the Feast of First Fruits celebrated exactly 49 days earlier (7 weeks X 7).

Until I read this passage, again, this time around, I had never noticed that the testimony of the apostles (and probably others) was actually divided into two parts. **Part 1** was a time of simply praising God for his wonderful acts of kindness. That is never a bad way to start off any gathering of his people. The apostles, probably assisted by the remainder of the 120 disciples, went out to the public area of the temple and scattered to different areas of it to talk to people. They had no mega-watt sound systems back then where just one person could speak to thousands.

After some undefined period passed, Peter took to the main stage. He focused the attention of everyone there on **Part 2** of why they had spread out to talk with their Jewish brethren.

By the way, these listeners were the most dedicated of the dedicated. Many of them had traveled many hard miles to get there, from Rome, Italy all the way along the eastern Mediterranean Sea to Jerusalem. Others came from the southwest, from as far away as Libya (just west of Egypt) in north Africa. None of them traveled on company credit cards and not one of them got any reward points for their mileage. They were there to honor God and to please him.

**First Gospel Sermon**

Peter and the other apostles and disciples began to preach the good news (i.e., the gospel account) of the coming of the Messiah. They persuasively told how he had walked and taught among them. But rather than receiving the great Messiah of Israel, the Jewish authorities had captured Jesus the Christ and severely abused him. Then, with hundreds of them chanting their hatred of Jesus, the leaders of the Sanhedrin turned him over to the Romans to be killed.

Peter and his friends told how the sinless Messiah had fulfilled all of the ancient prophecies about him. He had taught them the truth about God and his love for them. And he had voluntarily died a sacrificial death on that Roman cross, though he could have called upon his heavenly father to stop the torture. They said the redeeming blood of Jesus, the Son of God and God-in-the-flesh, gushed from his body because of them and for them as an offering of peace and atonement to Jehovah God.

The mass of Jewish listeners that day were stunned. They believed what the apostles had just said, and now they were 100% sure that this Jesus of Nazareth had been the Messiah for which they had hoped. They were deeply ashamed of their participation – vicariously or literally - in that miscarriage of justice. So the crowd, anguished with guilt, loudly pled for help.

Peter quieted the large crowd of Jewish men and told them what their only hope was to escape God's wrath. Please note he did not give them any of these false options:

(1) Put your faith in Buddha.

(2) Or put your faith in Allah, the god of the Muslim people

(3) Or think about the teachings of Confucius and meditate your way to salvation.

(4) Or consult your horoscope for further advice.

(5) Or plead that you are an agnostic and, therefore, clueless.

(6) Or put your faith in human philosophy and Humanism.

(7) Or try Yoga or Zen to will yourself into Paradise.

(8) Or put your faith in your ability to impress God by your accumulated spiritual knowledge (what you know) or by your perfectionist performances (what you do).

Hey, give us a break. Peter did not dish out any of those things. That's because there are no options, no Plan B. There is **one great, big truth** that he put on the giant screen:

**The one and only way to salvation<br>is by believing in Jesus as both<br>Lord and the son of God.**

What follows is not only what Paul and the other believers taught on that wonderful Day of Pentecost and birthday of the Christian Church, but also the consistent message taught throughout the New Testament. So please read it carefully.

"Each one of you must turn away from your sins and be baptized in the name of Jesus Christ, so that your sins will be forgiven, and you will receive God's gift, the Holy Spirit. For God's promise was made to you and your children, and to all who are far away – all whom the Lord our God calls to himself.

"Peter made his appeal to them and with many other words he urged them, saying, 'Save yourselves from the punishment coming on this wicked people.' Many of them believed the message and were baptized, and about three thousand people were added to the group that day. They spent their time in learning from the apostles, taking part in the fellowship, and sharing in the fellowship meals and the prayers" (Acts 2:38-42; **Good News Bible: Today's English Version**).

Oh, boy. Wouldn't you love to have been in that early group of Christians? Just imagine all the bear-hugs, kisses, handshakes, and shouts of hallelujah. At first, the converts were strictly men from Jewish backgrounds. But with the dynamic spread of the gospel, they soon welcomed women and non-Jewish people (often just called Greeks). Today, there is not a nation on our earth where the gospel has not gone and where there are not Christians living.

Pretty amazing stuff.

No wonder that the apostle Paul wrote to the body of Christ in the city of Rome and declared this: "I am proud of the Good News. The Good News is the power God uses to save every person that believes -- to save the Jews first, and also to save the non-Jews. The Good news shows how God makes people right with himself. God's way of making people right begins and ends with faith. Like the Scripture says, 'The person that is right with God by faith will live forever'" (**Holy Bible: Easy-to-Read Version**).

Here is a question which is super important to answer correctly:

**What are the elements that make up the gospel of Jesus Christ?**

I believe it is all about the cross and the blood of Christ, and that is certainly fundamental to understanding the "power" which draws or calls people to the Lord. The gospel also includes his status as the Son of God, as the crucified Messiah (or Christ), as the blood offering was a one-time sacrifice of atonement for our sins, and as the resurrected Lord and King who now reigns at the right hand of his heavenly father. He is just awaiting the appointed time for his return to earth and a final Judgment Day. Upon hearing that testimony and accepting it with total trust and faith, a person then is saved. He confesses that faith in Christ, repents of his past sins and commits spending his life pleasing God as much as he knows how. That normally includes being baptized soon as a testimony to and a symbol of his life changing faith-experience.

That's pretty much it.

You do not have to have a university degree in theology to understand the gospel and to share it with others. You do not have to have a high school diploma to understand the gospel and to respond to it with faith and obedience. You certainly do not have to be the legal age of 21 before you can read, understand, and obey the gospel by accepting God's unmerited gift of salvation and eternal life.

It just ain't that hard.

Well, that is how I would describe the gospel or Good News of Jesus. It is always better, though, to read it from the New Testament. The apostle Paul worked a long time in the city of Corinth, Greece as a tentmaker to support himself while he talked with everyone he met about Jesus. After he left the group of Christian there, he wrote back to them and encouraged this sometimes rowdy bunch of believers with these words:

"Now I would remind you, brothers, of the gospel I preached to you, which you received, in which you stand, and by which you are being saved, if you hold fast to the word I preached to you – unless you believed in me in vain.

"For I delivered to you as of first importance what I also received: that Christ died for our sins in accordance with the Scriptures, that he was buried, that he was raised on the third day in accordance with the Scriptures, and that he appeared to Cephas, then to the twelve. Then he appeared to more than five hundred brothers at one time, most of whom are still alive, though some have fallen asleep. Then he appeared to James, then to all the apostles. Last of all, as to one untimely born, he appeared also to me" (1 Corinthians 15:1-8; **English Standard Version** - ESV).

My friends, that in a nutshell is the gospel of the Lord Jesus Christ.

It summarizes the facts and purpose of his life and the spilling of his blood on the Roman cross. The gospel always points to Jesus as Savior and his bloody death on the cross as the single act of atonement by which we are made "at-one' or "right" with Jehovah God. Nothing else was worthy and important enough to satisfied God's standard of justice. That loving sacrifice alone, apart from any works or merit on our part, is what allows God's grace to declare us his righteous children.

Our belief must focus on Jesus and his cross, for our faith is meaningless without it. That is why our repentance or turning away from our sinful ways must always be related to the gift of his life for us. That's why our confession of and praise for Jesus as our Savior and the Son of God is pointless unless it relates to the cross. And our baptism is merely a hollow ritual in which we go down into the water a dry sinner and come up as merely a wet sinner if we don't understand its relationship to the cross. It all must be related to the blood of Christ on that awful cross.

The songwriter Isaac Watts was right on target when, way back in 1707 A.D., he wrote these words:

## When I Survey the Wonderous Cross
By Isaac Watts

When I survey the wonderous cross
On which the Prince of Glory died,
My richest gain I count but loss,
And pour contempt on all my pride.

Forbid it, Lord, that I should boast,
Save in the death of Christ my God:
All the vain things that charm me most,
I sacrifice them to His blood.

See, from His head, His hands, His feet,
Sorrow and love flow mingled down.
Did e'er such love and sorrow meet,
Or thorns compose so rich a crown?

Were the whole realm of nature mine,
That were a present far too small;
Love so amazing, so divine,
Demands my soul, my life, my all.

Yes, mankind had been wallowing in sin like pigs knee-deep in slop. They were desperately in need of someone to save them from themselves and from sin. So Jehovah God, in his own perfect timing, allowed his Son to give his life as a sin-offering on a vertical altar, the cross upon which he bled and died.

There you have the four basic ways God has given people in all cultures some amount of light. Probably most of us would agree that virtually everyone has had an opportunity to see God at some level by observing the order and beauty of nature and by simply observing how people behave. Some show they lean toward self-centeredness, and cruelty, while others are much more civil and helpful toward other people.

# Chapter 6

## The Process of Salvation, Part 1:
## By Grace Through Faith

What does God require of us to be able to serve him here on earth and to live with him forever? What was the answer that those Jews in the first century received with joy and gladness?

As we review the answer to that important question, we will see examples of how people were saved in the early days of the Christian church. We will look more in depth at several scriptures related to salvation. Keep this point in mind: there are, in fact, a few differences among those verses. The differences are more apparent than they are actual or real.

Whenever we find a New Testament verse requiring a certain condition for salvation (belief, for example in John 3:16), there can never be anything **_less_** than that condition required. But—and please underline this—there may be **_even more_** conditions set down by God in other verses which would also be required. That makes sense, doesn't it?

Let's start with a look at one of the Bible's most memorized and best-known verses. It is from the Gospel of John, chapter 3 and verse 16: "For God so loved the world that He gave His only begotten Son, that whoever believes in Him should not perish but have everlasting life." (**New King James Version** - NKJV)

If one should read this verse without considering related passages elsewhere in the New Testament he might conclude all God requires for him to be saved is to believe. Right?

And if you were really a legalist you might argue faith just means intellectually accepting the factual evidence regarding the life of Jesus and his sacrificial death for us. Yes, Jesus was born in Bethlehem. True, Jesus performed miracles. Sure, Jesus was a great teacher. And, yes, he fulfilled the prophecies made about the Messiah hundreds of years before. Right?

Wrong.

There is more to the process of salvation than both faith (or belief) in Jesus and an intellectual acceptance of the facts of his life and ministry.

## Love Is Superior to Logic

I saw a cartoon in our newspaper the other day which makes a good point about this logic business. That "Marvin" cartoon shows the little kid paralyzed with fear at the top of a slide. He cried out, "H-E-E-E-L-P! Somebody help me!!" Up walked a nerdy little kid with glasses and said, "What seems to be the problem, Marvin?"

Poor frightened Marvin replied, "I climbed up here, Warren, but I'm afraid of heights!" And his brainy pal Warren observes, "Well that wasn't a very smart thing to do." And this time Marvin loudly cries out, "Help from somebody who isn't an intellectual know-it-all!"

The trouble with majoring in deductive reasoning and minoring in syllogisms is that, if one is not very careful, it leads to spirit-choking arrogance ("I know what you don't; therefore, I'm a better Christian.") and exclusivity ("You are in error on x-number of doctrines, therefore I cannot have anything to do with you.").

My particular faith-heritage group has a long history of appreciation for philosopher **John Locke's** writings on logical reasoning. Two Presbyterian preachers, **Alexander Campbell** and **Barton W. Stone**, each left that heritage for what they first perceived as the more open and non-sectarian Baptist fellowship. These men were reformers or, more accurately, restorationists. They wanted to escape the maze of denominational creeds and divisions by leading people of all sects to renounce them and practice simple Christianity as Christians only (but not the only Christians – a big difference). The idea was to go forward together by going back to the basics of simple Christianity.

Alexander Campbell had a large following of people who liked his cut-and-dried logical mind, while Barton W. Stone's large number of folks liked his more emotional and charismatic leadership. Still, they loved each other as brothers in Christ because they agreed on the essentials of the gospel and practicing unity in diversity when it came to doctrine. By doing so, they were able to merge their efforts to restore simple Christianity as the norm.

> *With simple Christianity, the way forward is to go back to basics and to abandon churchianity.*
>
> *-- Stan Paregien Sr.*
>
> Graphic created by Stan Paregien Sr on Dec 15, 2020

In the end, people need the Good News and the leading of the Holy Spirit, not a lecture on the finer points of Biblical interpretation.

Christianity is, at its core, a matter of one's heart or attitude. In other words, our love for God is the underlying foundation of faith and whatever comes next. Long ago Moses instructed his brothers and sisters about the importance of obeying God out of love, not out of a reluctant sense of obligation. He said: "Listen, people of Israel! The Lord is our God. He is the only Lord. Love the Lord your God with all your heart, soul and strength" (Deuteronomy 6:4-5).

As Jesus went about teaching in his own days, some religious scholars (called Pharisees) were out to trick and shame him by asking hard questions. One of the toughest was, "Which command in God's Law is the most important?"

Rather than using his own words, Jesus answered by quoting their own scriptures. He replied, "'Love the Lord your God with all your passion and prayer and intelligence.' This is the most important, the first on any list. But there is a second to set alongside it: 'Love others as well as you love yourself.' These two commands are pegs; everything in God's Law and the Prophets hangs from them" (Matthew 22:34-40; **The Message**).

A few years after Jesus had ascended back to heaven, the apostle Paul echoed the Old Testament words and those of Jesus regarding the superiority of love over works and logic. In Romans 12:9-10, this former Jewish terrorist wrote: "9 Your love must be real. Hate the things that are evil. Do only the things that are good. 10 Love each other in a way you feel close to each other like brothers and sisters. You should want to give your brothers and sisters more honor than you want for yourself."

A few verses later, Paul said in Romans 13:8-10: "8 You should owe nothing to anyone, except that you will always owe love to each other. The person who loves others has done all that the law [of Moses – SP] commands. 9 The law says, 'You must not commit adultery, you must not murder anyone, you must not steal, you must not want what belongs to someone else' [Quote from Exodus 20:13-15, 17 - SP]. All these commands and all other commands are really only one rule: 'Love your neighbor the same as you love yourself."[Quote from Leviticus 19:18 – SP]. 10 Love doesn't hurt others. So loving is the same as obeying all the law."

Coloring by Peggy Paregien
Bradenton, FL - Sept., 2020

Wow. God's grace working through our faith in Christ's sacrifice on the cross. That fills our hearts with love. Then, that motivates us to love God in return, and to mirror the life of Jesus by loving others and doing good because we are saved (not to earn brownie points).

Paul had led the effort to evangelize the non-Jews in the area of the Roman province of Galatia. He had established several congregations in that area. Later, there were some legalistic Messianic Jews who came along and upset their thinking with the idea that to be fully Christian one must observe key parts of the Law of Moses. They argued it was necessary for them to perform the Jewish ceremony of circumcision on all adult males and on male babies on the 8th day of their lives. They wanted them to go back to religiously observing certain feast days and ritual cleansing.

All this was not merely a gesture of appreciation for the Jewish culture. It was, in fact, an effort to slide back into the mode of **law-keeping as a way of winning points with God**. The whole business was leading to bickering and heated arguments within the Christian family in that area.

The apostle Paul – himself raised as a strict Pharisee -- threw buckets of cold water on those flickering flames of false doctrinal teaching. He was as plain and as firm as possible, as shown in Galatians 5:1-17:

"1 Christ has liberated us to be free. Stand firm then and don't submit again to a yoke of slavery. 2 Take note! I, Paul, tell you that if you get yourselves circumcised, Christ will not benefit you at all. 3 Again I testify to every man who gets himself circumcised that he is obligated to keep the entire law. 4 You who are trying to be justified by the law are alienated from Christ; you have fallen from grace. 5 For through the Spirit, by faith, we eagerly wait for the hope of righteousness. 6 For in Christ Jesus neither circumcision nor uncircumcision accomplishes anything; **what matters is faith working through love** [emphasis mine, SP].

"7 You were running well. Who prevented you from obeying the truth? 8 This persuasion did not come from the One who called you. 9 A little yeast leavens the whole lump of dough. 10 I have confidence in the Lord you will not accept any other view. But whoever it is that is confusing you will pay the penalty. 11 Now brothers, if I still preach circumcision, why am I still persecuted? In that case the offense of the cross has been abolished. 12 I wish those who are disturbing you might also get themselves castrated!

"13 For you were called to be free, brothers; only don't use this freedom as an opportunity for the flesh, but serve one another through love. 14 For the entire law is fulfilled in one statement: Love your neighbor as yourself. 15 But if you bite and devour one another, watch out, or you will be consumed by one another.

"16 I say then, walk by the Spirit and you will not carry out the desire of the flesh. 17 For the flesh desires what is against the Spirit, and the Spirit desires what is against the flesh; these are opposed to each other, so that you don't do what you want. 18 But if you are led by the Spirit, you are not under the law" (**The Holman Christian Study Bible**).

## Don't Miss This
## Important Concept

**Paul's point is this: The person who abandons the New Covenant of salvation by grace through faith and reverts to practicing the Old Covenant and the endless rules and regulations which flowed from it is making a terrible mistake. If a Jew broke one part of the law, he was guilty of trampling and violating all of it. Then he had to make repeated sacrifices at the Temple. And the depressing, never-ending circle continued.**

**However, Paul shows how the free grace of God is constantly poured out to cover the sins of Christians who hold to their faith in the work (sacrifice) of Jesus for them. And because they boast about God's love, rather than their own imperfect religious performance, they prove their love for God and others.**

**Loving faith, completely apart from any works or law-keeping, fulfills both the heart and spirit of the Old Covenant under Moses and the identical heart and spirit of the New Covenant under Jesus.**

So, yes, faith in Jesus would be required of everyone seeking to walk with God. And people who lived in Old Testament times, those who lived in New Testaments and we today must be motivated to come to him because of both faith (deep trust) and love. These are mandatory, not optional, conditions for God to extend his grace and mercy. And under God's will for us today there are other conditions as well, none of which are to be seen in any way as a "work" of ours that would obligate God to save us.

Just to be sure we do not miss it. We are saved by grace through faith, not by earning reward points by our impeccable behavior or a boatload of good deeds. It just does not work that way.

**Hear ye, hear ye!**

Please pay attention to Paul's clear and powerful statement of how we arrive at salvation. This man ought to know. He was reared as a holiness Jew – my way of saying he was a member-in-good-standing of the party of Pharisees. To get into this exclusive Club, you had to prove you know the Law of Moses backward and forward, and you had to at least pretend like you never sinned like all those other normal folks.

Well, listen to Paul from **Romans 3:21-31** because this is the way God planned it from the beginning of time.

"21 God has a way to make people right without the law. And God has now shown us that new way. The law and the prophets told us about this new way. 22 God makes people right through their faith in Jesus Christ. God does this for all people that believe in Christ. All people are the same. 23 All people have sinned and are not good enough for God's glory. 24 People are made right with God by his grace (kindness). This is a free gift. People are made right with God by being made free from sin through Jesus Christ. 25 God gave Jesus as a way to forgive people's sins through faith. God forgives by the blood (death) of Jesus. God gave Jesus to show that he always does what is right and fair. God was right in the past when he was patient and did not punish people for their sins. 26 And God gave Jesus to show today that God does what is right. God did this so that he could judge rightly and also make right any person that has faith in Jesus."

There we have that foundational truth, again: **<u>Our loving God judges people by how they respond to the light (truth) they have been given. God is always is just and does what is right.</u>**

### Romans 3:27-31 - The faith-way stops all boasting

"27 So do we have a reason to boast about ourselves? No! And why not? It is the way of faith that stops all boasting, not the way of following the law. 28 Why? Because a person is made right with God through faith, not through the things he has done to follow the law. This is what we believe. 29 God is not only the God of the Jews. He is also the God of the non-Jews. 30 **There is only one God. He will make Jews right**

**with him by their faith. And he will also make non-Jews right with him through their faith. 31 So do we destroy the law by following the way of faith? No! Faith causes us to be what the law truly wants** [emphasis mine, SP]."

## Romans 4:1-25 – Abraham made right with God by faith

[NOTE: God had a unique relationship with a man named Abram ("father is exalted"). God told him to leave the Ur of Chaldees, where he was a wealthy and respected man, and to move far off to Canaan. God promised to make of Abram's descendants a "great nation." When the man believed him, God changed his name to **Abraham** ('father of a multitude'). Years passed and God reassured Abraham that the promise would come, and **circumcision** (when the foreskin of a baby boy's penis is cut off 8 days after birth) a sign of that special agreement made a special covenant (see Genesis 17:1-21). That promise was kept when Abraham was 100 years old, and that baby was named **Isaac**. Years later, God tested the depth of Abraham's faith, again. This time he told Abraham to take Isaac up to a mountain and to sacrifice his beloved Isaac on an altar. He took the boy there and was preparing the altar when God provided an alternate sacrifice, a goat. His faith got him through. He became known as "**the father of the faithful**." Religious Jews even today speak with awe of "**Father Abraham**" to indicate their connection to this man with a king-sized faith in God. – Stan Paregien ]

"1 So what can we say about Abraham, the father of our people? What did he learn about faith? 2 If Abraham was made right by the things he did, he had a reason to boast about himself. But God knew different. 3 That's why the Scriptures say, 'Abraham believed God, and because of this he was accepted as one who is right with God.' [Quote from Genesis 15:6 – SP]

"4 **When people work, their pay is not given to them as a gift. They earn the pay they get. 5 But people cannot do any work that will make them right with God. So they must trust in him. Then he accepts their faith, and that makes them right with him [Emphasis mine, SP].** He is the one who makes even evil people right. 6 David said the same thing when he was talking about the blessing people have when God accepts them as good without looking at what they have done:

7 'It is a great blessing
when people are forgiven for the wrongs they have done,
when their sins are erased!
8 'It is a great blessing when the Lord accepts people

91

as if they are without sin!'
[Quote from Psalm 32:1-2 – SP]

"9 Is this blessing only for those who are circumcised? Or is it also for those who are not circumcised? We have already said that it was because of Abraham's faith that he was accepted as one who is right with God. 10 So how did this happen? Did God accept Abraham before or after he was circumcised? God accepted him before his circumcision. 11 Abraham was circumcised later to show that God accepted him. His circumcision was proof that he was right with God through faith before he was circumcised. So Abraham is the father of all those who believe but are not circumcised. They believe and are accepted as people who are right with God. 12 And Abraham is also the father of those who have been circumcised. But it is not their circumcision that makes him their father. He is their father only if they live following the faith that our father Abraham had before he was circumcised.

"13 Abraham and his descendants received the promise that they would get the whole world. But Abraham did not receive that promise because he followed the law. He received that promise because he was right with God through his faith. 14 If people could get God's promise by following the law, then faith is worthless. And God's promise to Abraham is worthless, 15 because the law can only bring God's anger on those who disobey it. But if there is no law, then there is nothing to disobey.

"16 So people get what God promised by having faith. This happens so that the promise can be a free gift. And if the promise is a free gift, then all of Abraham's people will get that promise. The promise is not just for those who live under the Law of Moses. It is for all who live with faith as Abraham did. He is the father of us all. 17 As the Scriptures say, 'I have made you a father of many nations' [Quote from Genesis 17:5 – SP]. This is true before God, the one Abraham believed—the God who gives life to the dead and speaks of things that don't yet exist as if they are real.

"18 There was no hope that Abraham would have children, but Abraham believed God and continued to hope. And that is why he became the father of many nations. As God told him, 'You will have many descendants' [Quote from Genesis 15:5]. 19 Abraham was almost a hundred years old, so he was past the age for having children. Also, Sarah could not have children. Abraham was well aware of this, but his faith in God never became weak. 20 He never doubted that God would do what he promised. He never stopped believing. In fact, he grew stronger in his faith and just praised God. 21 Abraham felt sure that God was able to do what he promised. 22 So that's why 'he was accepted as one who is right with God'[Quote from Genesis 15:6]. 23 These words ('he was accepted') were written not only for Abraham. 24 They were also written for us. God will also accept us because we believe. **We believe in the one who raised Jesus our Lord from death. 25 Jesus was handed over to die for our sins, and he was raised from death to make us right with God** [emphasis mine, SP]."

## Romans 5:1-11 – We are now God's friends

"5 **We have been made right with God because of our faith. So we have peace with God through our Lord Jesus Christ. 2 Through our faith, Christ has brought us into that blessing of God's grace that we now enjoy** [emphasis mine, SP]. And we are very happy because of the hope we have of sharing God's glory. 3 And we are also happy with the troubles we have. Why are we happy with troubles? Because we know that these troubles make us be more patient. 4 And this patience is proof that we are strong. And this proof gives us hope. 5 And this hope will never disappoint us. We know this because God has poured out his love to fill our hearts through the Holy Spirit he gave us.

"6 Christ died for us when we were unable to help ourselves. We were living against God, but at just the right time Christ died for us. 7 Very few people will die to save the life of someone else, even if it is for a good person. Someone might be willing to die for an especially good person. 8 But Christ died for us while we were still sinners, and by this God showed how much he loves us.

"9 We have been made right with God by the blood sacrifice of Christ. So through Christ we will surely be saved from God's anger. 10 I mean that while we were God's enemies, he made friends with us through his Son's death. And the fact that we are now God's friends makes it even more certain that he will save us through his Son's life. 11 And not only will we be saved, but **we also rejoice right now in what God has done for us through our Lord Jesus Christ. It is because of Jesus that we are now God's friends** [emphasis mine, SP]."

Well, as farmers say, "It is time to shell the corn and show the cob." They mean it is time to get serious and down to the facts.

There was a time for each of us when we were an enemy of God. We were living only for ourselves and insisting on doing life our way. But when we were led by the Holy Spirit to a loving faith that Jesus is Lord and we embraced his voluntary sacrifice of his sinless human life for our salvation, our status changed in an instant. He took upon himself our sins and God himself declared us forgiven, righteous and saved. In addition, we were named **friends of God**.

## A Change of Status
## By Grace Through Faith

This faith-experience is similar in type to that which the Israelites had in the wilderness. We are reminded that the Jews wandering in the wilderness, centuries before us, underwent a spiritual baptism (I Corinthians 10:1-4). They were said to have been baptized unto Moses in the Red Sea and in the cloudy pillar which guided them by day (1 Cor. 10:2). They did not all physically go down into some creek or river and get dipped. But they were encouraged in their walk and their faith in Moses was strengthened.

Those wandering Jews, it is said, had a special relationship with none other than Christ himself. They experienced a symbolic baptism in the desert. And they feasted on spiritual food and drink provided for them by their real rock, the Christ.

Those people had placed their faith and trust in Moses. They were sort of joined at the hip with Moses. They often pledged their lives and resources to him as long as they lived. They considered themselves consecrated (or set apart) as his people.

In turn, Moses led them out of Egypt, through the Red Sea, and at Mt. Sinai delivered the Ten Commandments to them. And it was Moses himself in Deuteronomy 18:15 who endorsed the Messiah who was to come. Much later, in the First Century, the apostle Peter was preaching the gospel of Jesus to the Jews gathered in Solomon's colonnade in the Temple and quoted Moses in relation to Jesus (Acts 3:22).

There was, then, a transition of great importance when the people of Israel were hoping and looking for this Messiah predicted by the Law and the prophets. They should have easily shifted their faith and pledges from Moses to the Messiah, making them become sort of "naturalized citizens" under the New Covenant. They, Paul wrote, were natural branches in God's olive tree of righteousness – i.e., in Christ himself.

They did not need to be "grafted in" as was the situation with non-Jews. Where they had once followed Moses and the old covenant, they would change to following Jesus and his new covenant.

In 2 Corinthians 3:6-18, Paul describes the differences between the Old Covenant under Moses and the New Covenant under Jesus:

"6 He [God- SP] has made us competent to be ministers of a new covenant, not of the letter, but of the Spirit. For the letter kills, but the Spirit produces life.

"7 Now if the ministry of death, chiseled in letters on stones, came with glory, so that the Israelites were not able to look directly at Moses' face because of the glory from his face—a fading glory— 8 how will the ministry of the Spirit not be more glorious? 9 For if the ministry of condemnation had glory, the ministry of righteousness overflows with even more glory. 10 In fact, what had been glorious is not glorious now by comparison because of the glory that surpasses it. 11 For if what was fading away was glorious, what endures will be even more glorious.

"12 Therefore, having such a hope, we use great boldness. 13 We are not like Moses, who used to put a veil over his face so that the Israelites could not stare at the end of what was fading away, 14 but their minds were closed. For to this day, at the reading of the old covenant, the same veil remains; it is not lifted, because it is set aside only in Christ. 15 Even to this day, whenever Moses is read, a veil lies over their hearts, 16 but whenever a person turns to the Lord, the veil is removed. 17 Now the Lord is the Spirit, and where the Spirit of the Lord is, there is freedom. 18 We all, with unveiled faces, are looking as in a mirror at the glory of the Lord and are being transformed into the same image from glory to glory; this is from the Lord who is the Spirit" (**The Holman Christian Study Bible**).

God and the Holy Spirit call the unbeliever to walk by faith. After a person has been gifted with a loving faith in Jesus as Lord, the Holy Spirit leads or prompts the person to made a serious commitment to God. It is a personal acceptance of one's responsibilities to yourself, to your physical family, to your spiritual family (congregation or church), and to God himself. It is also a personal consecration or dedication of one's whole being and resources.

It also includes complete acceptance of the fact you will, like the Lord Jesus Christ, go through temptations, trials, and serious sufferings. Your ultimate goal is to follow the example of Jesus in being faithful . . . even unto death. And you realize that anything you may suffer for Christ just puts you one step closer to the rewards, joys, and glories promised by him.

## 1 Timothy 2:3-13

### (**Contemporary English Version**, CEV)

"As a good soldier of Christ Jesus you must endure your share of suffering. 4 Soldiers on duty don't work at outside jobs. They try only to please their commanding officer. 5 No one wins an athletic contest without obeying the rules. 6 And farmers who work hard are the first to eat what grows in their field. 7 If you keep in mind what I have told you, the Lord will help you understand completely.

"8 Keep your mind on Jesus Christ! He was from the family of David and was raised from death, just as my good news says. 9 And because of this message, I am locked up in jail and treated like a criminal. But God's good news isn't locked in jail, 10 and so I am willing to put up with anything. Then God's special people will be saved. They will be given eternal glory because they belong to Christ Jesus. 11 Here is a true message:

'If we died with Christ, we will live with him.
12 If we don't give up, we will rule with him.
If we deny
that we know him,
he will deny
that he knows us.
13 If we are not faithful,
he will still be faithful.
Christ cannot deny
who he is.'

## Romans 8:17-19 and 28-33

### (**Good News Translation**, GNT)

"12 So then, my friends, we have an obligation, but it is not to live as our human nature wants us to. 13 For if you live according to your human nature, you are going to die; but if by the Spirit you put to death your sinful actions, you will live. 14 Those who are led by God's Spirit are God's children. 15 For the Spirit that God has given you does not make you slaves and cause you to be afraid; instead, the Spirit makes you God's children, and by the Spirit's power we cry out to God, "Father! my Father!" 16 God's Spirit joins himself to our spirits to declare that we are God's children. 17 Since we are his children, we will possess the blessings he keeps for his people, and we will also possess with Christ what God has kept for him; for if we share Christ's suffering, we will also share his glory."

"28 We know that in all things God works for good with those who love him, those whom he has called according to his purpose. 29 Those whom God had already chosen he also set apart to become like his Son, so that the Son would be the first among many believers. 30 And so those whom God set apart, he called; and those he called, he put right with himself, and he shared his glory with them.

"31 In view of all this, what can we say? If God is for us, who can be against us? 32 Certainly not God, who did not even keep back his own Son, but offered him for us all! He gave us his Son—will he not also freely give us all things? 33 Who will accuse God's chosen people? God himself declares them not guilty! 34 Who, then, will condemn them? Not Christ Jesus, who died, or rather, who was raised to life and is at the right side of God, pleading with him for us! 35 Who, then, can separate us from the love of Christ? Can trouble do it, or hardship or persecution or hunger or poverty or danger or death? 36 As the scripture says,

> 'For your sake we are in danger of death at all times;
> we are treated like sheep that are going to be slaughtered.'

"37 No, in all these things we have complete victory through him who loved us! 38 For I am certain that nothing can separate us from his love: neither death nor life, neither angels nor other heavenly rulers or powers, neither the present nor the future, 39 neither the world above nor the world below—there is nothing in all creation that will ever be able to separate us from the love of God which is ours through Christ Jesus our Lord."

## Romans 12:1-2
## (The Message, MSG)

"1-2 So here's what I want you to do, God helping you: Take your everyday, ordinary life—your sleeping, eating, going-to-work, and walking-around life—and place it before God as an offering. Embracing what God does for you is the best thing you can do for him. Don't become so well-adjusted to your culture that you fit into it without even thinking. Instead, fix your attention on God. You'll be changed from the inside out. Readily recognize what he wants from you, and quickly respond to it. Unlike the culture around you, always dragging you down to its level of immaturity, God brings the best out of you, develops well-formed maturity in you."

I am convinced that God would justify and save such a person based on that wonderful act of faith in Jesus and loving commitment to him. How do I know? Because God said it, through the apostle Paul:

"And you were dead in the trespasses and sins in which you once walked, following the course of this world, following the prince of the power of the air, the spirit that is now at work in the sons of disobedience – among whom we all once lived in the passions of our flesh, carrying out the desires of the body and the mind, and were by nature children of wrath, like the rest of mankind. But **God, being rich in mercy, because of the great love with which he loved us, even when we were dead in our trespasses, made us alive together with Christ – by grace you have been saved – and raised us up with him and seated us with him in the heavenly places in Christ Jesus, so that in the coming ages he might show the immeasurable riches of his grace in kindness toward us in Christ Jesus. For by grace you have been saved through faith. And this is not your own doing; it is the gift of God, not a result of works, so that no one may boast. For we are his workmanship, created in Christ Jesus for good works**, **which God prepared beforehand, that we should walk in them**[emphasis mind – SP]" (Ephesians 2:1-10; English Standard Version).

Please note how the first third of the above passage describes how desperate the human condition was without God's grace through the gospel of Jesus. Paul told the folks there in Ephesus, "Friends, in your sinful lives you were as dead as a doorknob. You got exactly what you deserved and you were hopelessly stuck there."

Think about it: spiritually, they were dead. To be dead is to be void of life, without hope. What is there that a dead man can do about anything at all, much less finding a way to get "undead"? Or to put it as the late preacher Roy Osborne graphically put it many years ago, "Dead men can't climb ladders." In other words, they were lost and separated from God and their status would never, ever change unless Almighty God himself did something for them.

So there were the masses of humanity stuck in the graveyard of their own making. That is what they had earned by their sinful, rebellious lifestyle. That is also where people today who reject Jesus as the Son of God are living, right in their stinking, rotting, dead condition.

Whoa, hold the phone.

The last two-thirds of that quote from Ephesians suddenly changes from a tone of death and defeat to one of life, liberty, and victory. The difference is that these formerly "walking dead" folks heard and believed the great news – not just the good news – the amazingly great news that there was a way of escape for them from their awful condition.

No, God did not tell them that the good news was that he had created a do-it-yourself plan of salvation and he would give each of them a copy of the blueprint. And if they followed it exactly, with no mistakes, they could build themselves a ladder to get up out of the grave. Then they could drop by an Ace Hardware Store and pick up a few supplies, go back to their garages and build electric resuscitators which would bring them back to life. Then they could thank God for his ingenious plan and pat themselves of the back for flawlessly following the many pages of detailed blueprints. It was quite a plan, God's part, and man's part. Or maybe not so great.

Thankfully, God did not send a do-it-yourself plan of salvation to these folks who were dead, **dead**, <u>**dead**</u> in their sins. Instead, he sent salvation to them through a man, his beloved Son, Jesus the Christ. Yes, that son, the one their very own sins had condemned to the cross. The work of satisfying God's standard of justice had been accomplish, once for all people for all time, by Jesus dying for you . . . and for me.

Some may find this hard to accept, but God did not send the Bible to save us. Yes, I have faith that the 66 documents gathered and bound together as our "Christian Bible" contain the instructive and encouraging words of God. Frankly, some of the Old Testament narratives seem to have little relevance except to larger principles such as the wisdom in obeying God and the foolishness in rebelling against him.

And the Book of Revelation positioned at the back of our Bible, though I have studied it since my youth, often leaves me scratching my head when it isn't even itching. I do know this about the broader view of Revelation: (1) Jesus will come from heaven and return to get the redeemed children of God; (2) the saved will live with God for eternity, while the unbelievers from the creation of the earth to its end will be punished for not walking in the amount of light given to them; (3) that those who live in readiness to meet the Lord need not worry about the judgment; and (4) those who sometimes rave the longest and the loudest about their secret discoveries in Revelation are probably mistaken about other things, too.

There is an old bluegrass song named "I'm Using My Bible as My Road Map," and one of the verses goes like this:

"I'm using my Bible for a road map.
Ten Commandments they tell me what to do.
The twelve disciples are my road signs.
And Jesus will take me safely through."

The Bible is a precious book to me, as it has been to most of my ancestors going back several generations. The reason we love it is because it does a remarkable job of pointing people to the real Savior, to Jesus the Christ. Millions of people are doing as that old song said – using the Bible as a road map. But we do not put the Bible on a pedestal and worship it. (Not even the King James Version of 1611 A.D. Few people today could even read it much less understand that original KJV version. It belongs to trained medieval scholars and linguists.

We have the advantage today of many modern translations available in print, in cell phone apps, etc. Each one is just a helpful road map, leading to and pointing to the Son of God (Romans 10:17).

Decades ago, someone pointed out the message which rings out from the Old Testament is, **"Someone is coming!"** The first 26 documents of the New Testament shout with clarity, **"Someone has come!"** And the Book of Revelation, in particular, predicts with spectacular imagery, **"Someone is coming again!"** That "Someone," of course, was and is the Messiah or Christ, Jesus of Nazareth the Son of God.

You see, Jesus is our king and ruler, not the Bible. He, not the Bible, is our advocate before his father. Jesus paid the price for our redemption from sin with his blood on the cross; the Bible did not. Jesus, not the Bible, is our Savior and our only hope for eternal life with God. We must remind ourselves to keep our eyes upon Jesus.

Now as this great and wonderful news began to spread, those lost people gladly heard this account of how Jesus, their only Hope and Savior, loved them because God the Father had loved them that much. And God was offering to anyone who would accept it a free change of status, from death to life, with no human work required.

Because of God's grace and the work of Jesus on the cross, any person who comes to personally believe in Jesus as the Son of God can be justified (declared good and righteous by God) and forgiven of their sins and given the indwelling of the Holy Spirit himself to encourage, correct and comfort him until the Lord Jesus returns again. No wonder people often shout with joy upon first hearing the great and wonderful news of the gospel of Christ.

## The Multi-layered Process Of Salvation

The process of salvation involves several factors. It is not a simple six-layered cake, where you can take off each layer and do a spiritual examination and diagnosis. It is much more complicated, with various "moving parts" which may not happen in the exact sequence we might expect. Two or more factors may happen at the same time. We just need to be satisfied with the reality they do happen at God's own pace.

## God's Process of Salvation

| |
|---|
| Forgiveness by God's grace through faith in Jesus |
| Confession of your new relationship with Jesus |
| Power to turn away from sinful living (i.e., repenting) |
| Testimonial baptism to please God & share with others |
| Loving God, Loving all others, and doing good |
| Walking by the Spirit and sharing the gospel of Jesus |

Graphic created by Stan Paregien on Jan. 7, 2021

So, with that in mind, let's talk about that exciting moment when God declares that the new believer is a "righteous" person with his sins forgiven.

The fact is that when a person becomes a believer in the atonement work of Jesus, God makes that wonderful declaration then and there. At that moment, the new believer is certified as being right-with-God. His account is marked "Paid in Full." He or she is a member of God's family. He or she has eternal life. He or she is valuable and holy because Jesus paid his debt and God said it was so, regardless of the nature and number of his past sins.

The apostle Paul described this marvelous moment when he said this in Romans 3:19-16:

"19 Obviously, the law applies to those to whom it was given, for its purpose is to keep people from having excuses, and to show that the entire world is guilty before God. 20 For no one can ever be made right with God by doing what the law commands. The law simply shows us how sinful we are.

"21 But now God has shown us a way to be made right with him without keeping the requirements of the law, as was promised in the writings of Moses and the prophets long ago. 22 **We are made right with God by placing our faith in Jesus Christ. And this is true for everyone who believes, no matter who we are** [emphasis mine, SP].

"23 For everyone has sinned; we all fall short of God's glorious standard. 24 Yet God, in his grace, freely makes us right in his sight. He did this through Christ Jesus when he freed us from the penalty for our sins. 25 For God presented Jesus as the sacrifice for sin. People are made right with God when they believe that Jesus sacrificed his life, shedding his blood. This sacrifice shows that God was being fair when he held back and did not punish those who sinned in times past, 26 for he was looking ahead and including them in what he would do in this present time. God did this to demonstrate his righteousness, for he himself is fair and just, and **he makes sinners right in his sight <u>when they believe</u> in Jesus** [emphasis mine, SP]" (**<u>New Living Translation</u>** – NLT).

Let's be sure and get this important point. **The documents in the New Testament speak of the New Covenant but they are not the covenant.** The New Covenant between God and each individual cannot be chiseled onto tables of stone like the old one. The New Covenant cannot be printed and then sandwiched between covers of a book, but it is imprinted and engraved on our minds. It was not written on paper, papyrus, or even on space age materials. This covenant is also stoneless because it was not written on stone tablets like the old one.

Under the Mosaic Law, the tablets of stone containing the Covenant with Israel were placed in a fancy container called the **Ark of the Covenant**. It was holy to the people and to the priests. They never got to see the tablets or touch them because the Ark of the Covenant, containing the Ten Commandments, was securely kept in the Holy of Holies in both the Tabernacle and much later in the first Temple in Jerusalem. The Ark of the Covenant, along with the tablets, disappeared in about 587 B.C. Scholars seem to think that the Babylonians destroyed it. The Ark never appeared in the second Temple.

Instead, the New Covenant is written on our hearts by the Holy Spirit himself. While God's glory, his *Shekinah*, formerly rested over the Ark . . . now his code of love, grace and knowledge is present in the heart of each Christian. Instead of God temporarily residing in a Tabernacle or a fancy Temple, he now lives in the temple of our earthly bodies. That makes our inner man a sort of holy of holies for Jehovah, the one and only true God. And the Holy Spirit also occupies our hearts and bodies.

# Chapter 7

# The Process of Salvation, Part 2: Confession, Repentance & Baptism

We have seen that God's grace and the individual's faith in Jesus are the monumental elements in the process of salvation. Then came forgiveness and justification. And there are still more.

The moment you, in faith, make a personal consecration or dedication of your life to Jesus is when you know for certain God is at work in your life. He is making wonderful changes in your attitudes and behaviors. This breakthrough faith in Jesus opens your spiritual eyes and softens your heart. Then other amazing events take place.

## Confession

Confession is a practice which appears frequently in the context of individual and/or congregational worship in both the Old Testament and the New. Confession meant to make a heart-felt admission or profession of something one believes to be true. That was often seen where individuals and/or the nation of Israel confessed this or that to God. Often it was the confession of one's sins, weaknesses, fears, or one's praise and adoration for God.

In regard to the process of salvation, the sequence is to first believe and then to confess (John 1:49; 4:42; 9:35-38; Matthew 10:32-33). Confession is a testimonial to one's faith in Jesus. That implies one's acceptance of the authority of Jesus in one's life. Therefore, it is not something done before the faith-experience. Only after that event can one confess their unreserved faith in Jesus as Lord and Savior and as the Son of

God (Matthew 16:15-18; John 1:49; 11:27; 20:28; Acts 4:12; Romans 10:9-13; Philippians 2:11; 1 John 1:5-10; 4:2-31).

Some church folks encourage the unsaved truth-seeker to say, "The Sinners Prayer." However, there is no evidence anyone did that in biblical days. Nor are there any prescribed words for this personal confession.

"9 If you say with your mouth that Jesus is Lord, and believe in your heart that God raised Him from the dead, you will be saved from the punishment of sin. 10 When we believe in our hearts, we are made right with God. We tell with our mouth how we were saved from the punishment of sin. 11 The Holy Writings say, "No one who puts his trust in Christ will ever be put to shame." 12 There is no difference between the Jews and the people who are not Jews. They are all the same to the Lord. And He is Lord over all of them. He gives of His greatness to all who call on Him for help. 13 For everyone who calls on the name of the Lord will be saved from the punishment of sin" (Romans 10:9-13; **New Life Version** – NLV).

"2 This is how you know the Spirit of God: Every spirit that confesses that Jesus Christ has come in the flesh is from God, but every spirit that does not confess Jesus is not from God. This is the spirit of the antichrist, which you have heard is coming, even now it is already in the world" (1 John 4:2-3; **Holman Christian Standard Version** – HCSV).

The late William Barclay, in his book **The Letter to the Romans**, made a connection of confession with baptism. He wrote: "Baptism in the Early Church was intimately connected with confession of faith. A man was baptized when he entered the Church. And he was entering the Church direct from paganism. Baptism marked a dividing line in his life. In baptism a man came to a decision which cut his life in two, a decision which often meant that he had to tear himself up by the roots, a decision which was so definite that for him it often mean nothing less than beginning life all over again" (page 83-84; Fair Use Domain).

## Repentance

Remember that repentance flows from one's faith in Jesus. In fact, the New Testament lays down repentance as another condition of living in harmony with God.

Repentance as used in the Bible refers to when a person has a deep feeling of regret about his sins, a regret that leads to action in the form of a genuine change of heart and behavior. It happens when a person accepts God's offer of salvation from their past sins through the sacrificial death of Jesus on the cross. With love in his heart and trust in his mind, the believer wants to walk with God so strongly that he becomes sensitive to and obedient to the leading of the Holy Spirit in every decision he makes.

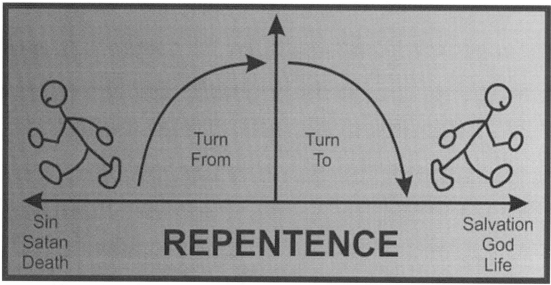

(Courtesy of ***Testimonies of His Goodness*** – Fair Use Domain)

In Acts 17:30, Paul said that God "now commands all men everywhere to repent" (The New King James Version). So here are the first two conditions required of each would-be-Christian: (1) a loving belief in Jesus as the son of God; and (2) a deep desire to repent of your sinful ways and, where possible, to apologize and make things as right as you can with anyone you may have mistreated.

> *A Christian is one who has confessed his faith in Jesus as Lord and Son of God, has repented of his sins, and lovingly tries in every way he knows to please God and be more like Jesus.*
> *-- Stan Paregien Sr.*
>
> Graphic by Stan Paregien Sr on Dec 15, 2020

In Acts 5, the apostles were again put in jail by the Jewish authorities for preaching the gospel and healing large numbers of sick people. They were hauled before the High Priest and the Sanhedrin, the ruling court regarding religious matters. He angrily reminded them the court had previously ordered them not to teach in the name of Jesus but, instead, "You have filled Jerusalem with your teaching and are determined to make us guilty of this man's blood" (Acts 5:27; **New International Version** – NIV).

The apostles, led by Peter, boldly answered: "We must obey God rather than human beings! 30 The God of our ancestors raised Jesus from the dead—whom you killed by hanging him on a cross. 31 **God exalted him to his own right hand as Prince and Savior that he might bring Israel to repentance and forgive their sins** [emphasis mine, SP]. 32 We are witnesses of these things, and so is the Holy Spirit, whom God has given to those who obey him" (Acts 29-32; NIV)

The disciples of Christ made it clear that, yes indeed, they were duty-bound to expose the Jewish authorities for their part in the persecution and execution of the long-awaited Messiah. **These apostles highlighted how the High Priest and his associates could find – as thousands already had – forgiveness of their awful sins by belief in Jesus as the Son of God and by their sincere repentance**. But the Jewish leaders would not accept it. Instead, they had the apostles beaten with whips and ordered them, again, to shut up about this Jesus. Then, powerless to do more, they released the apostles.

In Romans 2:4, the apostle Paul asks the unrepentant sinners in his day (as well as ours) this question: "4 Do you have contempt for God, who is very kind to you, puts up with you, and deals patiently with you? Don't you realize that it is God's kindness that is trying to lead you to him and change the way you think and act?" (**Names of God Bible** – NOG). Repentance is not an option; it is a God-given command.

The apostle John, writing late in his life, gave these encouraging words about this process of repentance, forgiveness, restoration, and sanctification. He reminded everyone that God is light (i.e., truth and kindness) with no hint of darkness.

"5 Now this is the message that we have heard from him and proclaim to you: God is light, and in him there is no darkness at all. 6 If we say, 'We have fellowship with him,' while we continue to walk in darkness, we lie and do not act in truth. 7 But if we walk in the light as he is in the light, then we have fellowship with one another, and the blood of his Son Jesus cleanses us from all sin. 8 If we say, 'We are without sin,' we deceive ourselves, and the truth is not in us. 9 If we acknowledge our sins, he is faithful and just and will forgive our sins and cleanse us from every wrongdoing. 10 If we say, 'We have not sinned,' we make him a liar, and his word is not in us. (1 John 1:5-10; **New American Bible, Revised Version** – NABRE).

That thought continued into Chapter 2:

"1 My children, I am writing this to you so that you may not commit sin. But if anyone does sin, **we have an Advocate with the Father, Jesus Christ the righteous one** [emphasis mine, SP]. 2 He is expiation for our sins, and not for our sins only but for those of the whole world. 3 The way we may be sure that we know him is to keep his commandments. 4 Whoever says, "I know him," but does not keep his commandments is a liar, and the truth is not in him. 5 But whoever keeps his word, the love of God is truly perfected in him. This is the way we may know that we are in union with him: 6 whoever claims to abide in him ought to live [just] as he lived" (1 John 2:1-6; NABRE).

## Baptism

Baptism is another "layer" or item related to the entire process of salvation. Our physical baptism in water is separate and different from the life-changing faith-experience discussed above. Christian baptism is a public, physical and visual confirmation of one's recent salvation by grace through faith in Jesus and accomplished by his blood-sacrifice on the cross to make possible the forgiveness of our outstanding debt of sin.

A new believer is baptized as soon as possible after their life changing faith-experience and salvation. The Bible shows that process repeated throughout the Book of Acts. On the Day of Pentecost when the full gospel was preached for the first time, the listeners were cut to their hearts by learning they had caused their own Messiah, Jesus the Christ, to be crucified. They begged to know from Peter and the other speakers, "What must we do to be saved?"

The good news was that they could have salvation based on their faith in the sacrificial death of Jesus Christ. The Spirit-anointed speakers on that Pentecost day had already convicted them of being personally responsible (figuratively – if not also literally) for the death of Jesus. They might not have personally captured Jesus or personally delivered him to the legal system for execution. But, clearly, they understood that sinless Jesus died for them. Jesus had to give himself as the perfect Lamb of God as a peace offering and sin offering to satisfy the justice of Jehovah God.

So, thousands of these Jewish men were already believers in Jesus as Lord. And then, the preachers on that day urged them to put that faith into action. Here are the apostle Peter's exact words to them as found in Acts 2:38-40 (ERV):

"38 Peter said to them, 'Change your hearts and lives and be baptized, each one of you, in the name of Jesus Christ. Then God will forgive your sins, and you will receive the gift of the Holy Spirit. 39 This promise is for you. It is also for your children and for the people who are far away. It is for everyone the Lord our God calls to himself.'

"40 Peter warned them with many other words; he begged them, 'Save yourselves from the evil of the people who live now!'"

There is no need to be hesitant or fearful of being immersed. Baptism in the first century was a simple ceremony, and it should be so today. It certainly can be done privately or before a great crowd. And, in the absence of another believer, the act may be performed by anyone willing to do it.

Normally, of course, another baptized believer -- a preacher, an elder, a Christian mother or father -- would perform the testimonial baptism. The act of baptism is not about who performs the baptism, but about honoring God's love and grace . . . about imitating the teachings and examples of Jesus and the early Christians . . . and about witnessing to both Believers and non-Believers that God has made an irreversible change in your status and in the direction of your life.

The New Testament does not prescribe any particular words to be said during the baptismal ceremony. If the person officiating wants to say a few words, let them be brief word pictures about the symbolism of the act. If the person being baptized was to say something, let it be about their love for Jesus or about their appreciation for those who helped him or her get to this moment in their life. Remember the abbreviation, "K.I.S.S."? In this case we'll say it means, "Keep It Short & Simple."

Baptisms have been done in most every conceivable venue. My maternal grandmother, Vada Walters (Cauthen), was baptized in a farm pond in Oklahoma in the wintertime – after they broke up the ice enough to do it. Brrrr. Others have been baptized in a comfortable, heated baptistry inside a church building. Some have been immersed in a clear mountain stream or a muddy river or in the pounding ocean surf. Actor and singer Pat Boone and his wife Shirley often baptized new believers right there in their swimming pool at their Hollywood home. Others have been baptized in a home bathtub or in a portable baptistry for use inside a prison.

Baptism follows repentance as spring follows winter, for it is a normal action and a further expression of one's faith in God and his son, Jesus the Christ. This act of obedience and testimony to God's grace is usually a complete dipping or immersion of the person in water. Most people see it as a beautiful symbol of the new believer's imitation of the death, burial, and resurrection of Jesus himself.

The late William Barclay was not only a minister in the Church of Scotland (Presbyterian) but he was a great Bible scholar who taught for years as a Professor of Divinity and Biblical Criticism at the University of Glasgow. He is best-known today for the popular commentaries he wrote in 1955 on the entire New Testament. In his book, **<u>The Letter to the Romans</u>**, he had this to say about Christian baptism:

"Commonly, baptism was by total immersion, and that practice lent itself to a symbolism which sprinkling does not so readily lend itself to. When a man descended into the water, and the water closed over his head, it was like being buried in a grave. When he emerged from the water, it was like rising from the grave. Baptism was symbolically like dying and rising again. The man died to the old life of sin and rose to the new life of grace. He went down into the water a man of the world and rose a man in Christ" (page 84; Fair Use Domain)

There was a novelty love song many years ago which celebrated love and marriage, as is seldom done in modern music today. One line stated, "Love and marriage, Love and marriage . . . go together like a horse and carriage."

Well, it is no accident that we see "faith" and "baptism" often discussed in various books of the New Testament. Then we see exceptions, such as John 3:16 where faith is mentioned but not baptism and in Acts 2:38 where faith is not mentioned but repentance and baptism are. Why is that?

There is no conflict or omission in either of those verses. A helpful rule of Biblical interpretation states, **"If any verse requires a condition for salvation, there can never be less than that required, but there may be more required in other Scriptures."**

For instance John 3:16 says nothing about repentance or baptism, but both actions are repeatedly mandated in other Scriptures. If we say that surely repentance is implied in John 3:16, then we can also say obedience (baptism) is also implied.

The late **Cecil Hook** preached in Texas and other places, but had a much wider influence because of his articles and books. We never met, but we corresponded a few times and I considered him a dear brother in Christ and an insightful encourager. Here is just one example, when he pointed out that conversion is a process of several elements which never really stand alone. He wrote:

"Baptism is symbolic of the whole change of the sinner into a new creature in Christ. It becomes . . . a literary device where the part is used to represent the whole. Belief is for the remission of sins. Confession is for the remission of sin. Repentance is for the remission of sins. Baptism is for the remission of sins. All of these combine in the whole process toward obtaining forgiveness" (**Free in Christ**, p. 76; Fair Use Domain).

Long ago, there was a gifted writer and speaker named **Alexander Campbell**. He was a deep thinker, a scholarly philosopher and theologian. He was a Presbyterian clergyman in Ireland, but still as a young man he came to the early American frontier of Pennsylvania, West Virginia, Kentucky, and Ohio. He later resigned from the Presbyterian Church and was appointed as a preacher in a Baptist collection of churches. In 1820, he agreed to debate a Presbyterian leader named John Walker on the ordinance of baptism and other topics.

In that debate, Campbell made a good case for the view that **baptism was a sign of something that had already taken place** (emphasis mine, SP), with no special link to the remission of one's sins. He argued that **baptism is a testimonial symbol in which one professes what he already possesses** (emphasis mine, SP; see **A Debate on Christian Baptism between John Walker (Presbyterian) and Alexander Campbell (Christian)**, pp. 56, 119-120, 136-38, 168-71 and 207).

Campbell also spoke of faith being the time when one's "real" conversion took place and when his faith secured one's pardon. Baptism, on the other hand, was the time when one was "formally" saved as an assurance of the remission of sins and certified one's pardon as having previously been given.

In other words, salvation takes place at the moment when a person is overwhelmed by his faith in the grace of God as shown by the blood-sacrifice of Jesus on a cross for the sins of mankind. At that moment he is added to the community of believers.

Who, then, is a Christian? One answer that seemed to be Alexander Campbell's favorite is this: **"A Christian is one that habitually believes all that Christ says, and habitually does all that he bids him"** (Quoted from an article titled "The Lunenburg Letter" on pages 498-499 of **The Encyclopedia of the Stone-Campbell Movement**. Fair Use Domain.)

My own answer to that question is this, as stated previously: A Christian is one who has confessed his faith in Jesus as Lord and Son of God, has repented of his sins and in love is trying in every way he knows to please God and be more like Jesus.

Later, in humble submission to the act of immersion, the person thus testifies to the change of status in his life – from a sinner to a saint – through the work of Jesus on the cross. It is his line of demarcation, where he once was on the Devil's side he is now on God's side. Baptism is his declaration of dedication, his proclamation of his position in Christ, his physical marker of his faith in Jesus, his judicial evidence of his conversion to the Christ, his opportunity to make his saving faith a faith seen by his society.

That is my position, also. And here is what changed my thinking. In the chapter titled "Examples of People Being Baptized," I discuss several examples in Acts. And when I was working on the example in Acts 10 where a Roman soldier named Cornelius and his household believed the gospel, they received the indwelling of the Holy Spirit, and then they were baptized, I had quite an epiphany regarding the timing of that process.

Peter elaborated on this event which marked the gospel being giving to non-Jewish people. He was with Paul and Barnabas and the elders in Jerusalem when he said of Cornelius and his people: "God chose me from among you to tell the Good News to those who are not Jewish. It was from me that they heard the Good News and believed. 8 God knows everyone, even their thoughts, and he accepted these non-Jewish people. He showed this to us by giving them the Holy Spirit the same as he did to us. 9 To God, those people are not different from us. When they believed, God made their hearts pure. 10 So now, why are you putting a heavy burden around the necks of the non-Jewish followers of Jesus? Are you trying to make God angry? We and our fathers were not able to carry that burden. 11 No, we believe that we and these people will be saved the same way—by the grace of the Lord Jesus" (Acts 15:7-11, ERV).

Notice he says, **"they heard the Good News and believed"** (verse 7), and God himself **"accepted these non-Jewish people"** and (verse 8) gave them **"the Holy Spirit the same as he did to us."** They eye-opening for me was when Peter said, "When they believed, God made their hearts pure" (verse 9).

Now here are three critical questions for you: (1) Exactly when were Cornelius and his people saved, before their baptism or during or afterwards? (2) How were they saved? (3) If Cornelius and his household were not saved until after they were baptized, doesn't that mean Cornelius and his family were unsaved, lost sinners when they received the gift of the Holy Spirit? Surely the answer is they were saved at the point of their faith.

Look at the text. Read it for yourselves. And believe it.

They were saved **"when they believed"** and that was before they were ever baptized. They were saved **"by the grace of the Lord Jesus,"** no doubt at the same moment they had faith in Jesus. So their salvation was given and received and certified by God himself.

Then each and every believer (no children involved), freshly saved by faith, received the gift of the Holy Spirit. And, finally -- in an act separate, and apart from that salvation experience -- every believer there stepped forward and was baptized as a visual, physical marker or testimony to their spiritual salvation experience which happened only minutes before.

I gladly confess to you that as I finished writing the above lines, I saw the simple salvation process more clearly than I ever have before. Praise the Lord! It clarifies for me so much of the books of Romans, Galatians, and Hebrews. It is liberating and exhilarated. I stand absolutely amazed at how I could have been so blind to something so obvious.

That is my position and I'm happy to share it. Some will argue, as I used to, that salvation occurs when a penitent believer comes up out of the waters of baptism and not before. I'm no longer interested in that discussion or any of the older ones, such as the one of how many angels can stand on the head of a needle.

When a person believes, repents, and is baptized I am happy for him, regardless of where in that process he believes he was saved. And I gladly welcome as brothers and sisters in God's family those who have accepted Jesus as the Son of God and Lord of their lives, have repented, but have not yet come to understand the value and purpose of baptism. One of the main reasons for writing this book is to take those people by the hand and introduce them to scriptures and ideas they may not have studied. I'll say it again: God is justice blended with love, so his judgments are always fair and just because – unlike any of us – he knows fully the heart and intentions of each person.

## Simple Christianity

Back to that crowd of Jewish men on the Day of Pentecost.

They heard the very first complete Gospel sermon. They were stunned by the message of God's love for them. And according to Acts 2:41-47 (ERV), this is the miracle of grace and faith that happened on that day and shortly afterward:

"41 Then those who accepted what Peter said were baptized. On that day about 3000 people were added to the group of believers.

"42 The believers spent their time listening to the teaching of the apostles. They shared everything with each other. They ate together and prayed together. 43 Many wonders and miraculous signs were happening through the apostles, and everyone felt great respect for God. 44 All the believers stayed together and shared everything. 45 They sold their land and the things they owned. Then they divided the money and gave it to those who needed it. 46 The believers shared a common purpose, and every day they spent much of their time together in the Temple area. They also ate together in their homes. They were happy to share their food and ate with joyful hearts. 47 The believers praised God and were respected by all the people. More and more people were being saved every day, and the Lord was adding them to their group."

In the seven verses above (Acts 2:41-47), we have one of the best descriptions ever given of **"Simple Christianity."** It was believers sharing the simple good news (gospel) of Jesus with sinners. It was an explosion of faith, repentance, and baptism by grace through faith and to the glory of no one but God. They were so excited with the good news that they met together as often as they could, whether in private homes or public places.

They prayed together, studied together, and ate together. That in itself was a Pentecost miracle, because – being from many nations – their skin and hair did not look alike. They did not dress alike, think alike, or even smell alike. Thanks to God's gift of unity by diversity, they enjoyed sweet fellowship with brothers and sisters in Christ. It was a hallelujah time.

This group of devout Jews became true believers in Jesus and the loving grace of God. More than 3,000 of them were baptized right there in the Temple courtyard pools. It was a public place where they were seen by God and everybody.

I never intended to spend so much time in this book talking about baptism. However, there are some more principles we need to understand about baptism.

## The Great Commission from Jesus

Jesus told his inner group of disciples to go, to teach, and to baptize. Those orders are often called "The Great Commission." The context for those marching orders is that he had just risen from the dead :

"16 Now the eleven disciples went to Galilee, to the mountain to which Jesus had directed them. 17 When they saw him, they worshipped him; but some doubted. 18 And Jesus came and said to them, 'All authority in heaven and on earth has been given to me. 19 Go therefore and make disciples of all nations, baptizing them in the name of the Father and of the Son and of the Holy Spirit, 20 and teaching them to obey everything that I have commanded you. And remember, I am with you always, to the end of the age'" (**New Revised Standard Version Catholic Edition** – NRSVCE.

Jesus did not call his people to fill pews in fancy cathedrals. Jesus did not call his people to bury deep in their hearts the stories of his life, ministry, death, resurrection, ascension and coming again. He did not create a new covenant and a new fellowship as a Country Club for people who want to play golf while the poor and the hurting folks walk the streets just outside their gated walls.

No. A thousand times, no.

Jesus makes it clear those eleven men were to spread the message of God's great love shown by the gift of his son's own life on the cross for the remission or removal of each believer's sins. They could not keep quiet about it. They did not keep quiet about it. Soon they had turned Jerusalem upside down as more than 3,000 Jewish men claimed this offer of salvation. The disciples were overjoyed to see people respond to the gospel, and those 3,000 went out and told more.

The Book of Acts repeatedly shows them going, them preaching the gospel message, and them immediately baptizing those who believed. So many of us grew up in churches where baptism was a given. When one accepted Jesus as his Savior, he also was baptized soon thereafter. It was cut and dried. No big deal. No serious questions.

Okay, then, just what is the hang-up for so many people today about the simple act of submitting one's self to Christian baptism as a loving act of obedience to God and a desire to please him?

Let's explore that together.

Bible scholars in most main-line denominations agree on many facets of Christian baptism. They agree that Jesus certainly demonstrated by his own baptism at the hands of John the Baptist that he wanted to please God in every way.

They agree that faith in Jesus as one's Savior is an absolute biblical requirement before anyone puts a toe in the baptistry. Otherwise baptism is an empty ritual which does nothing but make wet sinners out of dry ones.

In addition, theologians understand that God expects each baptismal candidate to have a commitment to turn from sin (we call that "repenting" or the act of "repentance"). The very first gospel sermon, found in Acts 2, told the lost listeners they should "repent and be baptized" (Acts 2:38). So at least the intention to change one's life, if not actual demonstrations of having done so, should precede baptism or be a timely activity.

Also, Bible scholars generally agree that the earliest converts experienced baptism as a complete immersion of the person in a stream or pool of water. That was the common method of baptism for many decades. Today, there is a diversity of scholarly opinions as to whether or not the actual mode used is crucial. So we have advocates for immersion, some for pouring, others for sprinkling, and many who argue that God never expressed a clear preference so they will not do so, either.

Well, let's go back for a moment to our previous discussion of the "Seven One's of Christian Unity." In their most basic form, they are simple enough even to be understood and affirmed by those who are hearing the gospel for the first time. And, yet, for those with greater spiritual maturity they are profound enough to sometimes stir up different opinions and ideas about their full application.

The fact is, all of us like to think of ourselves as "stronger believers" (in the way Paul uses the contrasts in 1 Corinthians 10:23--11:1; and in Romans 14:1—15:13). We are certainly free in our private study to explore the seven facets of unity in all the depth we desire. The God who created each of us and also created us with a brain could not object if we reach conclusions which others do not necessarily hold. And we may hold our conclusions as our personal opinions, pending further study.

However, sinful pride steps in when someone "discovers" something new to himself and then decides he must "convert" everyone else to the "correct" position. And then sin after sin is compounded if that person pushes his new favorite issue to the point where it (or he) causes confusion in the minds and hearts of "weaker" believers or even advocates shunning or disfellowshipping those who don't agree with him.

No disciple is ever to cause a division between God's children when the issue has nothing to do with the fundamentals of the gospel. It is far better that he continue studying his "new understandings" of whatever point of doctrine it may be. He should privately enjoy them, rather than causing any Christian to stumble in his Christian walk.

Let us always reflect the mind of Christ by showing Christian unity regarding matters of faith and facts. Let us display Christian liberty and freedom when we have differences of opinions about the facts. In all situations, let us show patience and love toward each other. And may we never, ever forget that Jesus is Lord. He alone is at the center of our thinking and actions, while anything else far in the background. And if we are now showing love to our brothers and sisters, we have neither God nor the Holy Spirit.

God's will for those who accept Jesus as their Lord is for them to validate or demonstrate their allegiance. And that includes a public statement of their faith, turning away from their sinful life, submitting to baptism to please God and to declare their allegiance to God's family, and more.

## What If a Person Refuses Baptism?

What if someone responds to the gospel message, affirms their faith in Jesus as the Son of God, understands God's expectation that they should be baptized . . . but the person refuses to do so.

The best-selling Christian author of all time, **Max Lucado**, has referred to baptism as the great divider. It divides the lookers from the doers. Or as Lucado described it, baptism separates the "tire kickers" from the "car buyers." That is a reference to all those casual lookers who wander through car lots and wander out without coming close to buying anything. There is a lot of truth in that statement.

The Lord did not appoint me a Judge, but like you I am a fruit inspector. And such an attitude of defiance suggests to me that person's heart was not right and his confession of faith suspect. If after further teaching and counseling, the person still refuses to obey, I am led to believe he or she was not really saved. Faith, after all, is the key which engages God's mercy and justification and then leads to humble obedience and such good works as peacemaking to God's glory.

Frankly, I cannot imagine a legitimate reason for a person of faith not being baptized as soon as possible. Most do obey that expectation of God's. And most see it, not as a sectarian rule or a burden, but as an act which in itself beautifully symbolizes the death, burial and resurrection of Jesus . . . as well as the candidate's own personal commitment to dying to sin and burying that wicked old life and to enjoying a resurrection to a new life in Christ.

Please let me state this as plainly as I can: Almighty God, according to his own plans and for his own reasons, freely offers to all his saving grace. He stands with hands outstretched saying, "My child, there are no strings attached, nor anything you can do to earn this gift. Jesus earned it for you by his work on the cross. So if you want it, take it right now by your faith, apart from any your works. You cannot merit my unmerited favor toward you."

Let's put all this in terms most anyone can understand. Some guy named Joseph J. Jingle has been raising seven kinds of hell ever since he was a teenager. At the age of

60, with sins of every kind being listed on his lifetime resume, he is so depressed he is thinking about suicide.

On this day, however, his next door neighbors, Kyle and Suzanne Smith stop by to pray with him and for him. He heart is primed for a change. They turn to the Gospel of John in their Bible and tell him the story of Jesus and his love.

Heck, ol' George had been trapped into going to church and had heard that story many times without being moved. This time it was totally different. He was grabbing for a lifeline. Right then and there, the Smith's led him in a prayer. They spoke to God like they were old friends. They told of George's life and his new openness. Then Kyle Smith said, "Lord, I'm gonna ask George to say what is on his heart today."

And, surprisingly, George spoke directly and plainly. Slowly, maybe, as he chose each word. He said, "Oh, Father, I have sinned against you. I've sinned against most everyone I have ever known, even my own family. So here and now I confess I need you. I am sorry for my sinful ways. I believe your promises about forgiveness and eternal life. And I see now how Christ died for my sins. So, God, I accept Jesus as my Savior and I ask for your mercy. In the name of Jesus Christ, amen."

Imagine, please, that in heaven Jesus the Son of God speaks as George's celestial advocate. "Father God, George is one of ours now." And God, looking at George's accounting ledger sheet, sees that it is full of sins written in red ink. There is not one thing on "Works" or "Assets" side of the ledge. Then God picks up a big rubber stamp and presses it down on George's ledger sheet. There are the words, big and bold **"DEBT PAID BY JESUS IN FULL, FOREVER."**

That is when another round of applause and praise broke out among the angels and the heavenly saints. It happens each time a soul is saved.

Oh, hallelujah!!

Well, friend, millions of believers over the years, in every corner of the world, have also accepted that free offer of forgiveness and eternal life. Then they obey him in every way they can, out of love and not fear. That is why they follow through on walking away from a sinful way of life.

That is also why they are baptized as soon as possible, to obey him because they are so thankful for their new status as a born again child of God. And they live for God the rest of their lives to their best ability and understanding. That is a wonderful and holy experience to have for yourself and to see others have it.

It reminds us of how old father Abraham, often called "the father of the faithful." By faith, he responded to God's request to move far away to a place not known by him. God promised that Abraham, an incredibly old man, would become the "father of many nations." Remember, Abraham did not say to God, "Well, I'll tell you what, I've got it pretty good right where I am with more animals than I can count. And this idea of me generating more children and descendants is a pretty good joke. So just count me out."

No, Abraham listened to God and believed him. Now read how Paul describes Abraham's attitude: "If Abraham was justified by works, he has something to boast about – but not before God. For what does the Scripture say? Abraham believed God, and it was credited to him for righteousness. Now to the one who works, pay is not credited as a gift, but as something owed. But ***to the one who does not work, but believes on him who declares the ungodly to be righteous, his faith is credited for righteousness***" (Emphasis mine. Romans 4:2-5; **Common English Version**). That is how each Christian is justified, too. It is by faith alone in the works which Jesus did for us.

## [NOTE TO OUR JEWISH FRIENDS:

*You might want to go back and read the last few paragraphs about Abraham. Later, it was through Abraham that circumcision (the act of cutting the foreskin away from a male's penis) became a revered mark of Jewishness for men. The point to remember here is that Abraham was justified long before the act of circumcision became part of the law of Moses. Abraham was justified by his faith, not by obedience in being circumcised.]*

God-seekers today hear or read the gospel. When those basic truths about Jesus take root in a person's heart, he or she believes it – emotionally and intellectually. At that marvelous moment, today's believer – like Father Abraham – is justified and saved by faith. Hallelujah. Praise God.

Later, the Jews saw a man's refusal to be circumcised as a despicable rebellion against God and all things Jewish. In much the same way in most Christian communities today, a believer is considered saved by faith prior to and during or after his baptism. But also, with time, anyone who understands God's purpose and desire for their baptism . . .. but refuses to be baptized is seen as an incomplete believer with an attitude which dishonors God and all those disciples who have been baptized.

The bad news, which is unthinkable for most of us, is that many others – far more than the number who accept the offer – spit in God's face and refused his free gift. They are bound to do life their way, and that was their choice. Unless they repent and turn to Jesus before they die, their destiny of isolation from God and his people will be sealed for eternity (read James 2).

## What Mode or Form of Baptism?

In my personal view, only baptism by total immersion clearly demonstrates the idea of a death, burial, and resurrection and so that is what I teach and perform. While I believe that baptism by immersion is God's will for all believers who have embraced the simple gospel of Christ, I understand that some have not yet come to understand the place of baptism in God's conversion process.

So if a penitent believer chooses to be sprinkled with water or to have a small amount of water poured on them, as a substitute for immersion, there are plenty of ministers who will do that for them. I am happy for them in wanting to draw closer to God and I pray for their continued spiritual growth. It is God's place, alone, to render any judgment on their status. God does not need our help or our legislation.

**Barton W. Stone** was a Presbyterian preacher who in 1801 led a huge "open air" communion service which brought 20,000 people together at Cane Ridge, Kentucky. Stone was the organizer but preachers from many sects preached for several days at this large campsite. Later, disheartened by the more than 10 distinctive and non-cooperating sects within the Presbyterian Churches in his area, he began to preach a dynamic way forward by going back to the basics of the Bible. He advocated giving up human names for the sects and just calling each other "disciples" or "brethren." He and another former Presbyterian preacher, Alexander Campbell, joined forces and created many congregations across the United States who wanted to go forward by going back to simple Christianity.

In 1831, just 13 years from his death, Barton W. Stone had these gracious words regarding those in his churches whose baptisms had been sprinkling or pouring but not immersion: "My opinion is that immersion is the only baptism. But shall I therefore make my opinion a term of Christian fellowship? If in this case I thus act, where shall I cease from making my opinions terms of fellowship? I confess I see no end. . . . **Let us still acknowledge all to be brethren, who believe in the Lord Jesus, and humbly and honestly obey him, as far as they know his will, and their duty [Emphasis mine, SP].**" (*Christian Messenger*, 1831, p. 19, 21.)

Another leader in the so-called "Restoration Movement," Alexander Campbell, was a prolific magazine editor and author. In answer to a writer's question as to how to identify a Christian except by his obedience to his commands [the context was the command to be baptized – SP], Campbell wrote:

"In no other way. But mark, I do not substitute obedience to one commandment, for universal or even general obedience. And should I see a sectarian Baptist or a Pedobaptist more spiritually-minded, more generally conformed to the requisitions of the Messiah, than one who precisely acquiesces with me in the theory or practice of immersion as I teach, doubles the former rather than the latter, would have my cordial approbation and love as a Christian. So I judge and so I feel. **It is the image of Christ the Christian looks for and loves; and this does not consist in being exact in a few items, but in general devotion to the whole truth as far as known** [Emphasis mine, SP].

"With me mistakes of the understanding and errors of the affection are not to be confounded. They are as distant as the poles. An angel may mistake the meaning of a commandment, but he will obey it in the sense in which he understands it."

Then in answer to the question of "Who is a Christian?," he wrote:

"Every one that believes in his heart that Jesus of Nazareth is the Messiah, the Son of God; repents of his sins, and obeys him in all things according to his measure of knowledge of his will" (*Millennial Harbinger* magazine in 1837, p. 411).

That is why I have said my personal view is this: A person is a Christian who has stated his faith in Jesus as Lord, has repented of his sins, and in love is trying to please God and be more like Jesus in the best way he knows.

That statement is non-judgmental, and simply states the obvious. It does no damage to any truth I currently hold, nor does it approve any errors that person may still hold. It holds open the opportunity for more study and prayer about baptism and other topics, but doing so within the family of God and without rancor.

For example, I have no doubt there are countless unimmersed Christians in virtually all of the mainline Christian bodies. Personally, I extend the hand of fellowship to many who are loving disciples of Jesus but who have never been immersed (baptized). Hopefully, many of them will decide to complete that part of their obedience to God.

In 1964, I joined several other college students to go off to North Augusta, South Carolina for a revival. One of our college professors, **Don Finto**, preached each night. We volunteers spent our days knocking on doors to invite local people to the revival. During that event, an elderly gentleman came to our revival at the local Church of Christ. He told us of his interesting faith journey. He was actually a member of a Methodist Church there in town.

Long ago, he had believed the gospel account and had faith in Jesus, so he was accepted into the Methodist Church. As he continued to study his Bible, the Holy Spirit's guidance led him to conclude that he needed to and wanted to obey God in one more detail. He wanted to be baptized by immersion. So he talked about it with his own pastor, who according to the **<u>Methodist Discipline</u>** could administer sprinkling, pouring or immersion as baptism. But for some reason, the pastor refused his request.

So this godly man went from denomination to denomination in town until a Baptist minister agreed to baptize him by immersion and did so. And the happy man continued his membership in the Methodist Church as an immersed believer. After he attended our revival and spoke with the preacher and the elders, this man decided to worship with that congregation. He was fully accepted as a brother with no regard for who baptized him.

Let's be clear on a few points about baptism.

**First**, **the person who is charged with baptizing a candidate should take a few moments to do a heart and mind check of that person**. No one should be baptized if he is too young to understand the commitment he is about to make. No one should be baptized who has a serious mental illness or is currently unstable, mentally, or emotionally. God's wonderful grace certainly covers such individuals. That pretty much eliminates baptizing (sprinkling or pouring water on) infants.

**Second**, **no one group of believers owns a copyright on baptism.** We should never speak of anyone having submitted to a "Baptist baptism," or a "Pentecostal baptism," or a "Presbyterian" baptism. That is a despicably sectarian desecration of a humbling act designed to honor Christ and please God.

**Third, when Jonathan Q. Public walks through our church house door, we welcome him as one who has received the Spirit of God.** If he professes to be a Christian, then we see him as having been called into the fellowship of God's people just as we have been (see 1 Corinthians 1:9). His fellowship or relationship with God is 100% unrelated to and unaffected by whether you or I "accept" him and "grant our fellowship to him." That is a "vertical" relationship between God and man. On the other hand, how I treat another child of God may be a mighty big disappointment to our heavenly Father.

**Fourth, regardless of who does the baptizing of a believer, the subject herself is thus "added to the church" of God (Acts 2:42).** She may have been immersed by an ordained minister of a Presbyterian Church, or a preacher for the Salvation Army, or the Church of the Brethren. God adds such a disciple to his world-wide, undenominational group of people. There is absolutely nothing sectarian about that. Now, before this person leaves the church building, she may be given a certificate of baptism that she is being added to the membership role of the Church of the Brethren or whatever. That is where the sectarianism creeps in.

I just cannot find in my Bible where God has set aside 40 acres in heaven for the Baptist Church, or the Church of Christ, or the Uncle of Luke Community Church. That ain't gonna happen. What will transpire is that the authentic lovers of God will be separated from unsaved church attenders in those human denominations and the saved will be ushered into heaven by a God who has an authentic love for them.

There is an old joke which fits in here, a funny story and yet a pathetic one. On Judgment Day, St. Peter was in charge of housing arrangements for the flood of saved people arriving in heaven. An architect who died a few years back had been placed in charge of designing the necessary housing. So he set up "cottages" designed much like common houses back home in the United States.

Anyway, large groups arrived and they were put in the first cottage. St. Peter gave some of them their assigned areas. He told this group to wait there until he assigned them. He told the Baptists to stay off in the master bedroom of the family home. He told the Pentecostal folks to take the guest room. He assigned he Presbyterians to the game room in the back. He told the Methodists to isolate themselves in the spare bedroom. Now before he let this bunch go, he asked them to be really quiet. And he explained, "You need to be very quiet all the time, because I put the Church of Christ folks in the basement and they believe they're the only family members in heaven."

Sorry, I just had to get that in. For one thing I still laugh at that old joke. You may substitute your own sect for the Church of Christ when you tell the story and your group will clearly understand it, too.

Again, as we see it, the way to go forward and out of our denominational mess is to go back to the basics. There were no Presbyterians, Mennonites, United Pentecostals, Calvinists, Lutherans or any such divisions for over 500 years after the Christian fellowship was established. And when it comes time for rewards and punishments, God will not see us as Disciples of Christ, Assembly of God, or Community Church. He will see us as individuals and judge us by what each of us did with the light we were offered.

**Fifth, there is nothing at all meritorious about the act of baptism.** It cannot be considered a "work" by the candidate because it is the person performing the baptism who is doing the physical action. The candidate is merely submissive. And, in the final analysis, it is not being "right" about every aspect of baptism which makes us one in the Lord. We are one -- bound together in a unity characterized by diversity -- because we have each accepted by faith the gospel – the amazing, grace-filled story of Jesus.

I must tell you this as forcefully as I can. My hope of eternal life is absolutely centered in the work of Jesus, not on anything I can do and it sure ain't centered on baptism. Jesus is the Lord of my life, not baptism       (sprinkling,    pouring    or    immersion!). When I became a Christian, I pledged my life and allegiance to Jesus Christ, not to baptism.

**Sixth, the highest possible motive for being baptized is simply because you want to please God in every way.** Whether a person even knows about the promises of forgiveness of sins or the gift of the Holy Spirit would not prevent those actions from happening. Whether the person believes his salvation was secured at the moment of faith or at the moment of coming up from the waters of baptism will not negate the reality of his salvation. And one does not have to have a complete System of Theology & Morality worked out in his head before being baptized. One just needs to grasp the basics of the gospel before baptism, then he can sort out the rest afterwards.

It is not a matter of knowing all there is about baptism that makes it important or valid; it is a matter of knowing enough about Jesus – that is, the basic gospel - to honestly confess him as your Lord and Savior. So when by the leading of the Holy Spirit and the study of the scripture one is baptized, that person is added by God to the fellowship of the saints (both living and dead). That person is inseparably linked with the one body or fellowship of Christ comprised of millions who have done the same thing since the First Century.

**Seventh, the only reason anyone should be baptized a second time is if a person firmly knows that when he was baptized the first time he really did not believe Jesus was the Christ (Messiah).** Some people have confessed that the only reason they were baptized the first time was to get their spouse off their back or for business reasons or to impress someone. In reality, that kind of person just went down into the water as a dry sinner and came up as a wet one. Nothing changed. It would be like some Roman Catholic priests who directed soldiers in old California to kill the natives who would not become Catholics. So a native would follow orders and save his life, but the ritual of membership without knowledge or dedication would not save his soul.

If that were really the situation, and now that person accepts Jesus as Lord, then he or she should be authentically baptized and welcomed into the family of God. Nor should a person ever be baptized again as a way to achieve forgiveness for sins which have happened since their original baptism. That situation calls for genuine repentance and for a renewal of one's dedication, not for a second baptism.

**Eighth, we all must be a bit cautious about what is said at a baptismal ceremony.** True Christian baptism is not a mystical, magical sacrament that automatically bestows blessings on a person who is without faith or without the ability to understand the act.

In my own faith-fellowship, the person requesting baptism walks to the front of the church building. There, an elder or a preacher might ask the person for an unscripted statement of his faith. More often, though, the member speaks quietly with the candidate. Then the member explains to the audience the person's desire and often calls on someone to pray for the person. Then, the church member and the candidate go to dressing rooms and change to baptismal garments. They go down into the baptistry and then someone draws the curtain so the congregation may see then.

Most often, the baptizer will raise his right hand straight up and say something similar to this: "John Brown, do you believe that Jesus is Lord and do you have faith in him as the Son of God?" After the candidate's positive response, the baptizer says, "Upon the confession of your faith in Jesus, I now baptize you into the name of the Father, the Son and the Holy Spirit." Except that virtually all of our ministers would add on the end of that statement " . . . for the remission of your sins."

There is even a theological phrase for that statement: **"the pastoral pronouncement."** Interestingly, we have no example in the New Testament of anyone having those exact words said over them. And there is no mention of the baptizer holding his hand up in a priest-like fashion. One might conclude, therefore, we ought to give baptizers a lot of slack in what they say and do.

Yes, one might conclude that . . . but one would probably be wrong. That sort of tradition has been stamped in our minds. We see photos, drawings, and paintings of baptismal scenes with the baptizer always looking solemn and raising that official right arm high in the air.

Even more odd, but far from funny, is how some preachers (in particular) have made it a church law that one must end the formulaic phrase with "for the remission of your sins." This argument seems to rest in a paranoid fear that the candidate will not remember the objective is the remission of sins. Such advocates often get more people to come down the isles by creating in them a doubt about whether baptism was authentic – i.e., "for the remission of sins."

**Al Maxey** is a long-distance, digital friend of mine. We exchange emails and other correspondence occasionally, but have never met in person. Al is both a preacher and an elder (presbyter) for a group of believers in Alamogordo, New Mexico. This man is a keen expositor of God's word. On Nov. 16, 2007, he wrote in his *"Reflections"* online newsletter an article titled, "Pre-Plunge Pronouncements." In in, he told how a young preacher got in trouble immediately after baptizing a candidate. The elders rushed up and told him he had goofed up the baptism by inadvertently leaving off "for the remission of sins." And they required him to repeat the pronouncement "the scriptural way" and to dip the person again.

Maxy further stated, "If a believer's eternal life is placed in jeopardy because some preacher fumbled his words in the baptistery, then maybe we should be stationing 'observers' at the four corners of the baptistery to make absolutely certain that all the 'rules of the ritual" are performed precisely according to the pattern. Not only the 'pastoral pronouncement' must be carefully reviewed, but also these observers must ensure that no toe, finger, or elbow pops out of the water during the baptism. And yes, baptisms have been repeated for this 'infraction' as well. By the way, as many of you undoubtedly know, there are indeed congregations that actually have such observers posted at the baptistery during each baptism. Such is the lunacy of legalistic patternism"

Al's concluding remarks are not only reasonable and Biblical, but they are also downright humorous. So here is what he said:

"I personally find nothing within the Scriptures that suggests anyone's baptism is rendered void or invalid due to the words spoken prior to immersion by the one performing that act. In fact, whether or not words are even **spoken** is irrelevant.

"It is the understanding and intent of the heart of the person being baptized that determines the validity of this act of obedient faith. I have heard it said (tongue in cheek) that even if a **mute monkey** performed the baptism, it would be just as valid if the heart of the penitent believer was right with the Lord as he submitted to this act. In other words, the person performing the baptism, and whatever he/she may or may not say just before, makes absolutely no difference whatsoever.

"We demonstrate **our own faith** by being immersed: visible evidence of a saving union we enjoy with the Father through the Son, and of the personal indwelling and empowering of His Holy Spirit. Whether the one performing the baptism utters the phrase 'Father, Son and Holy Spirit' or just 'Jesus Christ,' the reality is the same: we are united with **Them** through union with **Him**.

"How sad that so many fail to perceive and appreciate this marvelous relationship that is theirs because they are overly concerned and troubled, due to a legalistic background and upbringing, with the preciseness of some ritual, the details of which are neither specified nor prescribed in Scripture. The more spiritually perceptive we become, the less likely we are to obsess over such tedious tenets of traditionalism" (Fair Use Domain).

## Baptism and the New Birth

A devout, prominent Jewish leader named Nicodemus went to see Jesus one time at night. In my experience, preachers often delight in taking such a statement and psychoanalyzing to death. They find mystical meanings in questioning the cultural history of meeting at night back then, and speculate as to whether poor ol' Nic was ashamed or afraid to approach Jesus during the daylight lest his friends see him consorting with a radical.

Hmmm.

Maybe he just got lost in the maze of streets at night or just got out of a business meeting. It is all too much sweat over a too small a thing. Let's focus on the important discussion he had with our Lord. It started with a revealing statement of his apparent belief that Jesus was God-sent.

"'Rabbi, we all know you're a teacher straight from God. No one could do all the God-pointing, God-revealing acts you do if God weren't in on it.'

"Jesus said, 'You're absolutely right. Take it from me. Unless a person is born from above, it's not possible to see what I'm pointing to – to God's kingdom.'

"'How can anyone,' said Nicodemus, 'be born who has already been born and grown up? You can't re-enter your mother's womb and be born again. What are you saying with this 'born-from-above' talk?'

"Jesus said, 'You're not listening. Let me say it again. Unless a person submits to this original creation – the 'wind-hovering-over-the-water' creation, the invisible moving the visible, a baptism into a new life – it's not possible to enter God's kingdom. When you look at a baby, it's just that: a body you can look at and touch. But the person who takes shape within is formed by something you can't see and touch – the Spirit – and becomes a living spirit.

"'So don't be surprised when I tell you that you have to be 'born from above' – out of this world, so to speak. You know well enough how the wind blows this way and that. You hear it rustling through the trees, but you have no idea where it comes from or where it's headed next. That's the way it is with everyone 'born from above' by the wind of God, the Spirit of God.'

"Nicodemus asked, 'What do you mean by this? How does this happen?'

"Jesus said, 'You're a respected teacher of Israel and you don't know these basics? Listen carefully, I'm speaking sober truth to you. I speak only of what I know by experience; I give witness only to what I have seen with my own eyes. There is nothing secondhand here, no hearsay. Yet instead of facing the evidence and accepting it, you procrastinate with questions. If I tell you things that are plain as the hand before your face and you don't believe me, what use is there in telling you of things you can't see, the things of God'

"'No one has ever gone up into the presence of God except the One who came down from that Presence, the Son of Man. In the same way that Moses lifted up the serpent in the desert so people could have something to see and then believe, it is necessary for the Son of Man to be lifted up – and everyone who looks up to him, trusting and expectant, will gain a real life, eternal life'" (Gospel of John 3:1-15; **The Message** - MSG).

First, let's think about what happens in the normal human family. The husband and his lovely wife decide to have a child. Or, hey, it just happens. In the God-created process of procreation, the loving husband and his loving wife engage in sexual activity in a bed in the comfort of their own home. As that wonderful experience goes along, the husband's sperm ends up inside his beloved's vagina. The sperm, containing the "seeds" of new life, swim upward.

Let us say that "Sperm X" unites with an ovum, "Ovum A," and then attaches to the wall of his wife's uterus. That union begins to grow. Conception has happened. Nourishment continues from the mother's body. This is the point at which the prospective child has been "begotten." The process has started, though some problem could result in a miscarriage and no life birth.

It is the moment life has started, but it is some nine months before there will be a birth of their child. Please get this: the child in the womb is alive and sometimes kicking long before its actual birth when it is pushed out into the world. It is the very fact that it is healthy and alive that it moves toward the birth canal. Only then is there a live birth or a delivery.

The "begetting" (planting of the seed) normally begins in the privacy of a bedroom, never at the hospital where the "birth" (delivery) usually happens today. If it worked the other way, it would be a hot news item for the newspaper and TV reporters.

When the older Bible translations said that "Abraham begat Isaac" (Matthew 1:1-2), the writer meant that Abraham had impregnated his wife with the seed that finally grew and at delivery nine months later she was the one who gave birth to Isaac. And that actual birth changes everything, places the child in new relationships, with the prospects of great blessings and challenges and soon some responsibilities.

The process of the "New Birth" and becoming a spiritual child of God is similar in some ways to a natural, physical birth. First, let's deal with a normal fellow we will call "Edward."

The first step in the process of becoming a child of the King happens when the Holy Spirit of God "begets" a person through his reading or hearing the gospel message. He plants that seed or sperm of the kingdom into the person's heart. Now, just as with a human birth, the spiritual seed requires a gesticulation or germination period. Depending on the receptivity of a person's heart, that embryonic period may be quite short or last for years. Or it may stagnate and die. But with enough of a germination phase, then comes the actual delivery and birth of a baby Christian.

[NOTE: We are not speaking here of an infant or an older unbelieving child, because the New Testament gives no example of anyone—much less an infant or a person too young or too mentally challenged to decide for themselves—substituting a sectarian "sprinkling" or "pouring" for immersion. Just as in the case of an unbeliever participating in the Lord's Communion bread and wine, baptizing a person with no knowledge of the gospel, no understanding of or intention to repent from their sins and no faith in Jesus as their Lord and Savior is just an empty ritual signifying nothing.]

Before one is delivered into the new spiritual state he is begotten of the Spirit through the Word, which is the seed or sperm. The apostle John, when he was an old and wise leader, explained the process:

*"Everyone who believes that Jesus is the Christ has been born of God, and everyone who loves the parent [God –SP] loves the child. By this we know that we love the children of God, when we love God and obey his commandments. For the love of God is this, that we obey his commandments. And his commandments are not burdensome, for whatever is born of God conquers the world. And this is the victory that conquers the world, our faith. Who is it that conquers the world but the one who believes that Jesus is the Son of God?"* (1 John 5:1-5; **New Revised Standard Version**).

Please take a deep breath.

Really.

Now go back up to those important verses and read them, again. Slowly this time. Let the Holy Spirit speak to you through the Word of God.

# Faith in Jesus

So when does that spiritual "birth" take place? It happens when the very Word of God attaches to your receptive heart. It only happens when you -- overflowing with the incorruptible Word of God -- reach that point of faith when a spiritual light clicks on in your brain.

You know down deep you cannot make things right with God no matter how nice you act or how many good deeds you do. You clearly see that Jesus loved all of us – even you -- enough to die to make forgiveness of sin possible. It happens when that faith is strong enough you want to change your life and lovingly follow your Savior until the end of your life or until he returns in the end of time.

After that momentous life changing faith-experience, you are added to the world-wide family of God. It is not a sectarian Club or a Country Club where you pay your dues and play a few rounds of golf once in a while. It is not a place where you put down other believers because they don't know all you know or because they know a heck of a lot more than you.

And there is a wonderful change in your status. No longer milling with the lost and alienated, you stand with the saved of all ages. You inherit eternal life and neither the devil nor his evil angels can tear you from the arms of your loving heavenly Father. You are entitled to the same blessings available to Moses and Joshua and Ruth and Naomi and Peter and Paul and Lydia and Martha and Lazarus and Martin Luther, Billy Graham, Joyce Myers, Charles Stanley, David Jeremiah, and countless others, both those who are famous and those who in their past were downright infamous.

Likewise, you have many responsibilities here on earth just like the millions of your fellow believers around the world. You seek out other believers and meet regularly with them, sharing your victories and your failures. You practice a mutual ministry of teaching, correction and pure, sweet love. And you are on the receiving end of the same blessings. You look for opportunities to share the gospel of Jesus with people who are lost, and you look for ways to help those who are poor and need a hand up.

This relationship of living by faith in Jesus is more than commendable, it is a wonderful start. But there is more. There is the desire and commitment to obey God's commands even when we don't completely understand the why's and wherefores' of each.

## Repentance Results from Faith

The more you pursue maturity in your faith, the less you are attracted to the sinful pleasures around you. That is when your personal life is filled with sorrowful repentance and reformation, powered by the encouragement of the Holy Spirit within your heart. That means you are growing in the grace of God. And you follow a new compass in your journey through life, one which is set on living a holy life and a useful, productive Christian life.

This new life as a conscientious and sincerely penitent believer is a giant step, an especially important one. My understanding is that everyone in this position is my dear brother or sister in Christ.

However, they have not yet done all that the Bible tells them to do. And until I know differently, I prefer to believe their lack of complete obedience is due either to incomplete knowledge or to not having an opportunity. I do not like to think anyone has gone this far on their spiritual journey and would stop short because a parent or someone else might get angry at your new lifestyle. Who would think of refusing to be baptized because that would mess up their fancy hair style . But stranger reasons have been given.

Let me put it another way. My great-great grandfather **Jacob Mac Paregien** immigrated to the United States from Northern Ireland. That is literally all that I know about him prior to his arrival in the U.S.. Except that, like all immigrants, he had to file an application stating his desire to enter our nation and to become a citizen. When the ink dried on that document, he was a *prospective* U.S. resident with the possibility of becoming a resident and perhaps later to gaining actual citizenship. Only when the authorities approved his application – and not before -- did he become an ***actual*** resident of the United States.

Or better yet, let's go back to what happened to the apostle Paul in the city of Corinth. That town was a thriving commercial center and provided every act of sin one could imagine. Paul tried to preach the gospel of Christ to the Jewish people there, but they would not listen and even said awful things about Paul. In a different synagogue the leader, Crispus, invited Paul to his home. And all of the people living in his house believed in Jesus as Lord.

However, as Paul slept that night he had a disturbing vision. Luke the Physician, the writer of the book of Acts, described the event this way:

***"The Lord said to him, 'Don't be afraid! Continue talking to people and don't stop! I am with you. No one will be able to hurt you. Many of my people are in this city.' Paul stayed there for a year and a half, teaching God's word to the people"*** (Acts of the Apostles 18:9-11; <u>**Holy Bible: Easy-to-Read Version**</u>).

The sentence which jumps out at me here is when God tells Paul, ***"Many of my people are in this city."*** There was no outward indication of numbers of God-loving people. It was surprising news for Paul. Apparently, God claimed this unknown group of people within the city as "his" because, being all-knowing, he was sure Paul would eventually preach the gospel to them and their receptive hearts were ready to respond and accept Jesus as their Lord. They were, in a real sense, ***prospective*** brothers and sisters in Christ and people to be loved.

## Likewise, God Expects Penitent Believers to Be Baptized As Soon As Possible

Imagine a young sailor home on leave for 10 days and his first-time date at a party where alcohol is freely flowing. As the drinking gets more serious, another inebriated person yells out, "Let's all go down to the Justice of the Peace so Sailor John and his girl Mary can get married!" The loud crowd yells their approval and someone adds, "Yeah, I dare you to get married!" And, loaded to the gills with beer and hard liquor, they climb in cars and drive down to the office of the Justice of the Peace and the deed is done. Their sham marriage only lasts for a day or two before being annulled. Wouldn't we agree this "wedding" was a foolish thing as well as being a mockery of the holy, life-time commitment that marriage is supposed to be?

The same principle applies to the process of salvation. Certain elements and attitudes must be part of the process, otherwise it is a meaningless exercise. Any testimonial baptism must be preceded by the candidate hearing and believing the gospel facts (Matthew 28:18-20; Romans 1:16). He must come to that moment of faith and certainty that Jesus is the Son of the living God. Then, drawn by God's love and his own heart filled with loved, the candidate accepts God's grace-filled offer of salvation, forgiveness, and justification through his faith in Jesus.

I like the way that the late **W. Carl Ketcherside** described this process. In my particular faith-heritage, we were exposed to the idea that a person had to climb up a ladder with five rungs: (1) hearing the gospel; (2) faith in Christ as Lord; (3) confession of that faith; (4) repentance; and (5) baptism. Carl came to a new understanding of the grace of God in the early1950's. Later, he spoke before his home congregation and told them of his different interpretations and views. Here he describes part of that talk:

"I dealt with the 'five steps of salvation' and showed that we were not saved by climbing a little ladder into the kingdom. Rather we were drawn up by an 'escalator.' We simply took the step of faith and the grace of God, as an unseen power drew us up into repentance and immersion into the precious Lord. It was His power and not ours which accomplished His purpose and we never left the faith we had in the beginning to go on to the next step" (**Pilgrimage of Joy**, p. 6 of the online version at www.unity-in-diversity.org/Books/poj/page06.htm).

Almost immediately, this new Christian begins witnessing for Jesus. First, to please and obey God, he vows with the Spirit's help to change his sinful ways. Second, he proceeds with requesting that someone perform his water baptism. It is one of many new testimonies he will make as to his new relationship with God but also his new identity as a member of God's spiritual family. And third, he commits his life to living for Jesus and even suffering for him to the point of death if that becomes necessary. He makes up his mind to obey God to the full extent of his understanding and to encourage others to do the same (Hebrews 10:24).

The newborn child of God is set to begin an exciting journey. He has been saved by grace through faith, has been justified and received the indwelling of the Holy Spirit, has repented of his old way of life, and has been baptized to please God. Now he grows in the grace of loving God even more, of loving others (i.e., desiring the very best for anyone he meets), and of imitating Jesus in doing good and no harm wherever he goes.

The road rules are genuinely simple: Love God and his Word. Love God's people and be a peacemaker. Genuinely love non-Christians, even one's enemies. Live in harmony with all people so far as they will allow. Always try to please God in every way you know, and grow in grace so you mirror the image of Jesus more every day. Share the gospel, the story of Jesus, as you have opportunities to do so. Those virtues must form the basis of the Christian life, no matter one's spiritual age.

# Chapter 8

# Baptisms in Acts

Usually about this time or earlier, as new believers get deeper into the Word of God they begin to ask about this thing called baptism (from ***baptizo*** = literally to dip, plunge or immerse) but more generally to initiate or enroll a person into something). They read where Jesus was immersed by John the Baptist and that, in turn, Jesus actually told his closest disciples to go out and preach his gospel far and wide. And he told them when believers responded by faith in him, they were to immerse them in water: ***"He said to them, 'Go throughout the whole world and preach the gospel to all people. Whoever believes and is baptized will be saved; whoever does not believe will be condemned'"*** (Mark 16:15-16; <u>**Today's English Version**</u>)." Obviously, one who never comes to faith (believes) will not take the next step of being baptized.

Here is just a word of caution about these two verses. First, they are not found in the oldest manuscripts that we have in various museums around the world. The concepts are consistent with those found in other New Testament passages. Second, some have placed so much emphasis on the simple testimonial baptismal initiation that it overshadows the primary importance of whole-hearted love for and faith (trust) in Jesus as the Son of God. Their misplaced emphasis almost changes the message to "Go throughout the whole world and preach the gospel to all people and tell them baptism is essential to salvation."

The act of baptism did not originate with John the Baptist or with Christianity. The Jews performed a similar initiation ceremony long before Jesus was born of Mary. In Luke 7:30 the Jewish lawyers and Pharisees refused to submit to the baptism being done by John the Baptist, for they wanted nothing to do with this man's kind of "pre-enrollment" in the coming church or fellowship of Christ.

And as we read through the exciting book called The Acts of the Apostles, we repeatedly see new believers submitting to the simple act of baptism. They do it as a public testimony to their faith in Jesus. Remember earlier, we agreed that God does not have to repeat himself time and again for his command to be both true and binding on Christians. Once is all we need. Let's apply that principle here.

Jesus set the example himself by being baptized in the River Jordan, though he had nothing to repent of and therefore was not for remission of sins at all. It was a testimonial announcement of the beginning of his public ministry.

Later, Jesus ordered his disciples to baptize those who believed that gospel message. Isn't that enough? I would think so. However, for your further peace and conviction here are many more examples.

## *(1) In Acts 2, Peter preached the Good News and some 3,000 accepted Jesus and were baptized.*

They were initiated into the body of Christ as new believers. On this day, the complete gospel of Christ was first preached. Peter and the others told about his humanity and divinity, his life on earth, his voluntarily death on the cross for our sins, his resurrection and ascension, and his coming again. That was all they needed to know, right then, and they rushed forward to be immersed to please God.

Please note that nothing else has ever been added to this core gospel story. Because of that basic information, they repented of their sins and did what Jesus wanted them to do. This complete life changing faith-experience resulted in their salvation in their becoming children in God's family. The same simple process still applies today.

Here is how the writer of the Book of Acts, Luke the physician and evangelist, described that day: "Now when they heard this [the gospel – SP] they were cut to the heart, and said to Peter and the rest of the apostles, 'Brethren, what shall we do?' And Peter said to them, 'Repent and be baptized every one of you in the name of Jesus Christ for the forgiveness of your sins, and you will receive the gift of the Holy Spirit. For the promise is for you and for your children and for all who are far off [referring primarily to the Greeks, but also to you and to me! – SP] , everyone whom the Lord our God calls to himself. And with many other words he bore witness and continued to exhort them, saying, 'Save yourselves from this crooked generation.' So those who received his word were baptized, and there were added that day about three thousand souls" (Acts 2:37-41; **English Standard Version**).

Many people disagree as to the correct interpretation of the "for the remission of sins" portion of Act 2:38. Countless scholarly articles and books have been written about those words and scores of debates have been held by folks who have different opinions about them.

Much of the controversy hinges on figuring out how the Greek word, *eis* ("ice"), should be translated into English. Some argue the English text should read "**for.**" Others argue, adamantly, it should be translated "**because of.**" One's interpretation of that tiny word leads one to either conclude the point or moment of salvation takes place when one has that faith-experience or . . . that initial salvation takes place after one is baptized and rises to walk in newness of life.

You might think that sincere men and women should be able to come to an agreement . . . or at least disagree without being disagreeable and plain nasty toward each other. That is a reasonable line of thinking, but you would be wrong. Feelings have been hurt, relationships have been broken, and sects have formed around the various interpretations and applications of that little bitty word.

Well, I have no final answers to that controversy. However, I can share my personal experience and that might give you some insight to what this is all about. During my youth, in my own faith-heritage, that passage was always hammered into our heads that if the King James Version said "for the remission of sins" then that was the way it was. End of story. Except that as that conversion story in Acts 2 was told by our preachers, we were left with the impression that baptism was always linked with remission of sins and, therefore, . . . we were saved by and through the act of baptism. And we could mark the moment of our salvation by the exact second we came up wet all over from the baptistry. We just missed the point a wee bit, . . . like by a "country mile" as we used to say in Oklahoma.

Oh, yes, to be fair our preachers usually offered their "altar call" (we sure didn't call it that) by saying that salvation required (1) hearing the gospel; (2) believing the gospel story and having faith in Jesus as our Savior; (3) confessing our faith before others; (4) repenting of our sins; and (5) being baptized for the remission of sin.

So that is what I believed as I was growing up in a home where my mother was a dedicated Christian woman and my father was a consecrated smoker with no interest in religion. And in my 10th grade I accepted Christ and was baptized (immersed) "for the remission of my sins." I would not understand for several years after I started preaching that there are many more blessings or promises to those who are baptized to please God. Now I know better, and I will never again single out just one (such as "for the remission of sins") as being any more or any less important than the others.

It was not until about 1963 or so, in Nashville at Lipscomb University, that I began to sorta get the drift of what all this grace stuff and words like justification by faith meant. But the larger context of what I heard each day in chapel and what I preached on Sundays as a preacher-student at little country congregation was still typical, traditional "baptism for remission of sins" with a little grace sprinkled in.

Now it has been my experience that most Baptist churches will preach and interpret Acts 2:38 as meaning a person should be baptized "because they have been saved." That meant, unlike what I had absorbed in my own group, the Baptists pointed not to the act of baptism as the moment of salvation but to when the person believed in Jesus. That seemed pretty nebulous to me in those days.

Ironically, for a group of folks who taken their name from the act of baptism, the Baptists (who sometimes call themselves Baptist-Christians) by and large are dogmatic about it as a matter of church policy. They argue that baptism is not necessary for salvation, but it is necessary to be baptized by a Baptist minister in order to be considered for membership in their congregation. I see that as convoluted theology in which they make it harder to get into a Baptist congregation than it is to get into heaven.

To the best of my knowledge, most Baptist churches today would not accept me -- a baptized (immersed) believer for over 60 years and a Bible teacher, preacher and author for over 50 years -- without going through their ritual congregational requirement for church membership of being baptized again, only this time by a man of the right sect . . . and then I have to jump over the man-made hurdle of telling my conversion experience and being voted on by the congregation. I love my Baptist brothers and sisters, . . . as much in error as they are (oh, come on now, I'm mostly joking; I have enough errors of mine own). I was baptized in 1957 to please God and I just ain't gonna ever do it, again, for any sectarian reason.

For those who grew up reading one of the many revisions of the King James Version, you may notice in Acts 2:47 where it is said these Messianic Jews converted to Jesus on Pentecost were soon hit with persecution but they held strong. And in verse 47, even today's NKJV still says these devout people were "praising God and having favor with all the people. And the Lord added to the church daily those where were being saved."

Friend, the fact is when ol' Jolly King James of English authorized the original KJV the ancient texts they were translating made no such mention about anybody "being added to the church." That entire phrase is simply not there. But, given the influence of the Church of England, they mistranslated the verse by adding their view of God's family as a man-made and man-run organization rather than a divinely created fellowship. That unfortunate misinterpretation and improper insertion of the concept of a "membership" in a "high church" organization is a big deal because it is both disturbing and misleading. It is also counterproductive in the quest for simple Christianity.

So . . . **The Message** translates 2:47, "Every day their number grew as God added those who were saved." And **The Everyday Bible: New Century Version** translates the verse as, "The Lord was adding those people to the group of believers." And **Today's English Version** likewise simply says, "And the Lord added to their number day by day those who were being saved." The Lord God himself added the saved to his world-wide fellowship and, simultaneously, to each local group.

I know of a "Cowboy Church" out in Colorado where they do not have a membership role of any kind for their church. The pastor told me that God could keep track of that better than they could. So they simply accept into their community of believers all people who claim Jesus as Lord. Most go on to be baptized by immersion, right there in a horse watering trough in front of the podium (Hey, they are a cowboy community.). Those who have not reached that understanding are still welcomed as children of God.

## (2) In Acts 8:4-12, many people in the city of Samaria accepted Jesus and were baptized.

Here is how that happened. Persecution came upon the new Christians in Jerusalem. Most of them packed a few belongings and hit the road for other towns all over the area. Was that a bad thing? Yes and no. It was certainly a frightful time and a dangerous period for them, true. But this "scattering" of believers resulted in the rapid growth of the family of God as these eager new believers shared the Good News about Jesus in their new towns. We saw that same phenomenon after World War II when hundreds of our military people decided to return and preach peace and goodwill through Jesus to the very people they had liberated or even the same ones they had been fighting.

When the early disciples in Jerusalem fled, a brave evangelist named Philip went to the area called Samaria. He spent as much time as he could telling people about how the Messiah had come to earth, died on a cross for our sins, rose again and will one day return as King. And "when they believed what Philip was saying about God's kingdom and about the name of Jesus Christ, they were all baptized" (Acts 8:12; **Contemporary English Version**).

Although in this example, the important behavior of turning from sin (repentance) is not specifically mention, other examples clearly show that is simply part of the process of moving to a faith-experience, to a deep sorrow for our personal sins against the God we now love, submitting to the baptismal initiation into the family and living like a fully accepted child of God.

### (3) Also in Acts 8, a man named Simon—a man who made his living by witchcraft and sorcery—had a change of heart and was baptized.

Luke sums it up this way, "Simon himself believed and was baptized. He stayed very close to Philip. When he saw the miracles and the very powerful things that Philip did, Simon was amazed" (Acts 8:13). Another conversion, another immersion into the fellowship of Christ.

### (4) Again in Acts 8, a Jew from the nation of Ethiopia listened to the Good News of Jesus, developed faith in the Christ and asked for Philip to baptize him.

This unnamed man was an executive in the treasury office of Candace, the Queen of Ethiopia. Because he was in such close contact with the Queen and her court, this man had been castrated (his testicles had been removed) so there would be no hanky-panky, much less a half-breed child born into royalty. That act was standard procedure and such a man was known as a "eunuch." He was an important man back there and he was on business trip, personally driving a first-class chariot maybe with a specialized government license plate to let people know not to mess with him. Now he was way out in the desert returning from Jerusalem to his home in the nation of Ethiopia.

None of that made any different to Philip because an angel had told him to go make contact with the man and tell him about Jesus. Now this Ethiopian fellow, probably with very dark skin, was a religious Jew (not just a secular or cultural Jew) and was studying his personal and very costly copy of the Old scroll of the prophet Isaiah from the section we now label as Isaiah 53:7-8. Luke tells us what happened next: ***"Philip began to speak. He started with the same Scripture and told the man the Good News about Jesus.***

***"While they were traveling down the road, they came to some water. The officer said, 'Look! Here is water! What is stopping me from being baptized?' Then the officer commanded the chariot to stop. Both Philip and the officer went down into the water, and Philip baptized him. When they came up out of the water, the Spirit of the Lord took Philip away; the officer never saw him again. The officer continued on his way home, full of joy"*** (Acts 8:35-39; <u>**The Everyday Bible: New Century Version**</u>).

There are so many important points in those verses, so let's consider a few.

**(A)** Philip, like any perceptive teacher or preacher, got a feel for how much this person already knew about God. If he had been an alien sinner with no knowledge of the One True God, Philip would have started there. But this sincere man was much further along than that. So he started telling the man what he was lacking, and that was the wonderful and fresh news of the gospel of Jesus Christ.

**(B)** Their racial and cultural differences made no difference at all. True, they each were Jews. But they sure did not look alike or come from similar experiences or social standings. The man from Ethiopia was open to God's will, so Philip obediently explained how to come to faith in Jesus. Then he explained how to complete that process by submitting to a testimonial baptism. That whole process in just a few minutes ushered him into the fellowship of the new and fast-growing community of Christ.

**(C)** It did not take very long at all for Philip to explain the core gospel to this eager man. You see, friend, as I have stated above, the basic gospel facts are few and simple for even a person of limited education to understand. A bush woman in Australia can understand it. A man with a taco pushcart stand in Costa Rica can understand it. A man or a woman pulling a rickshaw in Japan or China or India can understand it in only a few minutes. Even a Ph.D. professor in Quantum Mechanics at Harvard University can grasp the good news.

It is in the understanding of those few facts combining with an open and receptive heart which provides the necessary ingredients for that "lightbulb" experience of reaching saving faith in Jesus. Hallelujah for those who are hungry for faith and for a gospel that is so powerful while being so simple. That is why the apostle Paul wrote, "I am not ashamed of the gospel of Christ, for it is the power of God to salvation for everyone who believes . . . . "(Romans 1:6; **The New King James Version**).

Now, after one's enrollment in the service of God, you have a lot of reading and praying to do to help you grow up from a "new baby in Christ" to a mature example and/or leader.

**(D)** Notice some more details about this wonderful event. It was the Ethiopian who spotted a small pond of water in the vast desert and begged for the privilege of being baptized right then and there.

Then make note of the simple statement that the two men both went down into the water. It would have been easier for them to stand on the edge of the water and for Philip to scoop up a small handful of water and then flick it on the Ethiopian in a "sprinkling" fashion . Simple, yes? Correct, I say no. Neither did Philip cup his two hands and scoop up enough water to have a "pouring" ceremony. Nope. That is not what they did.

They both no doubt shed their outer garments and waded waist deep, then Philip assisted in literally immersing or completely covering the believer with water. It was a simple but beautiful reenactment of the death, burial, and resurrection of Jesus . . . and a declaration of the Ethiopian's resolve to die to sin, to bury his old self-centered life and to live a new life under the command of his new King, Jesus.

Now, having stated what my person view of the beauty and logic of baptism by immersion, I want to add a word of caution as stated decades ago by a Bible scholar named **Edward Fudge**. He was a lawyer by trade and a preacher by profession. My ol' grandpa **Frank Paregien** used to say, "You can't be a used car salesman and a Christian both." My latter-day guess is he had a couple of bad deals with a used car salesman, and some of you may sorta bristle up when you hear the word "lawyer." But please hear Edward's words with an open mind and reflect on his question at the end:

"No New Testament passage explicitly defines baptism as immersion. That is its etymology, but etymology does not prove later usage. The evidence for immersion is certainly strong enough to justify our own practice. ***Is it really strong enough to rule out the practice of other Christians whose Greek scholars have a different view?***" [Emphasis mine -- SP - Edward Fudge in "Balancing Baptism" in ***Restoration Review***, Vol. 28, Number 3, March 1986]

"Ah, now there's the rub" as Shakespeare or maybe my kinfolk in Oklahoma might say.

**(E)** Oh, here is a good place to notice something else. There is no record here of Philip saying a word during this baptism. Maybe he did say a few words, maybe not. But it brings up the erroneous idea some folks have that a certified pastor or priest is the only one who can perform a baptism and he/she must absolutely say certain prescribed ceremonial words at a baptism. It is heart-felt, information-based faith in Jesus that is the saving factor here.

**(F)** When you read the four gospel accounts of the life of Jesus – as given by Matthew, Mark, Luke, and John – you will find countless examples of a particular story being given extended space and details by one writer, then shorter accounts with fewer details by one or more of the others. The same is true in the marvelous Acts of the Apostle. Luke the Physician is trying to get these thrilling events down on parchment. And he certainly believes his Christian readers know enough to supply certain basics when he does not mention them by name.

So here in this baptism of the Ethiopian, it is reasonable to assume – though Luke does not mention these – that he certainly developed a faith in Jesus, that he told Philip about it (confession) and that he intended to change his life (repent) – all prior to his baptism. (See related materials at Matthew 10:32; Romans 10:9-10; and in 1 Timothy 6:12.)

**(G)** Finally, please note the behaviors of the Ethiopian executive and of Philip the evangelist right after the baptismal initiation was completed. The Spirit of God led Philip away to another assignment, someone else who needed the gospel. Our late friend, Jimmie Lovell used to say, "No person has the right to hear the gospel twice, before every person hears it once." On the other hand, the man from Ethiopia got right back up into his chariot and hit the road for home. Only he was a changed man. He had become a disciple, a Christian. And he "was full of joy." And he had a story to tell as well.

In about 1850, an English preacher wrote a song based on this Ethiopian's exciting experience. Here is part of that song (rearranged by Edward Hawkins in the 1960s):

> Oh happy day.
> Oh happy day.
> When Jesus washed,
> Oh, when He washed
> Mmm, when He washed
> All my sins away.
> Oh happy day.

## *(5) Next we have the amazing conversion of a terrorist named Saul.*

When you think of Saul, think of a legalistic Jew who was a member of the sectarian Pharisee band. They knew the heathen Greeks, the agnostics and atheists, and the way-out Jewish faction called Christians were headed straight for hell at 150 m.p.h. And he not only knew that as a fact, but he was happy about it.

The first time we see him is in Acts 7 when Saul stood by cheering on a Jewish mob throwing rocks at Stephen for preaching about Jesus. Saul's adrenalin was skyrocketing as they bashed Stephen's brains and body to an unrecognizable pulp. They all thought they were doing God a big favor. Saul even congratulated his comrades on a job well done.

In fact, the Book of Acts tells us in 9:1-2 that Saul was set on helping these folks get to hell even faster. "All this time Saul was breathing down the necks of the Master's disciples, out of the kill. He went to the Chief Priest and got arrest warrants to take to the meeting places in Damascus so that if he found anyone there belonging to the Way, whether men or women, he could arrest them and bring them to Jerusalem" (**The Message**).

Nice guy this Saul. Well, on the outskirts of Damascus something happened that shocked Saul and everyone who knew him or even had heard about his viciousness.

Out of the clear blue, his eyes were hit by something like a laser beam. It was like a blinding flash of light you might associate with an atomic explosion. He fell to the ground, dazed, and scared out of his wits all the way down to his sandals. And to make matters much worse, he hears "I am Jesus, the One you're hunting down. I want you to get up and enter the city. In the city you'll be told what to do next" (**The Message** - MSG).

Yikes. Saul was out to terrorize or even kill the followers of this Jesus guy. And now this Jesus was giving him orders. And he had no choice but to follow them. What a revolting moment! What would his three Pharisee brethren, traveling with him, say about him now? It was not going to be good. But those three men, now able to see themselves, led the blinded Saul into the city of Damascus.

That is when Ananias, a follower of the Christ, got a direct vision from Jesus for him to find this wild man Saul and lay hands on him and give his eyesight back. Ananias had rather received orders to lay his hands around Saul's throat to choke him to death, but the Lord had clearly spoken. So Ananias did exactly as he was instructed. He said to this hated terrorist: "Brother Saul, the Master sent me. The same Jesus you saw on your way here. He sent me so you could see again and be filled with the Holy Spirit. No sooner were the words out of his mouth than something like scales fell from Saul's eyes -- he could see again! He got to his feet, was baptized, and sat down with them to a hearty meal" (Acts 9:17-19"; **The Message** - MSG).

This Saul, formerly a hater of all things Christian, dropped his Jewish name in favor of the Roman equivalent "Paul." And instead of persecuting Christians he became one of them and was often beaten and shunned because he was such an outspoken spokesperson for Jesus. (Luke tells other details about his dramatic conversion in Acts 22:6-21 and 26:13-23). He traveled widely preaching the gospel and baptizing those who had experienced life-changing faith Jesus. And Paul, like so many early courageous disciples, would eventually be killed for his faith.

This event has become "Exhibit A" or a "proof text" for those who hold to a sacramental view of baptism. They wind up endorsing in principle the erroneous view that the communion wine and bread are literally the blood and body of Jesus. It is the same logic or lack thereof.

Such thinking simple misses the heart of the gospel message. Salvation cannot be achieved by human merit or works. If we are ever saved, it will be only by God's grace. It is his grace which leads us to faith in Jesus as our hope of glory. It is this abiding faith which God accepts by which he grants us the **reality of salvation** and the benefit of our Lord's blood-sacrifice. It is only by this faith that we acquire the benefit of being washed in the blood of the Lamb.

On the other hand, **baptism is a physical and visual symbol of testimony to our new relationship as a child of God.** Some have compared it to the symbolism of a wedding ring. You see, there is no miraculous chemical transaction stirred up in the baptismal waters to literally wash any filth on the candidate clean just because of that dipping process. Baptism is a symbolic testimony to the believer's recent change of life through faith in Jesus.

### *(6) In Acts 10, we have a Roman soldier named Cornelius who placed his future and his faith in Jesus and was baptized into our Lord's body of believers.*

Cornelius was a professional soldier in the Roman army, the sometimes brutal occupiers of the area we know today as the Holy Land. We know nothing of his childhood or youth, but one most unusually feature stands out. He was a devout Jew, both of a lover of Yahweh (the Jewish transliteration of God) and of the people of God. This good-hearted soldier, a ruler over 100 men, lived in Caesarea. He and his whole family, apparently including any older children at home as well as his household servants, worshiped the one true and living God.

One day an angel knocked on his door and ordered him to send two of his men to the city of Joppa with orders to bring back a man named **Simon Peter**. While the messengers were on their way, back in Joppa the Spirit of God was softening Peter's heart toward the idea of a faith which would include not just Jewish people but people of every nation. While Peter was praying, the Lord sent him a vision in which a bag of both approved kosher food (ceremonially approved) and food which no rule-keeping Jew could eat. Three times the angel dangled that odd combination of food in front of him and told him three times not to think of anything God had cleaned as being ceremonially unclean.

While poor ol' Peter was pondering this strange vision, the three men arrived and informed him that **Captain Cornelius** of the Roman army wanted him to travel with them back to Caesarea. So the next day Peter and few of his fellow believers went with the three messengers to Caesarea, none of them knowing what was in store. Lo and behold, when they arrived at the home of Cornelius he had gathered several folks together to hear whatever Peter might have to say. They had no idea what his message would be. So they . . . and Peter . . . had a shock coming.

Luke described the fantastic meeting this way: "Peter began to speak. 'I now realize that it is true that God treats everyone on the same basis. Those who fear him and do what is right are acceptable to him, no matter what race they belong to. You know the message he sent to the people of Israel, proclaiming the Good News of peace through Jesus Christ, who is Lord of all.

"'You know of the great event that took place throughout the land of Israel beginning in Galilee after John [the Baptist – SP] preached his message of baptism. You know about Jesus of Nazareth and how God poured out on him the Holy Spirit and power. He went everywhere, doing good and healing all who were under the power of the Devil, for God was with him. We are witnesses of everything that he did in the land of Israel and in Jerusalem. Then they put him to death by nailing him to a cross. But God raised him from death three days later and cause him to appear , not to everyone, but only to the witnesses that God had already chosen, that is, to us who ate and drank with him after he rose from death. And he commanded us to preach the gospel to the people and to testify that he is the one whom God has appointed judge of the living and the dead. **All the prophets spoke about him, saying that all who believe in him will have their sins forgiven through the power of his name** [emphasis mine, SP].'

"While Peter was still speaking, the Holy Spirit came down on all those who were listening to his message. The Jewish believers who had come from Joppa with Peter were amazed that God had poured out his gift of the Holy Spirit on the Gentiles also. For they heard them speaking in strange tongues and praising God's greatness. Peter spoke up. These people have received the Holy Spirit, just as we also did. Can anyone, then, stop them from being baptized with water? So he ordered them to be baptized in the name of Jesus Christ" (Acts 10:34-48; **<u>Today's English Version Bible</u>**).

Sorry that was such a long passage. However, it has several points of truth we must briefly mention.

**First**, when God tells you to do something—even when he does not explain why—you better get your action shoes on and do it.

**Second**, there are good people – even deeply religious people – out there just waiting for someone to come and explain the way of the Lord more perfectly.

**Third**, pay attention to what Peter was slow to learn: God loves everyone and his family circle includes people of every color, nation, occupation, and language. So don't ever put down a person who is different from you. And lest we forget, never say anything degrading about a Jew or Jewish people. They are still special people in God's sight. Remember, too, Jesus was born as Jew, lived as a Jew, and died as a practicing Jew.

**Fourth**, Peter was talking to people who did not yet have faith in Jesus so he kept his message focused on the core gospel message. He did not spend any time on "church doctrine" that is important after conversion and vital for grown, but he kept it on the gospel and what was necessary for the New Birth.

**Fifth**, God doesn't have to follow man's "patterns." This was an unusual event, unique in the fact that God's vision specifically told Peter to eat snakes, etc., that God had previously forbidden Jews to eat. Then, the second unusual thing (at least to folks in my faith-heritage) was that Cornelius, his family and friends received the Holy Spirit . . . and then they were baptized. Heck, everyone (in my group) knows that the order in Acts 2:37-38 is **first** baptism and **then** the Holy Spirit. But here, again, was God . . . being God and not subject to criticism by those he created.

**Sixth**, Peter elaborated on this event which marked the gospel being giving to non-Jewish people. He was with Paul and Barnabas and the elders in Jerusalem when he said of Cornelius and his people: "God chose me from among you to tell the Good News to those who are not Jewish. It was from me that they heard the Good News and believed. 8 God knows everyone, even their thoughts, and he accepted these non-Jewish people. He showed this to us by giving them the Holy Spirit the same as he did to us. 9 To God, those people are not different from us. When they believed, God made their hearts pure. 10 So now, why are you putting a heavy burden around the necks of the non-Jewish followers of Jesus? Are you trying to make God angry? We and our fathers were not able to carry that burden. 11 No, we believe that we and these people will be saved the same way—by the grace of the Lord Jesus" (Acts 15:7-11, ERV).

Notice he says, "they heard the Good News and believed" (verse 7), and God himself "accepted these non-Jewish people" and gave them "the Holy Spirit the same as he did to us" because in his eyes "those people are not different from us" (verse 9).

Now here are two critical questions for you: (1) Exactly when were Cornelius and his people saved, before their baptism or was it afterwards? (2) How were they saved?

Look at the text. Read it for yourselves. And believe it.

They were saved "when they believed" and that was **before** they were ever baptized. They were saved **"by the grace of the Lord Jesus,"** no doubt at the same moment they had faith in Jesus. So their salvation was given and received and certified by God himself.

That is why I have say my personal view is this: A person is a Christian who has stated his faith in Jesus as Lord, has repented of his sins, and is lovingly trying to please God and to be more like Jesus the best way he knows.

That statement is non-judgmental, and simply states the obvious. It does no damage to any truth I currently hold, nor does it approve any errors that the other person may still hold. It holds open the opportunity for more study and prayer about baptism and other topics, but doing so within the family of God and without rancor.

Then, separate, and apart from that salvation experience, every believer there stepped forward and was baptized as a visual, physical marker or testimony to their spiritual salvation experience which happened only minutes before.

I gladly confess to you that as I finished writing the above lines, I saw the real and true salvation process more clearly than I ever have before. Praise the Lord! It clarifies for me so much of the books of Romans, Galatians, Hebrews, and the Gospel of John. It is liberating and exhilarated. I stand absolutely amazed at how I could have been so blind to something so obvious. I guess that comes from reading the scriptures with "sectarian lenses."

I believe that we are saved by God's grace at the moment we have faith in and acceptance of the atoning blood-sacrifice of Jesus on the cross. At that very moment, God declares us righteous in his eyes. We are saved, we are redeemed, and we are forgiven of all our sins. We are adopted into God's family, his spiritual household that is composed of all those who have ever been saved. And the Holy Spirit enters the temple of our body as a comforter, enlightener, guide, and when necessary, a corrector.

Other related factors in salvation come into play, sometimes very quickly.

**Confession** is a practice which appears frequently in the context of worship in both the Old Testament and the New. Confession meant to a heart-felt admission or profession of something one believes to be true. That was often seen where individuals and/or the nation of Israel confessed this or that to God. Often it was the confession of one's sins, weaknesses, fears, or one's praise and adoration for God.

In regard to the process of salvation, the sequence is to first believe and then to confess (John 1:49; 4:42; 9:35-38; Matthew 10:32-33). Confession is an act of faith, just like repentance and baptism. It is a testimonial to one's faith in Jesus. That implies one's acceptance of the authority of Jesus in one's life. Therefore, it is not something done before the faith-experience. Only after that event can one confess their unreserved faith in Jesus as Lord and Savior and as the Son of God (Matthew 16:15-18; John 1:49; 11:27; 20:28; Acts 4:12; Romans 10:9; Philippians 2:11). There are no prescribed words for this personal confession.

"9 If you say with your mouth that Jesus is Lord, and believe in your heart that God raised Him from the dead, you will be saved from the punishment of sin. 10 When we believe in our hearts, we are made right with God. We tell with our mouth how we were saved from the punishment of sin. 11 The Holy Writings say, 'No one who puts his trust in Christ will ever be put to shame.' 12 There is no difference between the Jews and the people who are not Jews. They are all the same to the Lord. And He is Lord over all of them. He gives of His greatness to all who call on Him for help. 13 For everyone who calls on the name of the Lord will be saved from the punishment of sin" (Romans 10:9-13; **New Life Version** – NLV).

We must include **baptism** in the multi-layered process of salvation. We have no choice in the matter. Baptism was a direct command from Jesus to his apostles. They, in turn, preached the gospel and baptized those who believed it and encourage all those new believers to do the same. And they did.

Following the conversion examples in Acts, a new believer today should be baptized as soon as possible after their faith-experience. We are physically baptized in water to please our Father and in obedience to the words of Jesus. **We are baptized because we are already children of God by grace through our faith-experience**.

In this additional act of faith, our testimonial baptism, we tell the world about our new relationship with God and other believers. We see baptism as an action of faith, not works. Our faith for salvation is centered in Jesus, not in baptism. Therefore, we cherish baptism is an important symbolic event - "An outward sign of an inward grace," as some say. But we reject the erroneous idea of elevating baptism to a ritual with mysterious sacramental powers present in the water. We see it as no more important and no less important than one's confession or repentance.

Of course, I know there will be plenty of people within my own faith-heritage and elsewhere who will be offended at my conclusions. I've been down that lonely road before. All I can say is this: for the first 45 years of my life I had a lot of help reaching the wrong conclusions. I was taught early on and constantly reinforced over the years with the idea that most of the evangelical world got it all wrong. That included Billy Graham, Charles Stanley, Oral Roberts, etc.. I am ashamed of that narrow mindedness. I repent of that kind of lame theology, and I vow before God to accept as my spiritual kinfolk anyone he accepts as his children.

I stand on the above paragraphs as being what I believe today, pending further prayer and study.

## (7) In Acts 16 we read about the conversion of a merchant in the city of Philippi.

Oh, and did I mention this prominent businessperson was a Jewish woman named Lydia? She was a successful seller of "purple cloth" (i.e., bolts of cloth which had been stained with the fairly expensive color associated with royalty). We know that she was a worshiper of Jehovah God, the one true and living God, though the text is unclear whether she was an actual Jew. But the spirit of God made sure that she connected with Paul, Silas, and Luke in the city of Philippi. Here's how the physician described what happened next:

"On the Sabbath day we went out the city gate to the river. At the river we thought we might find a special place for prayer. Some women had gathered there. So we sat down and talked with them. There was a woman named Lydia from the city of Thyatira. Her job was selling purple cloth. She worshiped the true God. Lydia listened to Paul. The Lord opened her heart. She believed the things Paul said. She and all of the people living in her home were baptized. Then Lydia invited us into her home. She said, 'If you think I am truly a believer in the Lord Jesus, then come stay in my house.' She persuaded us to stay with her" (Acts 16:13-15; **Holy Bible: Easy-to-Read Version**).

That brief account is amazing in several ways.

**First,** Paul and Silas and Luke forsook the traditional Sabbath synagogue meeting for a chance to refresh themselves in prayer down by the river. There are certain times and circumstances when such a "retreat" for the normal routine of life can be beneficial. And this occasion was certainly that.

**Second**, they joined in with a group of women who had already started their own prayer circle.

**Third**, Lydia had already discovered Yahweh, the true and living God, but the Lord opened her heart to the gospel of Jesus.

**Fourth**, Paul wasted no time sharing the core gospel with these women who were eager to draw nearer to God. This was the moment when Paul "begat," as it were, the women with the seed of the gospel. And it took hold immediately and brought about a desire to be part of this Jesus movement or fellowship. That was the point of their faith-experience and the moment of their salvation.

**Fifth**, Lydia and the other believing women in her household quickly submitted to the simple testimonial baptismal, certifying their intent to live for Christ. Then they were on equal footing with Paul, Silas, Luke, and the thousands of new converts across that part of the world. They had been born again and were members of the spiritual family of God because their faith, their confession of their belief and turning from sin were all anointed by the grace of God.

## (8) Still in Acts 16, we have a midnight jail house conversion.

Ah, yes, Philippi, a city of gracious people just waiting to hear the gospel and to welcome the evangelists with open arms. Mmmm, not entirely. Before long Paul, Silas and Luke were in deep doodoo, to use a little known theological phrase.

They barely had time to celebrate the conversion of Lydia and her female friends when suddenly some irate Jews began stirring up the crowds against these men. Even some local small-time government leaders riled up the mob so much they tore off the trio's outer robes and brutally beat them with heavy rods. Then they threw the bruised and bloodied men into a nasty, dark jail cell.

There is no account of what the mob said as they high-fived each other and walked toward the nearest pub to gloat. But it must have been something like, "Now that'll teach 'em a danged good lesson. They won't say another word about this heretic Jesus in our town ever again."

Wrong. Really, horribly wrong.

Here's what happened next, according to Luke's account: "About midnight Paul and Silas were praying and singing hymns to God, and the prisoners were listening to them, and suddenly there was a great earthquake, so that the foundations of the prison were shaken. And immediately all the doors were opened, and everyone's bonds were unfastened. When the jailer woke and saw that the prison doors were open, he drew his sword and was about to kill himself, supposing that the prisoners had escaped. But Paul cried with a loud voice, 'Do not harm yourself, for we are all here'"(Acts 16:25-28; **<u>Holy Bible: English Standard Version</u>**).

Whoa, wait a minute. These men were still hurting from their beatings. And then Paul and Silas start singing duets of Jewish hymns? And they prayed aloud, both giving thanks for the opportunity to suffer for the cause of Christ and praying for their new converts and all the prospects in Philippi? Yes. And note that the other prisoners, perhaps there for far more serious crimes, were listening to the songs and the prayers. Amazing.

Then the truly miraculous happened, or as a hard-nosed scientist might say "An unusual coincidence took place." Whatever. What we know is an earthquake shook the jail and joggled open all of the jail doors. When the poor jailer jumped up and saw the doors swinging in the breeze, he knew he would be dead meat as soon as the Roman officials arrived. It was a capital offense for a jailor to let a prisoner – much less a jail full of prisoners – get loose. And the Romans had perfected the art of squeezing every ounce of pain out of a man before death mercifully came.

So Paul, Silas and Luke yelled "Yahoo!" and ran down the street and out of town like Olympic sprinters. Right? Nope. Didn't happen. Read Luke's account:

"And the jailer called for lights and rushed in, and trembling with fear he fell down before Paul and Silas. Then he brought them out and said, 'Sirs, what must I do to be saved?' And they said, 'Believe in the Lord Jesus, and you will be saved, you and your household.' And they spoke the word of the Lord to him and to all who were in his house. And he took them the same hour of the night and washed their wounds, and he was baptized at once, he and all his family. Then he brought them up into his house and set food before them. And he rejoiced along with his entire household that he had believed in God" (Acts 16:2934; **<u>Holy Bible: English Standard Version</u>**).

Notice how similar the jailor's question is to that of the multitudes on the previous Day of Pentecost who asked Peter, "Brothers, what shall we do?" And the response this night in jail was the same as that day in Jerusalem. They were to have faith in Jesus, turn from their sins, tell people about their love for Jesus and . . . oh, yes . . . be baptized into the growing and soon to be world-wide fellowship of Christ. So this humble jailor and those members of his household who were old enough to decide for themselves were immediately baptized. And God added him to the countless number of saved people.

Do you see a consistency here in all of the conversions we have discussed so far? Do you understand that their faith was in Jesus -- not in baptism, not in their ability to turn from their sinful, self-centered lives, not in their great knowledge of religion, not in messengers like Paul or Silas or Peter or in Ananias. Their hope for eternal life, their desire for forgiveness hinged on their faith in Jesus. That was the moment in which they were saved. That set about the flow of God's healing grace upon them, along with all the blessings which rapidly come with it (the gift of the Holy Spirit, remission of sins, adoption as God's children, etc).

Let me point out a couple of things. Some Bible scholars have honestly concluded that, given the secure circumstances and the time of night, Paul and Silas might have baptized the jailor and his house members by some other mode of baptism, perhaps "sprinkling" or "pouring." My guess is they had enough water for the preferable full-immersion testimonial baptisms, maybe at nearby watering troughs. But, when you get right down to it, the Bible text gives no indication of how much water was available.

In this case I defer to my Christian brother, **Al Maxey**, in his well-worded personal conclusion, with which I agree:

"My own personal understanding is that the spiritual meaning of this event is of greater significance than the physical mode. My preference would be immersion (as that lends itself better to the figure of a burial), however I would never suggest that another mode invalidated one's baptism, since I find nowhere in Scripture where such is even hinted at. Some may assume God would be displeased with another mode, but there is absolutely nothing in God's Word where such is declared. Thus, we should be careful, lest we condemn that which God has not." –Al Maxey, "Twenty Questions About Baptism," *Reflections* (online blog), Issue 642 – Dec. 19, 2014.

And, again, Al Maxey wrote:

"We humans tend to take far too far the particulars of our rituals, even to the point of suggesting any departure from what we regard as 'the pattern' will result in eternal damnation. I personally doubt our Father is all that concerned with legalistic particulars pertaining to some religious rite. He focuses on the heart, while we tend to fuss and fight over forms. Although my preference, based on my understanding of Scripture, is full immersion, I would never condemn another who may not have that same understanding.

"If a penitent believer submits to baptism, and his/her form or mode differs from mine, yet their heart is totally committed in love and faith to their Lord, and they submit to this rite to please Him, then I would say their baptism is just as valid as mine.

"Man obsesses over the externals; the Lord observes the intent of our hearts. Thus, I would respond to this question by saying that whether or not one is 'biblically baptized' is not so much determined by the form or mode of that rite, but by the heart of the one submitting to it. It is the latter, not the former, in my view, that determines divine acceptance or rejection of such evidentiary acts" ("Twenty Questions About Baptism," **Reflections** online blog, Issue 642 – Dec. 19, 2014).

I am more than willing to let God sort out the facts and the intentions involved, knowing that our loving God always does what is just and right.

Well, there is even more.

## *(9) In Acts 17, we have conversions in the city of Thessalonica.*

Luke wrote, "After Paul and Silas had passed through Amphipolis and Apollonia, they came to Thessalonica, where there was a synagogue of the Jews. And Paul went in, as was his custom, and on three sabbath days argued with them from the scriptures, explaining and proving that it was necessary for the Messiah to suffer and to rise from the dead, and saying, 'This is the Messiah, Jesus whom I am proclaiming to you.' Some of them were persuaded and joined Paul and Silas, as did a great many of the devout Greeks and not a few of the leading women" (Acts 17:1-4; **New Revised Standard Version**).

As it later turned out, many of the townspeople in Thessalonica got upset with the preaching of the gospel. But that is beside the point, which is that the Holy Spirit through the gospel story of Jesus used Paul and Silas to win the hearts and minds of a number of believers there. No doubt, these people came to faith in Jesus, turned away from their pagan way of life, confessed their love for Jesus and were immersed just like all of the others.

## *(10) Also in Acts 17, we have conversions in the city of Berea.*

Luke states, "As soon as it was night, the brothers sent Paul and Silas away to Berea. On arriving there, they went to the Jewish synagogue. Now the Bereans were of more noble character than the Thessalonians, for they received the message [i.e., the Gospel of Jesus – SP] with great eagerness and examined the Scriptures every day to see if what Paul said was true. Many of the Jews believed, as did a number of prominent Greek women and many Greek men" (Acts 17:10-12; **New International Version**).

So here we have the same sequence of events. As was typical of their habit, Paul and Silas went right to the Jewish synagogue and began telling their people how the Old Testament documents were being fulfilled in the life and ministry of Jesus and, most importantly, how they could receive forgiveness of their sins and be admitted to the fellowship of the Christians. Not only did many of the Jewish people respond to the gospel but so did many of the non-Jewish Greek men and women. Everything was going very well.

That is until those frustrated and angry Jews back in the city of Thessalonica found out about the success of Paul and Silas. They hotfooted it over there to spread false rumors and break up this growing celebration.

Luke informs us that, for Paul's own physical safety, "the brothers [i.e., the new converts there at Berea] immediately sent Paul to the coast, but Silas and Timothy stayed at Perea. The men who escorted Paul brought him to Athens and then left with instructions for Silas and Timothy to join him as soon as possible" (Acts 17:14-15; **New International Version** - NIV).

## *(11) And in Acts 17, we have conversions in the great city of Athens.*

Athens was a tough nut to crack. It was an ancient city in which every kind of idea and philosophy and religion could be floated out and have it examined. It was guaranteed to be picked to pieces by learned men and by old men at the local coffee shops. There were wierdo man-made idols of every description on virtually every street corner. They might have scared away some Christian preachers, but to Paul that was like saying "sic 'em" to a dog. He jumped into the philosophical waters with both feet.

Luke says, "So he [i.e., Paul – SP] reasoned in the synagogue with the Jews and the God-fearing Greeks, as well as in the marketplace day by day with those who happened to be there" (Acts 17:17; **New International Version** - NIV).

Finally, after a while, the leaders invited Paul to stand up share his ideas with them. So this lonely disciple stood up and eloquently discussed the one true and living God. And he pointedly explained that God now calls on all people to repent from their sins because one day in the future this same God "will judge the world with justice by the man he has appointed [i.e., Jesus – SP]. He has given proof of this to all men by raising him from the dead."

As might be expected, some of the people sneered and rejected Paul's words. But, and listen closely to Luke's words, "A few men became followers of Paul and believed. Among them was Dionysius, a member of the Areopagus, and a woman named Damaris, and a number of others" (Acts 17:34; **New International Version** – NIV ).

The family of God was growing all over the region, spreading like wildfire. And in just a few years the story of Jesus would have spread to all the nations of the known world. Amazing.

## *(12) In Acts 18, we read where Paul moved on to the city of Corinth in Greece and established a fellowship of believers there.*

Paul took up his tent-making trade to pay his own expenses. And he worked in that business with **Aquila and Priscilla**, a Jewish husband and wife who had arrived in Greece after the Roman emperor Pontus had ordered all Jews to leave Rome, Italy. As he had opportunity, Paul talked with people about Jesus. And every Jewish Sabbath day he made it a point to meet with them in an effort to convert them. And that process accelerated when his friends Silas and Timothy arrived from Berea.

Luke tells the rest of the story this way: "Paul then moved into the house of a man named Titus Justus, who worshiped God and lived next door to the meeting place. Crispus was the leader of the meeting place. He and everyone in his family put their faith in the Lord. Many others in Corinth also heard the message, and **all the people who had faith in the Lord were baptized** [emphasis mine, SP].

"One night, Paul had a vision, and in it the Lord said, 'Don't be afraid to keep on preaching. Don't stop! I am with you, and you won't be harmed. Many people in this city belong to me.' Paul stayed on in Corinth for a year and a half, teaching God's message to the people" (Acts 18:7-11; **Contemporary English Version**).

The same gospel was preached. The same responses were made. People believed in Jesus, changed their lives, and immediately underwent the baptismal ceremony.

## (13) In Acts 19, we have the conversion of some men at Ephesus.

You will recall that a man called John the Baptist had been picked by God to go around the nation of Israel for the purpose of telling them that the Messiah, Jesus the Christ, would soon begin his public ministry in that area. He preached his heart out with a message for them to repent of their sins and to be baptized before the arrival of the Son of God. Hundreds and hundreds of people believed John and submitted to his baptism.

Luke picked up the story right there. "Paul was visiting some places on the way to Ephesus. There he found some followers. Paul asked them, 'Did you receive the Holy Spirit when you believed?'

"They said, 'We have never even heard of a Holy Spirit!'
"So he asked, 'What kind of baptism did you have?'

"They said, 'It was the baptism that John taught.'

"Paul said, 'John's baptism was a baptism of changed hearts and lives. He told people to believe in the One who would come after him. That One is Jesus.'

"When they heard this, they were baptized in the name of the Lord Jesus. Then Paul laid his hands on them, and the Holy Spirit came upon them. They began speaking different languages and prophesying. There were about 12 men in this group" (Acts 119:1-7; **The Everyday Bible: New Century Version**).

The main problem here seems to be that the baptism of repentance that John the Baptist preached had people looking forward to the coming of the Messiah and the New Covenant. By the time of the events in Acts 19, Jesus had appeared as the Chosen One – the Messiah – and the Old Covenant had been fulfilled and cancelled. The New Covenant of grace and love replaced it.

These men were certainly lovers of God and trying to obey him to the best of their knowledge. But Paul quickly found out these men did not even know the full gospel story. This Messiah they were looking for had come, he had lived on the earth and taught the truth about God. Jesus had voluntary died on a Roman cross for our sins, died and was placed in a cold tomb but three days. Then he arose victorious over both death and sin, and soon had ascended back to heaven to await the wonderful time of his return on judgment day.

So when these men heard these facts of the full gospel, they placed their complete faith in Jesus as their Savior. This was their life-changing faith-experience. And . . . just like all the examples we have seen previously . . . , they gratefully underwent Christian baptism as a marker or testimony of their recent faith experience in Jesus as Lord.

All of the above New Testament conversion accounts are consistent in the process of the New Birth we've been discussing. The germ or seed of the gospel "begets" the person with an open heart, and as that person learns more and more about the gospel of Jesus the Holy Spirit is at work to bear fruit. So when that moment of absolute faith was reached, people responded by pledging to change their sinful lives and to follow whatever Jesus wants them to do.

Yes, I believe it is important for every person of faith to obey Jesus in being baptized, just as countless millions of believers have done over the centuries. But we must not think that there is some magic chemical in the waters of baptism or that words spoken over a person being baptized have some *hocus pocus* power. No, not at all. When you come up from the waters of baptism, it is an emotional high for sure. But there is just not a thing in baptism which can change your behavior. From start to finish, it is the grace of God at work in your life that is the sparkplug. Our testimonial baptism always follows devout faith and repentance.

One other thing about baptism: this simple faith-based, grace-promised act of baptism is a physical assurance to the believer of God's love. Immersion is a physical act in which the water covers your whole body, gets you wet and you can smell and taste the water and touch it with your fingers. It is somewhat like eating the bread of the communion or drinking the wine, so far as being a physical experience. And a very meaningful event.

Years ago, my wife and I had a dear friend who was a dyed-in-the-wool Southern Baptist. She sometimes poo-pooed the importance that people in my own faith-heritage gave to the act of baptism. But one morning we were all having coffee and sharing what we remembered about our respective conversions. When we asked her whether she knew exactly when she was saved, she casually said: "Oh, honey child, yes sir. I remember I was baptized by Brother So-and-So after his sermon on the first Sunday morning in March of 1958 ." Then, realizing what a sincerely important emphasis she had just put on her own baptism, she sheepishly said: "Doggoned if I didn't hang myself by my own tongue." And we all giggled and smiled at her own revelation.

Well, the song below speaks of the confidence and trust a believer has that God is, that God is just, and that God loves us as his dear children. **Fern Jones** wrote this little song and soon thereafter sold it to singer, songwriter, and politician **Jimmy Davis** of Louisiana. He recorded it in 1955 and had a big hit with it. Here is just the first verse and the refrain:

### I Was There When It Happened
By Fern Jones & Jimmy Davis
There are some people who say we cannot tell
Whether we are saved or whether all is well.
They say we only can hope and trust that it is so
But I was there when it happened and so I guess I oughta know.

Yes I know when He saved me (saved my soul),
The very moment He forgave me (made me whole).
He took away my heavy burdens,
Lord He gave me peace within (peace within).
Satan can't make me doubt it (I won't doubt it).
It's real and I'm gonna shout it (I'm gonna shout it).
I was there when it happened and so I guess I oughta know.
(Fair Use Domain.)

Now, let's look at one other question before we leave this topic. Some people ask, "Is baptism always necessary for salvation?" I used to answer that enthusiastically in the affirmative. Now I answer it with the negative. No, there are some exceptions.

I have already defined a person who is a disciple of Christ this way: A person is a Christian who has stated his faith in Jesus as Lord, has repented of his sins and in love is trying the best way he knows to please God and to be more like Jesus.

I did not mention baptism in that statement and, therefore, it means a person would be saved before baptism. That does not take away the importance of that act of faith.

I believe that we are saved by God's grace at the moment we have faith in and acceptance of the atoning blood-sacrifice of Jesus on the cross. At that very moment, God declares us righteous in his eyes. We are saved, we are redeemed, and we are forgiven of all our sins. We are adopted into God's family, his spiritual household that is composed of all those who have ever been saved. And the Holy Spirit enters the temple of our body as a comforter, enlightener, guide, and when necessary, a corrector.

Now, having said that, I must add that it does not negate the fact that a new believer is expected to repent of his sins. Right? Of course, he must. And then he is expected to be baptized. Right. Yep, that's right.

Well, almost all who stress the importance of baptism would admit the ordinance certainly does not apply to anyone too young or too mentally challenged to understand the gospel and the subsequent pledge to the New Covenant. And the fact is that God, as God and in his wisdom and kindness, may excuse others because of extenuating circumstances. That is up to him and I will not speculate as to what his other exceptions might be. **Remember this: Our loving God always does what is just and right.** Never doubt that.

So why do some people spent so much time and energy trying to downgrade the act of baptism when we know that Jesus commanded it and so did the apostles?

In the final analysis, I find it wasted effort to continue arguing about whether salvation comes before baptism or after it. In the natural scheme of things, a new believer is expected to be baptized soon after their faith-experience. So we're talking about a gap of maybe an hour or maybe a few days, during which I do not believe their eternal destiny is in danger if they cannot get into the baptistry because of their death.

Furthermore, I am of the opinion that God is not as concerned as we are as to whether the person being baptized actually knows that salvation came at his moment of faith – before baptism – or will come after rising from the water. What is critical is for the believer to be convinced that Jesus came to earth to show us how to really live, gave his life on the cross and was resurrected to give us hope and power in our lives, and promised to come back to take us home with him to God the Father. He should stand assured that baptism is not a work of man, but man's act of faith in the grace of God. Now that is the gospel, the good news, in any language!

# Chapter 9

# Blessings Beyond Belief

One is not a Christian just because they were born in the United States. Contrary to what many say, the United States has never been a "Christian nation." You see, our founding fathers were wise enough to put statutes in our constitution about the separation of the church and the government. In other countries, the Presbyterian (Church of Scotland) is the official religious body of that nation. The Church of England (Episcopalian) is the official there and has special standing over other religions. And in Costa Rica, the Catholic Church is that country's official religious body with special privileges. Not so in the United States, and that is a good thing.

One is not a Christian just because his family has had their own pew at the Holier Than Thou downtown church for a hundred years. Passively sitting in a church building no more makes one a Christian than sitting inside a chicken house makes you a chicken. You are not a disciple of Jesus Christ because you use his name when you hit your thumb with a hammer, nor just because you dress up the kids and go sit in a church building on Easter or on Christmas Eve. Certainly not if you are just a **"Buzzard Believer."** What is that you ask? It is the person who only goes inside a church building when there is a funeral service for someone he knows.

You are certainly not a Christian just because you are not Jewish. At one time, there were many within the sect of Orthodox Jews who often thought of anyone who was not a Jew as a heathen Gentile or , even worse, as a Christian. They pretty much used the terms interchangeably. More than likely it was because the super-ritualistic Orthodox Jews had so little contact with any non-Jewish people. So they drew the broad and erroneous conclusion that "they all look alike," so to speak.

Okay, enough of that. Here is how I see the Bible itself displaying and therefore defining who is really a Christian. A Christian is one who displays these characteristics:

(1) He is mature enough to evaluate for himself the basic gospel account of the life, death, and resurrection of Jesus.

(2) Based on that evaluation, his heart is filled with love and his brain is filled with deep-seated faith that Jesus is the Christ (Messiah), the Son of God. This is his "light bulb" moment when he makes a calculated choice to accept God's offer of grace and forgiveness. He allows the Holy Spirit to dwell within his body and submits to his leadings.

(3) His loving trust motivates him to want to show his love for God by pleasing him in every way he can, to the best of his understanding.

(4) Similarly, that loving trust leads him to have genuine remorse for his own sins and to change his life. Churchy folks call that repentance.

(5) He imitates all the early Christians in being baptized to please God, and does so as soon after his salvation-experience as possible.

(6) He commits the rest of his life to loving God, loving people in God's world-wide family, being a peacemaker, telling others about Jesus, and looking for opportunities to do good to all people.

Really, each one of those characteristics is a reflection of that person's trust in Jesus and his sacrifice on the cross. Just as faith is not a meritorious work, neither are the acts of obedience, repentance, confession, baptism, loving others and doing good. They are simply responses to and expressions of faith. Faith is the "battery" which is essential to each and every one.

Please remember that these factors in the process of salvation should be viewed as integral parts of the whole. They must not be viewed as a ritual checklist of items required for admission to the kingdom of God. Some people will experience this process more slowly than others, just as people move through the five stages of grief at different speeds.

When all is said and done, we will be saved not by a divine blueprint or scripted plan but by a man who was and is the Son of God – Jesus the Christ (Messiah). We are not saved by correctly answering a 100-item test on theology, nor are we saved by living an absolutely mistake-free and sin-free life. "Nothing in my hand I bring, simply to Christ's cross I cling," to paraphrase an old gospel song.

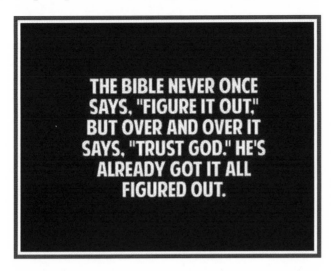

THE BIBLE NEVER ONCE SAYS, "FIGURE IT OUT," BUT OVER AND OVER IT SAYS, "TRUST GOD." HE'S ALREADY GOT IT ALL FIGURED OUT.

Can you name all of the blessings which God gives to the new believer? If you have been a Christian for a few years and still cannot name each and every God-bestowed blessing when you first believed, does that mean your previous baptism was null and void?

Unfortunately, many sectarian preachers and church leaders over the years used highly emotional language and skillfully framed logic to manipulate sincere truth-seekers into being "re-baptized" when there was no basis in scripture or in early church practices for such a thing.

First, let's examine some of the God-bestowed blessings which the new believer is promised. These blessings are listed in no particular order of importance nor order of occurrence.

But what is crucial is getting three facts right about them: (1) the candidate does nothing which would "earn" him or her these blessings, rather it is their simple act of submission and contrition; (2) the candidate does not have to fully understand any of these blessings in order to enjoy them; and (3) our loving God himself graciously and immediately bestows these blessings on the new believer no matter how theologically sophisticated or ignorant they may be.

## (1) One blessing God gives is remission of sins followed by his declaring us righteous in his eyes.

Jesus told his inner band of disciples, "'Go into all the world and preach the gospel to every creature. He who believes and is baptized will be saved; but he who does not believe will be condemned'" (Mark 16L:15-16; **The New King James Version**).

In the second telling in Acts of the conversion of Saul (i.e., Paul), it is the apostle himself relating the story. Luke records his words this way: "In that city was a man named Ananias, a religious man who obeyed our Law [the Old Testament laws – SP] and was highly respected by all the Jews living there. He came to me, stood by me, and said: 'Brother Saul, see again!' At that very moment I saw again and looked at him. He said, 'The God of our ancestors has chosen you to know his will, to see his righteous Servant, and to hear him speaking with his own voice. For you will be a witness for him to tell everyone what you have seen and hear. And now, why wait any longer? Get up and be baptized and have your sins washed away by praying to him.' (Acts 22:12-16; **Today's English Version**).

In Romans 3:22-26 (ERV), the apostle Paul clearly states that it was the holy blood-sacrifice Jesus made for us which gives us any standing before God. Our best works are creations of junk, so far as earning any favor from God. Instead, when God sees a person come to faith in his Son, the debt of sin has been paid for us and he says, "Welcome to our holy family. Jesus made it possible and I declare it to be so." Read this scripture carefully:

"22 God makes people right through their faith in Jesus Christ. He does this for all who believe in Christ. Everyone is the same. 23 All have sinned and are not good enough to share God's divine greatness. 24 They are made right with God by his grace. This is a free gift. They are made right with God by being made free from sin through Jesus Christ. 25-26 God gave Jesus as a way to forgive people's sins through their faith in him. God can forgive them because the blood sacrifice of Jesus pays for their sins. God gave Jesus to show that he always does what is right and fair. He was right in the past when he was patient and did not punish people for their sins. And in our own time he still does what is right. God worked all this out in a way that allows him to judge people fairly and still make right any person who has faith in Jesus."

## *(2) Another blessing God graciously gives is making us as alive as the risen Christ.*

In Colossians 2:11-15 (**The Message** version), Paul discussed that new status.

"Entering into this fullness is not something you figure out or achieve. It's not a matter of being circumcised or keeping a long list of laws. No, you're already in – insiders not through some secretive initiation rite but rather through what Christ has already gone through for you, destroying the power of sin. If it's an initiation ritual you're after, you've already been through it by submitting to baptism. Going under the water was a burial of your old life; coming up out of it was a resurrection. God raising you from the dead as he did Christ. When you were stuck in your old sin-dead life, you were incapable of responding to God. God brought you alive – right along with Christ! Think of it! All sins forgiven, the slate wiped clean, that old arrest warrant canceled and nailed to Christ's cross. He stripped all the spiritual tyrants in the universe of their sham authority at the Cross and marched them naked through the streets."

## *(3) Another blessing God gives is freedom from the powerful grip of sin.*

In Paul's day some of the converts in Rome, Italy were badly mixed up about the grace of God. Some people thought they should just "party" like fools so the grace (kindness, favor) of God would be poured out that much more on them. Here are the wise words of Paul, both for them and for you and me today:

"So do you think that we should continue sinning so that God will give us more and more grace (kindness)? No! We died to (quit living) our old sinful lives. So how can we continue living with sin? Did you forget that all of us became part of Christ Jesus when we were baptized? We shared his death in our baptism. So when we were baptized, we were buried with Christ so that we could be raised up and live a new life. This happened the same as Christ was raised from death by the wonderful power of the Father.

"Christ died, and we have been joined with Christ by dying too. So we will also be joined with him by rising from death like Christ rose from death. We know that our old life died with Christ on the cross. This happened so that our sinful selves would have no power over us. And then we would not be slaves to sin. Any person that has died is made from free from sin's control (power).

"If we died with Christ, we know that we will also live with him. Christ was raised from death. And we know that he cannot die again. Death has no power over him now. Yes, when Christ died, he died to defeat the power of sin one time – enough for all time. He now has a new life, and his new life is with God. In the same way, you should see yourselves as being dead to the power of sin. And see yourselves as being alive for God through Christ Jesus"(Romans 6:1-11; *Holy Bible: Easy-to-Read-Version*).

## (4) Another blessing God gives by his grace is the washing of regeneration and renewal of the Holy Spirit.

In his brief letter to Titus, Paul asked him to remind the local disciples there of certain things:

"Remind them to be submissive to rulers and authorities, to be obedient, to be ready for every good work, to speak evil of no one, to avoid quarreling, to be gentle, and to show perfect courtesy toward all people. For we ourselves were once foolish, disobedient, led astray, slaves to various passions and pleasures, passing our days in malice and envy, hated by others and hating one another. But when the goodness and loving kindness of God our Savior appeared, he saved us, not because of works done by us in righteousness, but according to his own mercy by the washing of regeneration and renewal of the Holy Spirit, whom he poured out on us richly through Jesus Christ our Savior, so that being justified by his grace we might become heirs according to the hope of eternal life. The saying is trustworthy, and I want you to insist on these things, so that those who have believed in God may be careful to devote themselves to good works. These things are excellent and profitable for people" (Titus 3:1-8; **The Holy Bible: English Standard Version**).

The phrase "washing of regeneration" is often mistakenly interpreted as something done in the act of baptism or as a result of it. Over a hundred years ago, Bible scholar Adam Clarke issued this warning about that interpretation: "Baptism is only a visible sign of the cleansing, purifying influences of the Holy Spirit. Baptism changes nothing; the grace signified by it cleanses and purifies. They who think baptism to be regeneration neither know the Scriptures nor the power of God, therefore they do greatly err" [**Clarke's Commentary**, vol. 6, p. 657].

Actually, the constant focus in this section of Scripture is on what God in his grace has done for us, not what we have done or ever can do for him. God was the activator. He was the saving force or agent. Like running a beat-up junky old car though a skilled restoration body shop, God applied his love and justifying power of regeneration to our sinful lives so completely as to make us new creations in Him and hosts in our bodies to the ever-renewing work of the Holy Spirit himself.

It is the Comforter who cleanses our hearts, motivates us to serve the living God, and renews our love for Jesus fresh every morning like the dew on the grass. This passage speaks of the spiritual overhaul which God performs on our hearts, souls, and minds, with no hint of it being a literal washing with water or being performed in a baptistry. Instead, it is an on-going, perpetual renewal of our inner person.

## (5) Another blessing God allows us to be born of the Spirit.

In a night-time discussion with **Nicodemus**, a devoted follower of the sect of Judaism known as Pharisees, Jesus plainly told him:

"'Truly, truly, I say to you, unless one is born again he cannot see the kingdom of God.' Nicodemus said to him, 'How can a man be born when he is old? Can he enter a second time into his mother's womb and be born?' Jesus answered, 'Truly, truly, I say to you, unless one is born of water and the Spirit, he cannot enter the kingdom of God. That which is born of the flesh is flesh, and that which is born of the Spirit is spirit. Do not marvel that I said to you, 'You must be born again.' The wind blows where it wishes, and you hear its sound, but you do not know where it comes from or where it goes. So it is with everyone who is born of the Spirit'" (John 3:3-8; *The Holy Bible: English Standard Version*).

## (6) Another blessing God gives is his acceptance of our appeal for a good conscience.

The apostle Peter in 1 Peter 3 frankly talks about the trials all Christians will face, but reminds of why we are grateful when we suffer for God's sake.

"For it is better to suffer for doing good, if suffering should be God's will, then to suffer for doing evil. For Christ also suffered for sins once for all, the righteous for the unrighteous, in order to bring you to God. He was put to death in the flesh, but made alive in the spirit, in which also he went and made a proclamation to the spirits in prison, who in former times did not obey, when God waited patiently in the days of Noah, during the building of the ark, in which a few, that is eight persons, were saved through water. And baptism, which this prefigured, now saves you –not as a removal of dirt from the body, but as an appeal to God for a good conscience, through the resurrection of Jesus Christ, who has gone into heaven and is at the right hand of God, with angels, authorities, and powers made subject to him" (1 Peter 3:17-22; **New Revised Standard Version**).

The above is a long and complicated passage. So let's get to the point Peter is making. When Noah and his immediate family were loading the creatures two-by-two, the rain was pouring down around them. If they had not obeyed God and built that huge ark (ship), they would have drowned for sure. The ark itself, along with the occupants, were "saved through water" in the sense that it was that flooding water which literally lifted the water-tight ark up on top where it floated on the raging sea. Plainly, it was God's grace and power at work in that act. And Peter simply uses that same analogy about the Christian baptismal initiation that came in his own day.

In a way, today's believer is "saved by the waters of baptism" (to use Peter's own words) but only because it is actually God's grace and power at work in that act made possible by the death, burial, and resurrection of Jesus. That is one powerful image and we personally rejoice whenever we know a lost person has been adopted into the King's family.

## (7) God gives to each new believer the gift of the Holy Spirit and adopts him into the body of Christ (i.e., the fellowship of all believers).

After his resurrection and his pending ascension to heaven, Jesus had told his inner core of disciples to remain in the city of Jerusalem until they were "imbued" with something from "on high." They did not know exactly what he meant, but they did exactly as he ordered.

Then on the feast day of Pentecost, they were all shocked to the bottoms of their sandals by what happened to them. Suddenly, a rushing and roaring wind filled the house where they had gathered. That was strange enough. But then amazement took over as every one of the believers looked around at each other and saw something like flickering flames on every person's head. This was not going to be like anything they had experienced before.

Then, with no warning, each believer began to speak in some kind of foreign language or tongue unknown to them. It would be like a deacon's meeting on Thursday night and all of a sudden ol' Harold was speaking Swahili, while Jack was speaking French, and Walter was thundering away in some Brazilian tribal dialect.

Only in this case, each believer in that house in Jerusalem spoke in his own native tongue. Many, many of them. And the absolutely amazing part is that they could all understand what they were saying. Their subject to a man was what wonderful things God had been doing.

A short time later, Peter and the eleven other apostles walked outside to the common area where a large and joyous Pentecost celebration was going on. The apostles spread out and each began telling a large section of the crowd about the gospel of Christ and how they had actually turned the Son of God over to the Romans and had him executed for no legal reason. Their hearts were sad and broken over their sins.

Luke records, "Peter's words pierced their hearts, and they [the Jews – SP] said to him and to the other apostles, 'Brothers, what should we do?'

"Peter replied, 'Each of you must repent of your sins, turn to God, and be baptized in the name of Jesus Christ to show that you have received forgiveness of your sins. Then you will receive the gift of the Holy Spirit. This promise is to you, and to your children, and even to the Gentiles – all who have been called by the Lord our God.' Then Peter continued preaching for a long time, strongly urging all his listeners, 'Save yourselves from this crooked generation!'

"Those who believed what Peter said were baptized and added to the church that day – about 3,000 in all" (Acts 2:37-41; **New Living Translation**).

Wow, what a list of blessings which they received and so may we today.

Country music giant **Hank Williams** (1923-1953) wrote a song in 1948, "I Saw the Light." This stanza expresses what these folks on the Day of Pentecost must have experienced after they had repented and had been baptized into Jesus:

> I saw the light, I saw the light.
> No more Darkness, no more night.
> Now I'm so happy, no sorrow in sight.
> Praise the Lord, I saw the light.

It is a sin of gross sectarian inconsistency to make any one of the above seven blessings "the gold standard" for whether a person's baptism was invalid. Yet there are those who would not accept another baptized believer because he or she cannot recall that one item (usually "for the remission of sins") as being "the reason" they were baptized and refuse the right hand of fellowship until they parrot the party line with the right words. Or they throw a "hissy fit" if the person who is doing a baptism does not exactly repeat their traditional phase. All of that when the Bible itself does not prescribe any specific words when one is immersed.

Think about this: When someone honestly says, "I just want to be baptized to please God" isn't that the most basic and best reason of all?

So, my friend, please allow me to ask you the most important question you will ever hear. Are you absolutely sure you are right with God?

I cannot answer that question for you. Your parents, friends, church folks and even your preacher cannot answer that question for you.

Maybe this will help. Do you love God and want to be with him for the rest of eternity? Are you so ashamed of your sins that you would do anything for complete forgiveness and peace of mind? Do you sense the Holy Spirit leading you toward God and giving you a better understanding of his Word? Do you believe beyond any doubt that Jesus is Lord. And more than that, do you claim Jesus as your Lord and as your Savior? Friend, if so, you are not far from the Kingdom.

When a person becomes a sincere Christian, there will still be moments when doubts and fears and negative self-feelings creep into your heart. You see, the Devil may have lost you but he is sly enough to do whatever he can to get you back on his side.

The Word of God is always a powerful antidote for Satan's poison. Read and believe with all your heart these encouraging words from the Apostle John:

"Little children, let's not love with words or speech but with action and truth. This is how we will know that we belong to the truth and reassure our hearts in God's presence. Even if our hearts condemn us, God is greater than our hearts and knows all things. Dear friends, if our hearts don't condemn us, we have confidence in relationship to God. We receive whatever we ask from him because we keep his commandments and do what pleases him. **This is his commandment, that we believe in the name of his Son, Jesus Christ, and love each other as he commanded us.** (Emphasis mine,

SP) The person who keeps his commandments remains in God and God remains in him; and this is how we know that he remains in us, because of the Spirit that he has given to us" (1 John 3:18-24; **Common English Bible**).

Remember this well: the good news of salvation through Jesus is the basis for your faith. Your faith is not in your church or your congregation or your preacher or any TV evangelist. Your faith is not in the Bible itself, nor do you worship the Bible. Your faith in not in your limited ability to perform a do-it-yourself repentance from all your sins. Your faith in not in some special H20 in a baptistry or lake or river. Your faith is in Jesus, the Son of the living God, and all your heart and devotion belong to him.

So right now, today, you are in good company – with the redeemed of all nations. You have placed your faith in Jesus. You have turned away from your sinful way of life. You have confessed that he is your Lord and Master. You have by grace been added to God's community or family. And you have been baptized in water as a physical marker testifying to your status as a child of God.

Friend, you are not a Methodist-Christian, an Episcopalian-Christian, a Catholic-Christian or a Church of Christ-Christian. You are a child of the King, filled with the Holy Spirit, born-again to be a peacemaker both among all the Christians scattered in all the sects or denominations and with people of good will everywhere.

Or as the Apostle Paul said to new believers in the city of Corinth, Greece many centuries ago:

"Therefore, if anyone is in Christ, he is a new creation; the old has passed away, and see, the new has come! Everything is from God, who has reconciled us to himself through Christ and has given us the ministry of reconciliation. That is, in Christ, God was reconciling the world to himself, not counting their trespasses against them, and he has committed the message of reconciliation to us.

"Therefore, we are ambassadors for Christ since God is making his appeal through us. We plead on Christ's behalf: 'Be reconciled to God.' He made the one who did not know sin to be sin for us, so that in him we might become the righteousness of God" (2 Corinthians 5:17-21; **Holman's Christian Standard Bible**).

# Chapter 10

## Slow Descent into Churchianity

All digressions begin with one small step in the wrong direction.

Sometimes the spiral downward starts with something so innocuous as a believer saying, "What would be wrong with us doing such-and-such?" The question is suspicious on its face. Since when do God's people adopt ideas and programs just because there is no flashing red stop sign?

Shouldn't the questions really be, "Does God's word shed any light on this matter? Would it bring honor to our Lord? Would it be bring greater unity to his people or less? Who would be genuinely blessed by it and who might be negatively impacted? And will it siphon money, people and resources from what we are doing now?"

Back in the first centuries of simple Christianity, there were a significant number of times when a congregation took a step in the wrong direction. Most often, leaders who were more spiritual in their thinking interceded and helped the body do a course correction that got them back in step with God.

We see that happening in Acts 15. Some long-time Jews who became Christians took a step toward requiring new believers to religiously keep certain Jewish holy days, dietary restrictions, and ceremonial rituals such as circumcision of boy infants. Fortunately, the leaders in Jerusalem succeeded in teaching them that it would be unwise to take that step, both in the case of Jewish converts and non-Jewish converts.

The basic method of evangelism and church growth after the day of Pentecost was for a believer to go out and find someone to tell about Jesus. That might have been an encounter between a Christian and a non-believer at a well where they watered their animals. That Christian might find two farmers working at the edge of their field and stop to visit with about Jesus. Sometimes a Christian or two would have an opportunities to visit a large family in their home and discuss Jesus with them.

There were seldom any large gatherings. Evangelism at that time meant each Christian finding opportunities to share Jesus with other folks. A soul-winner named Jack Exum wrote a book one time titled, **The Glory of the Ordinary**. It motivated ordinary folks to talk about Jesus with other ordinary folks – their relatives, neighbors, and business associates. And that person-to-person evangelism which spread the gospel message like wildfire in dry brush.

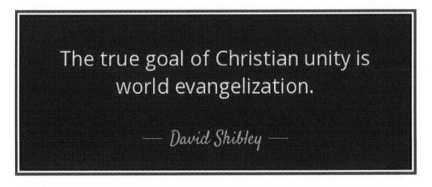

The true goal of Christian unity is world evangelization.

— David Shibley —

Eventually, over time, the change-agents gained influence and/or decision making power. And the slide downward had begun.

It sorta happened like this. A particular group of 10 believers met in John Smith's house. But the group was becoming too large for intimate sharing. Somebody came up with the idea of buying a regular place to meet, one that could handle maybe two or three times the number of disciples in their current group. That way they would have room to grow in one place, rather than simply birthing another house church in a different area of town.

So somebody else came up with the idea of forming a committee to find a suitable building, to get enough benches or chairs, to take care of on-going expenses and be a standing committee for if or when they needed to get an even larger building. And so it happened.

With the additional growth, they became a cell with about 40 members. They discovered they were way too large a group to allow each and every brother and sister to share a scripture or give a witness or lead a prayer. That's when they became acutely aware of socially acceptable time restraints for their meetings.

Then, Eureka! Some well-meaning Christian came up with another idea. "Since we cannot all share – and some just are not good speakers, anyhow – let's have Brother George do most of the preaching and teaching. He is a fine speaker and is bound to attract more people to our assembly. Heaven knows, we need a few more working adults to help share in the expenses of maintaining our new . . . eh, . . . let's call it, 'our church house.'" Amens were loud and clear. And so it was.

Later, a deacon at the Temple Street Church came up with a solution for their now crowded "sanctuary" (they had never described Bill's house or Suzy's barn or a meeting under a shade tree as a "sanctuary" before). The deacon, a mechanical engineer and a time-and-space analyst by profession, enthusiastically said:

"Instead of sitting in one big circle, we can get a bunch more people seated by putting seating tightly together, with folks facing the front. Maybe five rows with 12 people to the row. That way ol' Brother George can stand at a lectern at the front, like they use in synagogues, and still be heard by all of us. Heck, we don't need to look into everyone's face, anyway." And so it happened.

Never mind that it ripped the heart out of any face-to-face, honest-to-God communication with each other. Now they were locked in place with one person speaking at the front and the rest of the believers looking at the backs of the heads of everyone else. That is just as deeply depressing here and now. Lord, deliver us from this logistical nightmare.

In that regard, I must tell you about a time in the early 1980's when the importance of seating arrangements was really driven home to me. I was attending a church seminar in Fullerton, Calif., and my assigned roommate was a bright young fellow from Cincinnati. His name was **Mark Taylor**, then fairly new to his job as editor of a magazine titled **Lookout**. We hit it off and were enjoying the classes at our seminar. But one morning, I read about a religious meeting that night at a mega-church in Anaheim, right across from an entrance to Disneyland. I told Mark about it and we both got excited and decided to skip our own meeting to attend the other one.

Well, we arrived that night in a church building that probably seats 2,000 or so. And it is arranged "in the round," totally. There was not even a podium on the platform. Whoever spoke, had a portable microphone, and walked in circles on the stage to eye-ball everyone. Anticipation was flowing like a 220 electrical current. Then two men were called up on stage and introduced.

The first man was none other than **Charles "Chuck" Colson**, the man who had been a confident to and enforcer for the president of the United States, Richard Nixon. He had been in the highest circle of power in Washington. Now he was an ex-felon who had served time in prison for his part in the Watergate Scandal. But he had become a born again believer there and started a prison ministry from the inside.

The second man to take the stage was **Eldridge Cleaver**. He was the polar opposite of Colson, growing up in poverty and powerlessness. He spent time in three prisons: Soledad, Folsom, and San Quinten. He came to believe in armed violence as the best agent to fight racism. He joined the Black Panthers Party specifically because they were armed and ready to fight. In 1968, just two days after Martin Luther King, Jr. was murdered, Cleaver and the BPP armed themselves with shotguns and M16 rifles. They confronted the police in Oakland, Calif., and one BPP member was killed, two officers and Cleaver were wounded. Cleaver fled and lived overseas for seven years. In the early 1980's, he became a convert to Christianity.

So, . . . and here is my point . . . we all sat with amazement as these two radically different men – formerly adversaries - hugged each other. Each had been saved by Jesus and now they were brothers in the family of God.

Wow, I get shivers just thinking back about it. And that night, as I looked    around, I could see men and women all over that audience openly crying with joy and hugging each other. I heard loud shouts of "Amen" and "Hallelujah" all around that platform. It was a visual and auditory confirmation of something powerful happening. And I still do not believe that a traditional seating arrangement could allow such a response. We desperately need to revise the seating arrangements in auditoriums and classrooms so we can clearly see each other and respond to those visual communications.

Okay. Are you beginning to image and feel just how easy it is to "improve" things until we don't even recognize them? Do you see how one step in the wrong direction, or even just a step slightly off course, can result in a dramatic missing of the mark?

That's what happened when the panel of Elders asked Brother George to step down from his voluntary preaching ministry. They wanted to hire that dynamic, young Brother Jason to move down from up yonder to become their very first full-time, paid preacher.

Oh, that Jason was like a young Billy Graham. He packed so many people in, the Elders decided to triple the size of the building and to add a wing of small rooms where they could have formal Bible studies according to ages. When people objected to being assigned to a particular classroom by age, some deaconess suggested assigning people by weight. But there were no Amens to that.

Also, some of the sisters said the preacher's shabby clothes were a disgrace. Rather than giving him a raise or new clothes, they hand-made two really luxurious robes. They also persuaded him to agree to alternate in wearing one of the beautiful and oh so distinctive robes over his regular clothes when preaching.

The ladies also came up with the idea of making a kind of special white collar for their preacher to wear during the week. One brother said, only halfway jokingly, the dog collar would be so noticeable the preacher couldn't sneak up on people anymore. But the ladies insisted the big white collar identify him as their official minister when he was out and about town.

One old saint said he kinda liked the good old days of "mutual ministry." That was when each and every Christian was thought of as a minister of Christ and each shared in the teaching and encouragement ministries. He said, "That worked pretty darned good for decades. After all it was drawn from Paul's words to the Christians in Corinth, Greece. Remember, he said in 1 Corinthians 14:26:

"'26 So, brothers and sisters, what should you do? When you meet together, one person has a song, another has a teaching, and another has a new truth from God. One person speaks in a different language, and another interprets that language. The purpose of whatever you do should be to help everyone grow stronger in faith" (**J.B. Phillips New Testament**)'." That elder brother's idea was never even brought up for a vote because it was considered too old fashioned.

## Preaching the Gospel to the Saved Rather than the Lost & Neglecting the Doctrinal Edification of the Saints

Sometime along the way we started using our congregational meetings for evangelism of the lost (who were seldom in those meetings) and choked off the original emphasis on mutual edification – using our meetings with fellow believers as invaluable time to encourage one another with useful applications of doctrine. So we had concocted a time to preach the gospel to people who were not there and to neglect those believers who were begging for mutual edification on doctrinal topics.

**James S. Woodruff**, who preached for a large congregation in Searcy, Arkansas for many years, wrote a fine book titled **The Aroma of Christ**. In it he voiced this same analysis:

"Too long has today's well-established socially acceptable church stifled its outreach by limiting the proclamation of the message to one focal point (the church pulpit). Such an approach is founded on a misconception of the weekly Christian assembly. It is believed erroneously that the thrust of the Christian assembly should be toward the unsaved instead of toward the saved. This, in the light of practicalities, is impractical. There is no scripture that authorizes turning the Christian assembly into the church's evangelistic tool. Nor is there any logic that would justify ignoring the legitimate needs of the vast majority while purporting to fill the needs of oftentimes only a straw man; for too often the non-Christian is not even present" (**The Aroma of Christ**, p. 21. Fair Use Doctrine).

Others, including author **Hollis L. Green** in his book **Why Churches Die**, have pointed out that first century believers did their gospel preaching in the marketplace and the workplace, not in their private assemblies in their homes. In their homes, they used the doctrines of the apostles to bless and edify each other.

Woodruff quoted with approval Green's statement that **the church building "is probably the greatest single hindrance to world evangelism . . . . It places too much responsibility on the professional clergy and fails to advance the priesthood of all believers"** (emphasis mine, SP - **The Aroma of Christ**, p. 22 – Fair Use Domain).

By then, the first century tradition of chanting psalms and hymns was extinct. It had been the practice in the early church as they met in small groups for any and almost every person to sing a solo or to sing (chant) the words as a group. Before long, their choral-only praises by one or all was being supplemented with flutes and lyres.

Then as bigger buildings demanded dramatic preachers who could attract crowds, they took the additional step of taking the singing largely away from the congregation and increasing the theatrical presence of a well-trained choir and professional musicians.

Sadly, it is not unusual today to walk into a large sanctuary where they have earplug stations set up at the back. It is a brazen warning that your ears are about to be assaulted with music that is so high-decibel that it is dangerous. Worshippers can conveniently grab a throw-away-set of earplugs and brace their ears for the high-octane, high decibel music awaiting them. There just seems to be something in the DNA of most musicians that loud is good and LOUDER is even better.

Regardless, it all works against the idea of simplicity. Often, the congregants are so bombarded by the musical volume they cannot even hear themselves sing – not that they are given many opportunities today. Gee, don't they have volume controls on instruments anymore?

I have gone to more churches than I can recount where the drummer is ostracized and quarantined. It seems like cruel and unusual punishment to lock the drummer into a plastic box. Of course, maybe there is extra padding in there who he won't hurt himself with all his flailing around. There he is in isolation, but I guess he is wearing that set of earphones so even he cannot hear his thumping and clanging.

Then, once at a Christmas concert at First Baptist Church in Edmond, Oklahoma, I saw a drummer right in there with the other musicians. No plastic box, no massive earphones. Nuttin' but him and his chops. Later, I was told the secret. Don't let this get out . . . but . . . . his drum set had a *v-o-l-u-m-e c-o-n-t-r-o-l* . . . and the sound man was brave enough to actually control the drummer's enthusiasm. That was another Christmas miracle.

Back to the descent into the swamp of complex churchianity.

Soon, the main leadership role shifted from a plurality of elders in each independent congregation to the concentration of influence and power in one person. Yep, the prominent man in the pulpit was given more and more power. Decisions were no longer made openly and with the mutual consent of the people but behind closed doors.

Simultaneously, it was no longer enough for congregants to speak of "Brother Edwards" as their preacher, minister, or pastor. No, they wanted more in the way of a status symbol. So they began anointing their local preacher-teacher as "Reverend" and then as "The Right Reverend." I always have wondered what became of The Left Reverend, but that is another story.

And then a particularly gifted preacher was asked to serve as the leader of two other small churches in the area (or just assumed the role). And then over a district . . . and then a state. More exalted titles were created such as "District Superintendent," "Bishop," "Archbishop," and "Chief Bishop." And then . . . , well, you know how complex and convoluted denominational power hierarchies are today.

There are "mega-churches" in many places around the world, including in the United States, Mexico, and South Korea. In many instances, "The Pastor" reigns supreme over at least 20,000 members scattered around in dozens upon dozens of "campuses" and held together by the modern technology of simultaneous transmission of sermons by "The Pastor" to every location. And so it has become.

Oh, say, . . . there is that other thing. Who would believe that anything so simple as a church name would become so divisive and sectarian? We're talking here about whatever the assembled group wants to call itself.

Back in the early days, when a group of believers met at Mel and Petunia Cumquat's house, between themselves they just called it "the meeting." Or maybe "the meeting at Cumquat's house." Or maybe "Comquat's house on Straight Street." When they stopped meeting in houses and starting meeting in their own "church building," often they hung a simple sign over the door saying something like "Center Street Chapel" or "Oak Grove Assembly Meets Here."

Many, many years later, the situation had morphed to one of pride in labels. "We are the Baptist Church" or "We are the very first congregation of the Methodist Church in Dallas," which officially became "First United Methodist Church in Dallas, Texas, and later joined a group of other Methodists to become "First United Methodist Church in Dallas, Texas." I have never heard of a group that claimed, "We are the First Divided Methodist Church in Dallas," but – hey – it could still happen.

That is a brief bird's eye-view of how simple Christianity can become so complex in just a few generations that it becomes dysfunctional.

Now that you see the process and understand at least part of the problem, what solutions do you see? How can average Christians reclaim their heritage? What can you do, specifically, to get others to join you in a return to greater simplicity?


NOTE:

Some of you may want to read more about the historical drift away from simple Christianity in the early centuries. Here are my recommendations:

Rutz, James H. **The Open Church: How to Bring Back the Exciting Life of the First Century Church**. Auburn, Maine: The Seedsowers, 1992. This easy-to-read paperback is long out of print. However, you are likely to find a used copy online through Amazon.com or one of the many online used book dealers.

George, Bob. **<u>Classic Christianity: Life's Too Short to Miss the Real Thing</u>**. Eugene, Oregon: Harvest House Publishers, 1989.

Towns, Elmer. **<u>Core Christianity: What is Christianity All About?</u>** Chattanooga, TN: AMG Publishers, 2007.

Stott, John R.W. **<u>Basic Christianity</u>**. Downers Grove, IL: Inter-Varsity Press, first edition in 1958 and second edition in 1971.

Stott, John R.W. **<u>Christian Basics</u>**. Grand Rapids, MI: Baker Books, first edition in 1991 and second edition in 1999.

Well, this "church sign" pretty much sums up how things are today. It is all about Churchianity with cafeteria-style choices. It is so funny, I laugh until my stomach hurts. And it is so pathetic and so anti-simple Christianity that it makes me sad enough to cry.

# Chapter 11

# How Simple Christianity
# Flourishes

Alright, time for a reality check.

Did you care enough about this subject to actually open up a Bible and read the Gospel of Luke, The Gospel of John, and The Acts of the Apostles?

Did you?

Those Biblical documents contain life-changing, generation-changing information . . . if taken seriously. So I sincerely congratulate you if you read those documents before continuing here.

If you did not, please reconsider.

You see, I do not want you to accept a single idea which I present in this book if you cannot find it in your Bible study. I am just an ordinary Christian with a deep desire to share the wonderful truths I have found in the Bible.

Okay, then, let's move right along.

The following story is a "composite" account of how ordinary people, like you and me, often have come to know Jesus as their Lord and Savior. It tells how they seek to live out their lives concentrating on practicing simple Christianity. They focus on the essential basics of the faith, those unity-building principles which are universally accepted in mainline Christianity. The man's name is made-up because it is the process of discovery we want to emphasize. And it rings true.

Edward Marsoni (as we are calling him) was 23 years old and a hard working plumber. He had little or no knowledge of God. He cussed all the time and lived to party on the weekend. He usually got drunk or high and went to bed with any female who was available and willing at closing time of the bar.

"All the gals really do get prettier at closing time," he liked to say. He was living a godless, high-risk life and could not care less.

One Saturday morning, he woke up in a cheap motel about 9 a.m. with a pounding headache and a faint recollection of some red-headed gal going to bed with him. But what's-her-name was long gone.

Unlike other days, he felt depressed in a world spinning around his head. He hid his out-of-control lifestyle from his relatives back home because he knew he was living a trashy life they would not approve.

Edward noticed a Bible on the nightstand and, out of curiosity, he opened it up and landed on the first chapter of The Gospel of John. He began to read about this guy named Jesus. "Pretty amazing man," he says to himself, "if this is all true." And he continued to read, right through the Acts of the Apostles.

Edward was stunned by the faith of the early Christians who became followers of the resurrected Jesus, regardless of the persecution. These men and women witnessed to others with one united message: **Jesus is both Lord and Christ**. He died upon a Roman cross because of their sins against God, and by the giving of his life and blood made forgiveness available to all who believe in him. They pointed toward Jesus and invited people to come to him.

"Even I can understand that," Edward beamed. Also, Edward noticed that the clear response to that gospel preaching in Acts, time and again, was for new believers to be baptized into the name of Jesus soon after their conversion.

He begins wondering whether God could possibly forgive all the crap in his life, much less love him.

"But hold on. That man in Acts named Saul was actually something of a terrorist the way like to beat up on Christians. And he stood there cheering the crowd of his fellow Jews as they stoned a Christian named Stephen. Then he accepted Jesus as his Lord and was baptized, completing changing his life. I have done a lot of bad things, but I've never done that. Why couldn't I get right with God, too? Maybe today?"

So Edward showered, got into his car, and drove toward his house. No loud, thumping radio music this time. He was still thinking about Jesus and his love for everybody. A few blocks before he gets home, he noticed a house with a cross hanging in a window. Impulsively, he stopped and knocked on the door and in a minute or so the door opened and a 50-ish man stood there in his workout clothes.

"Mister, " Edward began, "I need real badly to talk to somebody who is a Christian. Is that cross in your window just a decoration or are you a Christian?"

"Why, yes, I'm a disciple of Jesus. My name's Jim. Come in and let's talk."

Jim, as it turns out, was a commercial photographer. He and his wife accepted Christ as Lord and Savior early in their long marriage. So Edward opened up and told him about how he had just this morning come to believe in Jesus by reading the Gospel of John and the Acts of the Apostles.

"I don't want to go on living like I have been, and I believe in the Jesus of the Bible. So I want to do exactly what those sinners in the Book of Acts did to get right with God. I figure I can't go wrong with that. I believe that Jesus is Lord. So I'm looking for somebody to baptize me into the name of Jesus."

After a moment of congratulating the young man on his decision, Jim led them in prayer and said: "Edward, I have a swimming pool in my back yard. If you are serious about your faith in and love for Christ, I'd be honored to baptize you right now."

The older man excused himself for a moment, went into his bedroom and changed into a swimming suit. And he came out carrying another swimsuit to fit Edward and gave him a few minutes to change. Then they went out and walked down into the pool until they were waist-deep in the water.

"Oh yes," Edward smiled and said, "I remember how that preacher Phillip met the Ethiopian guy and told him about Jesus. And kinda like me as I recall, Phillip and that man stopped by a pool along the road and went into the water and the Ethiopian was baptized. There was nobody else around then, either. Just like now."

Jim replied, "You're right on target, Edward. And in that passage, we do not read where Phillip made any fancy ceremony about it. They both knew what they were doing. So I am just going to say that the angels are rejoicing at this moment. Since you have faith in Jesus and his blood sacrifice, and you want to obey God's will in your life, I baptize you into the name of God the Father, God the Son, and God the Holy Spirit."

The moment Edward came up from the water, he yelled: "Thank you, Jesus!" And Jim hugged him and said, "Amen, brother. Welcome to the family of God the universal, undenominational body of Christ."

The two men dried off with towels, went inside the house and changed clothes, then sat down for cups of coffee and some heart-to-heart talk.

Jim leaned forward and said, "Edward, now that you've become a child of God through the same New Birth process experienced by the first-century Christians, you will want to grow and mature in your knowledge of Jesus and of his ethics and doctrine."

"Oh, yeah," Edward said with enthusiasm. "I want to be more like my Savior. What can I do?"

"Well, I'll tell you brother," Jim say as he leaned over and looked into Edward's eyes. "Part of the good news of the gospel is that when Jesus returned to heaven, he did not leave us by ourselves. Part of Peter's wonderful promise to the Jews was that when they accepted Jesus they would be given 'the gift of the Holy Spirit' to inspire and motivate them to live for him."

Jim reached over to his Bible on a countertop and opened it to Acts 2:38. He placed his Bible where Edward could follow along.

"See right here, Edward, Peter told this large crowd of Jewish people about how their sins had caused the death of Jesus, their own Messiah (or Christ). And that hit 'em like a baseball bat. So they yelled out, 'Okay, we believe. How can we escape punishment for our guilt and unbelief?' And Peter told them to turn from their sins, from their attempts to earn their salvation by religious works, and to continue their faith-commitment by being baptized. By God's amazing and unmerited favor or grace, they would be founding members, as it were, of this new Jesus community of believers and would be forgiven of their past sins and given the person of the Holy Spirit to walk with them. You see, the Holy Spirit is both a mentor and comforter to us in our Christian life."

Edward had trouble taking it all in. After a few moments he said, "Man, I had no idea about all that. It is more wonderful than I could have imagined."

Jim refilled their coffee cups and said, " Well, your first step is to prayerfully accept the Holy Spirit into every corner of your heart. He will help keep you on the right track. And when you pray, Jim, pour your heart out in your own words. We're even promised that the Holy Spirit will help us communicate with our heavenly Father when we just can't find the words."

"Your second step is to begin your own personal Bible study. But keep in mind that Christianity is not some kind of intellectual exercise. The Bible is not a law book of do's and don'ts. And your increasing knowledge does not put more points on your heavenly scoreboard. We do not worship the Bible; we worship Jesus, the man the Bible helps us find. Learning more of the Bible is important, but only to extent that it helps you know Jesus better and helps you have a deeper relationship with him.

"So, third, you need to work on your own spirit or attitude. And at the very heart of that and all of Christianity is the idea of loving God and loving other people. No one lived this aspect out better than Jesus. He loved each of us and all of us when we were over on the Devil's side doing devilish, stupid stuff. Then Jesus loved us enough to die for us. Most of the apostles loved Jesus so much they wound up being killed because they refused to renounce their faith in him. And over the centuries, ordinary men and women like us have loved him enough to live their lives for him and, when necessary, to suffer and even be killed in his name."

Edward lowered his head, took a sip of coffee and confessed: "Jim, I gotta tell you. I had been a rounder most of my life. I was a party guy and I put my needs in front of everyone. My faith is new and maybe a little shaky right now. But I love Jesus and I ain't turning back no matter what. Is my next step to join some church? My mother is a Baptist and my father is Episcopalian, but heck, they won't even go to church together."

Jim knew exactly how he felt. His own mother and father never reconciled their religious differences before they died. She had been a Catholic and he had been a deacon in a Methodist Church.

Jim looked into the young man's eyes and said, "Edward, you're gonna find out that just being with other believers and sharing our respective failures and successes is important. It is a vital part of becoming a mature Christian. Or, as I like to put it, that is how you finally give up the baby bottle and diapers and you put on your man-pants and eat real food. That is my hope for you, my friend. Now, may I share some more faith-building information with you."

Edward had tears in his eyes as he said, "Brother, I feel like I just came out of a walk across the desert and I found a clear mountain stream. I am still thirsty, so let help me drink some more."

Jim smiled broadly and said, "Good deal. Here are some things you should know about our family, our spiritual family that is. The body or fellowship of Christ was established on the Day of Pentecost in about 33 A.D. by the preaching of Peter and the other disciples. Other than the phrase 'Jesus is Lord,' the early Christians had no creed books . In most cases, they did not even have a full collection of those documents we call the New Testament. They certainly had no clerical system, so believers encouraged each other in what we would call today 'mutual ministry.'

"They met in homes or public places, but no congregation owned a 'church building.' Small groups in many nations gathered together on Sundays and shared verbal stories they had learned from earlier believers. They ate and drank the communion elements or Lord's Supper in memory of Jesus and looking forward to his return. Each congregation was independent, so they chose their own leaders to shepherd them. It was very simple and all focused on Jesus. That was how this Jesus movement spread so rapidly throughout the known world."

Edward had never heard that concise history of the early church, but he liked the sound of it. "That all seems pretty simple to me."

"Yep, it sure was," Jim agreed. "Their teaching and preaching was all about Jesus. But as centuries went by, local teachers were replaced by a professional clergy. And certain congregations began thinking that their own way of doing church was not only right for them but the only way church could be done. So they separated from those who did not agree in every point with them. Sad, but true.

"Others decided to emphasize a certain doctrine or a certain leader, as with those who idolized Martin Luther and even against his wishes established the Lutheran denomination. The idea of liberty in Christ, as taught and practiced in the early days, got lost in sectarian bickering and fighting and power grabbing. That is a capsule version of how the Jesus community—the universal body of Christ—fractured into groups which often do not have any contact with each other. That sectarian spirit certainly worked against the unity which Jesus prayed they would have."

Edward let that dark bit of history sink into his brain. He leaned back and stretched his arms, then set straight up and rapped his fingers on the table.

"If I get you right, Jim, here I am a guy who just wanted to be a Christian like the people in the Book of Acts. And I did what the Bible says the early Christians did to be saved and give my life to Jesus. And now I have to go out and join a church which has strayed a heck of a long way from simple Christianity. Is that what you are telling me? If so, that just makes me want to just stay at home in my man cave and worship Jesus there by myself."

This young man, a brand new Christian, was visibly moved and upset by what he had heard. But Jim had shared that information right up front because Edward probably would have been confronted with the facts the first time he went through a church house door.

"Look, brother, I know that was a bit of a shock to you. So I wanted to be with you when you realized it for yourself. While there is that bad news, there is an awful lot of good news for you.

"Let's look right here in Chapter 2 of the Book of Acts. Here is where Peter and the other disciples told people the gospel story for the very first time. Well over 3,000 people came to believe in Jesus as Lord and Savior. Then Peter and the others told those told those new believers they also needed to repent and be baptized.

"Over here in Acts 2:41-42, we read about the amazing results of their preaching: 'Then those people who accepted what Peter said were baptized. About 3,000 people were added to the number of believers that day. They spent their time learning the apostles' teaching. And they continued to share, to break bread, and to pray together.' (**The Everyday Bible: New Century Version**).

"That's not all, Edward, in Acts 2:44-47 we get a clear snapshot of how the first Christians where so happy in their united Jesus community. And we see some of what they did. 'All the believers stayed together. They shared everything. They sold their land and the things they owned. Then they divided the money and gave it to those people who needed it. The believers met together in the Temple every day. They all had the same purpose. They broke bread in their homes, happy to share their food with joyful hearts. They praised God, and all the people liked them. More and more people were being saved every day; the Lord was adding those people to the group of believers' ."(**The Everyday Bible: New Century Version**).

"Holy smoke!" Edward blurted now. "Now that's the kind of people for me. I like that plain and simple Christianity. But where can I find such a group and become a member of it."

Jim grinned at his young friend's words and then said: "Edward, let me ask you a few questions about what you just read in Acts. These 3,000 Jews who believed and were baptized and were added to something, was that something the Church of Peter or the Baptist Church or maybe the Methodist Church? Would you read what it says right there."

Edward found the spot and read, "About 3,000 were added to the number of believers that day . . . " And he said, "I guess they didn't have denominations yet, so they were added to that group of Christians. Right?"

Jim shook his head in the affirmative and pointed down to the end of verse 42 and suggested, "Read this part, too."

Edward read, "More and more people were being saved every day; the Lord was adding those people to the group of believers."

"Same thing," Edward concluded. "They didn't join some sect or denomination. They didn't really join anything because it was the Lord who added them 'to the group of believers'."

"Bingo!" Jim said with obvious approval. "With your faith commitment to Jesus today -- just as the first Christians did – the Lord God himself added you to his family, the body of Christ or the church of God. That is the church role that really counts. Simple, wasn't it?"

"I love this simple stuff," Jim said with a laugh. "I just wish I'd done this five years ago. And I can hardly wait to tell some of my friends and relatives about this. I bet they'll like this simple Christianity, too."

Jim said, "Your enthusiastic faith is just like what the first century believers had, too. They did not wait for some preacher to spread the word about Jesus for them. They were on fire for him, too. And that is exactly why the Bible says, 'More and more people were being saved every day; the Lord was adding those people to the group of believers.' You see, Edward, for many centuries nobody needed a degree in theology or a certificate from any group to share the Good News. That was the way of simple Christianity.

"So let me tell you this: you are a disciple, a follower of Christ, a baptized believer with the Holy Spirit now living in your heart. And God added you to his family.

"Now the term 'family of God' means all those around the world, living or dead, who have done the same thing. We cannot even begin to estimate that number and will not know until we all get to heaven. But you need to start getting acquainted with your new brothers and sisters right here is this area. You need their encouragement and they need yours. And remember, you must accept as your dear brother or sister anyone whom God has added to his group of believers. Wherever God has a child, you have a brother or a sister. We must not deny our family ties.

"Now, if you go out and ask to be a member of the True Vine Church down the street, you would be adding a status. If they accept you, and they might not if you do not agree to accept their denominational creed book word-for-word. Just warning you, my friend. If you do that, then you would be a Christian + a True Viner. They may or may not allow others you believe are members of God's family into their human organization.

"If you tried to join a Baptist congregation and were successful, you would be a Christian + a Baptist. But first they would probably require (1) that you relate an acceptable conversion experience; (2) that you receive a favorable vote from their membership; and (3) that you be baptized, again, to be a member of their human organization. If you want to be an Episcopalian, then they would require you to affirm your belief in the old (but not found in our Bible) 'Apostle's Creed' and may or may not accept your baptism.

"At the polar opposite of such man-man rules and rigid sectarianism is the simple Christianity we've talked about today. For example, my wife and I are part of a growing number of believers who firmly believe in being Christians, only. We are not Baptist-Christians or Presbyterian-Christians, just plain Christians with a name which honors Jesus Christ.

"We don't promote or approve division in the body of Christ. We are Christians, only; but we are certainly not under the delusion we are the only Christians. That would be stinkin' thinkin'.

"Of course, we know and love as God's people a lot of Born Again folks who, for one reason or another, have added a human membership in the Assembly of God or the Methodists or the Church of What's Happening Now. Whatever. Their status with God is in his hands, not in our hands. Because we are not called upon to judge the spiritual standing of any person. We just make it our mission to love God, to love his people both in and out of his family, and to do good as often as we can in every way we can. It is a simple way, not an easy way."

Edward seemed to absorb every word Jim spoke like a new-bought sponge. "Wow, I like it. Simple Christianity is what I want. So where do I get it? Jim, where is that Jesus community here in town where you two worship?"

Jim cautiously looked around, then leaned over and whispered, "Edward, . . . can you keep a secret?"

"Of course I can," Edward replied.

Jim leaned back over and whispered, "So can I."

And he sat there smiling at Edward.

"I don't get it, Jim. Aren't you going to tell me?"

The older man reached out and touched the young man's shoulder. "Sure, I'm gonna tell you. But even Christians can have a little bit of fun, you know.

"There are many groups across America and the world who have embraced the concept of simple Christianity. That means letting the Bible and the Holy Spirit be our guide, not some sectarian creed book. It means looking at the practices of the Bible congregations, each one imperfect in some ways (divisions, immorality), and following only the God-approved practices.

"It means accepting individual freedom and responsibility for personally reading the Bible and applying its principles, according to our best understanding, while allowing each other some slack in our conclusions. Lots of folks today are doing that very thing. Some of those congregations are quite large, while others are quite small and their practice of that concept may differ a bit from ours. But that is okay. That's what liberty and freedom in Christ is all about.

"A very small part of this area's Jesus community is a group of folks who meet . . . in the room next to us, in our den. Right now, we have about a dozen of us. We come from several denominations and even a couple who were Jews. Our den will only hold about 25 people. So when our group adds another six or seven people we will help several of them establish a similar group in one of their homes. We have 'birthed' two other groups who are meeting elsewhere. But we all try to get together at a park or someone's large backyard for worship and fellowship each 5th Sunday. Kinda simple, but we love it.

"And we encourage our folks to love on other people and do service projects with people of faith in the mainline denominations. We may not like their mandatory creeds and control by a denominational headquarters off somewhere, but we appreciate the individuals themselves. That is how a lot of us started out. Now we are trying our best to please God with this simple kind of Christianity. Edward, we would be delighted for you to be with us this Sunday morning at 10:00 a.m. Can you make it?"

Edward stood up and as he was shaking hands with his new friend he said, "Jim, my brother, I thought you'd never ask. Count me in."

*****

Well, friends, that is how simple Christianity often reproduces itself and is spread around the world.

Are you ready for the simple Christian life? If you take up that challenge, you will discover this amazing truth: **Less can really mean more. And the way forward is to return to basics.**

Right now, please take a break. Maybe talk a long walk and prayerfully consider your current spiritual state.

# Chapter 12

# What to Do After
# Being Saved?

John Q. Public put a lot of effort into pursuing the girl of his dreams. John's sweetheart was Mary Lou Doe, a lovely redhead who had just graduated from high school and was about to start college. She turned heads wherever she went, and he was a handsome dude with a mile-wide smile. They met at a Christian Singles luncheon at his church and immediate hit it off.

So ol' John put on his track shoes and chased after her for two whole years. He took her to movies. He took her to music concerts. He started attending her church with Mary Lou and her family. He bought her outrageously large boxes of candy and dozens of bouquets of flowers during that courtship. And, most important, he spent a considerable amount of time getting to know her. They took quiet walks along the riverside, prayed with each other, and sat on park benches talking for hours about their romance and their dreams and goals.

Finally, both John and Mary were convinced this was true love. Or, as we sometimes jokingly say, "He chased her until she caught him." The date was set for an intimate marriage ceremony at a 1880's style, white bandstand in the park. The marriage came off without a hitch, and they honeymooned on one of the Florida Keys (islands). Then they settled into their married life, with John working as a management intern in a large bank and Mary Lou resuming her courses at the university nearby.

Two years into their marriage, as Mary Lou began her senior year in college, trouble knocked on their apartment door. John was having to work late almost every day, and he spent almost as much time each day with another management intern who was a young, blond lady with a great personality. She was not hard to look at or talk with, either.

Mary Lou would come home to an empty apartment, fix enough supper for both of them, but ate hers alone and hit her textbooks until nearly midnight every night. Seldom did John and Mary take walks together, except to get the groceries. They had neither the extra money nor the time to attend music concerts. And being tired most of the time, it was easy for each to criticize and snip at each other. They were in deep trouble and hardly knew it.

Sound familiar? Been there and done that?

Yes, most of us have at one time or another. John and Mary needed to slow down and spend lots of quality time together, just like they did before they married.

The fact is, sometimes a person who is on the road to faith in Jesus works much harder to get into the family of God than he does to maintain that relationship. Sad to say, but it is true.

Take a guy we'll call Oscar Lydell Andersen, for example. He earnestly prayed every day for God to help him escape his sinful and self-destructive, self-centered lifestyle. Then he heard about the gospel of Jesus Christ and began to research and read about it. Oscar bought his own Bible, the first person in his unbelieving family to have one. He reads it, thinks long and hard about this man Jesus who it is said is the Son of God.

Oscar talks with a couple of his friends who are Christians, but he is confused because one tells him to do this to be saved and the other tells him, no, you must do that. Each invites him to join his respective denomination and to avoid all others like the plague or Corona-19 Virus.

So poor Oscar doubles down to see what the Scriptures really say. And, after months of searching and praying and studying, he kneeled outside in his backyard one day and said, "Alright, Jesus I believe and trust you are the Son of God. Now I'm ready to follow you, to change my stupid ways, and do whatever God wants me to do. And, dear God, I believe you will keep your promises."

A week later, he woke up one morning and, even though it was raining outside, he smiled with joy and enthusiasm at this new day. And the reason was because last Sunday he had found a gospel-believing, gospel-preaching group of Spirit-led people meeting in a rented hall just a few blocks from his home. They helped him fully accept the Lord Jesus, praising his statement of faith and his intention to leave his life of lust and greed and selfishness behind.

Then they all went down to a pond in the nearby park and one of the Christian men, a trucker by trade, baptized him into the name of the Father, the Son, and the Holy Spirit. And, just like the Ethiopian convert in Acts 8:26-40 who after his faith-testimony in baptism went on his way rejoice, the whole group rejoiced and hugged Oscar like he had never been hugged before.

A few days later, Ray Dominguez, the fellow who had baptized him, called Oscar, and asked if he could drop by that evening for a visit with him. Oscar gladly accepted, eager to get acquainted with other believers. So Ray knocked on his door that evening and they chatted about their respective backgrounds and jobs. Then Ray turned the subject toward their spiritual lives.

"Oscar, my brother, I'm here tonight because I love you in the Lord. We've gotta watch each other's back, 'cause we all need to grow stronger in our faith and walk. I am four years into my journey with Jesus. I'm not bragging about it, just explaining the fact that I am today much better and stronger believer than I was that first year.

"Frankly, when I made my faith-commitment I was totally on fire for the Lord. I wanted to tell everyone the Good News. I wanted to read the Bible from cover to cover. I visited everybody I knew who was in a hospital or nursing home. I even helped some folks in my neighborhood I wouldn't have been caught dead with before I found the Lord.

"Then ordinary life crept in, with this problem and that crisis, and I started slipping away from my relationship with God. I didn't meet with the brothers and sisters for fellowship and worship on a regular basis, and I went back to an old habit or two that were not in keeping with who I really was. That being a child of God.

"So one day an older sister in our Christian community came over and prayed with me and for me. She told me she had been on that same roller coaster ride after she had been a Christian for a while, but another believer stepped up and became her spiritual mentor. And that got her back on solid ground.

"I guess what I'm saying, Oscar, is that you need to make your relationship with God and with his people the number one priority in your life. Being new in the faith, as you are, you must spend time alone building your spiritual muscles. Ask the Holy Spirit who now dwells in you to help you pray. Ask him to open your eyes to the truths in the Bible which are really good for you right now.

"Then, besides loving God and obeying him and working for him because of his favor (not to win his favor), get to know your brothers and sisters in the body of Christ. They can be a great encouragement to you, my brother. And guess what? They will be delighted and encouraged by your presence at our meetings. Relationships. Man, don't miss any chance you have to praise the Lord together. Now I better get on home and love on my own family."

Oscar looked into the eyes of his short, rather husky, darker skinned new friend in Christ. He smiled and said, "Ray, what you said makes sense to me. I don't know what Jesus has in store for me, but I want to be strong for the journey and the adventure. Thank you, brother, for caring enough to come over and talk. I'll see you at the next meeting."

And so the baton is passed from person to person. It often works that way in the family of God, in what we enthusiastically call simple Christianity.

Now, that spiritual growth we are talking about sometimes involves your physical muscles. Maybe there is an elderly person in your group or neighborhood who could use your help in mowing her yard or fixing a leaky faucet. Maybe there's a house being built nearby by Habitat for Humanity and you could help paint or spread cement. Maybe there are a couple of kids in your group of Christians or just in your acquaintance who have never been fishing and would get a thrill out of you helping them one afternoon to catch a fish.

Maybe another Christ-honoring and gospel-preaching church of God's is have a special Bible seminar and needs some folks who will take a bunch of flyers and hand them out around the neighborhood. The opportunities to bless other people by using your own muscle power are limitless. Just be more like Jesus. Go about doing good, not just talking about it.

Always keep in mind, though, you are using those muscles for the glory of the kingdom and not so people will say what a great guy you are. Nor are you earning any "Merits" in God's Book of Life for your work. God loved you even while you were wading in your personal cesspool of sin and now you are loving him back because he saved you from all of that.

The apostle Paul had a special place in his heart for the people and the leaders (elders or shepherds) of the congregation in the city of Ephesus. He reminded them of some basic principles of simple Christianity, facts which he had told them before. Here is part of what he said:

"God, who is rich in mercy, out of the great love with which he loved us even when we were dead through our trespasses, made us alive together with Christ – by grace you have been saved – and raised us up with him and seated us with him in the heavenly places in Christ Jesus, so that in the ages to come he might show the immeasurable riches of his grace in kindness toward us in Christ Jesus. For by grace you have been saved through faith, and this is not your own doing; it is the gift of God – not the result of works, so that no one may boast. For we are what he has made us, created in Christ Jesus for good works, which God prepared beforehand to be our way of life" (Ephesians 2:4-10; **New Revised Standard Version**).

**Dr. John Mark Hicks**, a respected Bible scholar at Lipscomb University in Nashville (my ***alma mater***, by the way), in 1994 explained Ephesians 2:10 (the last sentence in the quote, above) this way:

"We are not saved because we work, but we work because we are already saved. Ephesians 2:10 is a comment on the relationship between works and salvation, as if Paul wishes to clarify or head off misunderstandings of his point in verses 8-9. We are saved by grace through faith--not of ourselves or our works, but as a divine gift so that no one can boast. This is true because, as verse 10 says, we are created for good works, and not because we do good works. Rather, we are God's work--we are God's doing, his creation. We work the works of God because we are God's work of salvation--new creatures in Christ.

"As one looks at the structure of the text, 'works' follow salvation. God saves us by grace, not works. But he saves us so that we can do good works. Works are the result of salvation. We are his creation for good works. Paul's order is clear: Grace, faith, salvation, works. It is not: grace, faith, works and then salvation. Works are not a means to salvation, they are the evidence of salvation already received. Works are evidence of God's work of creating us. They testify that we are God's new creation; they testify to our salvation--they do not create the salvation" (Fair Use Domain).

Amen to that.

Anybody who has a name that sounds like some kind a sweet chocolate stands high on my list of esteemed people. Well, really, one of those who is up near the top of my list also happens to be one of my generations great Christian thinkers and writers. I'm talking about the late Edward Fudge. He was a lawyer by trade and a disciple of Christ by faith and conviction. Here are a few of his thoughts about the relationship between faith/and/or trust and obedience. His brief essay is titled, "Obedience and Trust as Fruit and Root," and it first appeared on his **Grace Digest** online magazine on Jan. 8, 2015 (http://gracedigest.com/2015/01/18).

"When I was a child, we often sang a hymn that admonished us to 'trust and obey,' assuring us that 'there's no other way to be happy in Jesus.' The two verbs go together: we obey because we trust, and because we trust we obey. Trust and obedience are well-suited companions, but more. Related, but more. They live in symbiotic relationship, each nourishing and being nourished by the other, each simultaneously drawing life from and contributing life to the other.

"Trust initiates obedience, activates and motivates it. Obedience expresses, affirms, and confirms trust. Neither is found in its mature state without the other. **Hannah W. Smith**, the Quaker universalist author of the spiritual classic, **The Christian's Secret of a Happy Life**, had it right when she wrote: 'Perfect happiness is perfect obedience to one in whom you have perfect trust.'

"Of course, not everyone appreciates such nuances and niceties. We all have heard some for whom obedience seems to have gobbled up anything even slightly resembling trust. They argue that anyone who enjoys God's fellowship, either now or forever, must somehow merit his favor. Their confusion is called 'legalism,' and it leads sober- minded people either to self-deception or to despair.

"There are other folks so infatuated with what they call trust or faith that they rarely mention obedience at all. They seem quite confident that God's grace makes obedience all but superfluous. Their confusion is known as 'antinomianism.' Think of legalism and antinomianism as deep ditches on opposite sides of the gospel road. Each ditch is hazardous to spiritual health. Both need to be warned against and to be avoided at all costs" (Fair Use Domain).

Wise words, don't you think?

# Chapter 13

## Simple Christianity Means
## Being Christians, Only

Simple Christianity involves our embracing the truth that no matter how "right" we are on this or that doctrine, we are Christians, only. But we are definitely not the only Christians. Not by a country mile.

Frankly, I grew up in a very conservative church in a small farming town in southern California. So that concept in the previous paragraph was as foreign to me as using Chinese chopsticks to eat with. Christians in other denominations besides our own? No way, José. We were taught that other folks – like Baptists, Methodists, Presbyterians, and Pentecostals – were in error on a bunch of doctrines and we should consider them a great evangelistic field ready for the harvest by corrective teaching from us, the Only True Christians in town. Hey, if I'm lyin', I'm dyin', as the late comedian Jerry Clower was fond of saying.

These same preachers and Bible class teachers never brought up even the possibility that the people in our congregation and our entire sect of the church of God just might be wrong on a point or two. I was vaguely aware some of "our" congregations would not recognize or have fellowship with others who used the same name we did above the church house door.

Only when I was off in college did I learn that, in fact, our sect of the fellowship of the firstborn itself was fractured into about 20 sub-sects, none of which would do anything with each other. Except maybe to occasionally conduct a public debate with one other.

"And Jesus wept," the Scripture records as his reaction to the death of his friend Lazarus. By my college days, I was sure that Jesus must have shed many tears over such in-fighting by children of God.

Jesus also told both his inner core of disciples and the skeptical Pharisees to wake up to the fact that their little group was not the full extent of those in his fellowship. Or to go back to his Shepherd analogy, he told them he had other sheep in different folds or places. This point is critical to understanding the universal nature of his body which has been sliced and diced by sectarianism. So carefully listen to Jesus himself:

"'I am the good shepherd. The good shepherd gives His life for the sheep. But he who is a hireling and not the shepherd, one who does not own the sheep, sees the wolf coming and leaves the sheep and flees; and the wolf catches the sheep and scatters them. The hireling flees because he is a hireling and does not care about the sheep.

"'I am the good shepherd; and I know My sheep, and am known by My own. As the Father knows Me, even so I know the Father, and I lay down My life for the sheep. And other sheep I have which are not of this fold; them also I must bring, and they will hear My voice; and there will be one flock and one shepherd'" (John 10:11-16; **The New King James Version**).

The Apostle John then moves the conversation forward to the Jewish Feast of Dedication (now more commonly called Hanukkah) held in the winter in Jerusalem. He tells how Jesus continued that Shepherd analogy when confronted by certain Jews right there in the splendor of Solomon's Porch. They demanded for him to say whether he was the hoped for Christ (or Messiah). Here is what he said to them:

"Jesus answered, 'I told you, but you don't believe. Everything I have done has been authorized by my father, actions that speak louder than words. You don't believe because you're not my sheep. My sheep recognize my voice. I know them, and they follow me. I give them real and eternal life. They are protected from the Destroyer for good. No one can steal them from out of my hand. The Father who put them under my care is so much greater than the Destroyer and Thief. No one could ever get them away from him. I and the Father are one heart and mind' (John 10:25-30; **The Messenger -** MSG).

Alright, that's a lot. So please take a moment and slowly read John 10, again, to drink in both the plain words and the spirit of the words.

Here are the main points of what Jesus said:

(1) Jesus is the one and only Shepherd of his sheep.
(2) Jesus, as their protector and Shepherd, was going to die to save them.
(3) Jesus knows each one of the sheep in "Fold A" and they know him.
(4) Jesus has other sheep in even more "Folds" and he will save them, too.
(5) All the sheep who hear his voice and follow him, regardless of Fold, will be part of one universal flock and under one Shepherd, Jesus our Lord.
(6) Some sheep are lost because they will neither hear Jesus' voice nor follow him.
(7) Jesus provides all of his sheep who hear his voice and follow him with eternal life and eternal protection against being taken away from God by the Evil One.

Again, those who hear the voice of Jesus and follow him are in his communion, his fellowship, his world-wide family. Yet, we humans sometimes divide ourselves into exclusive groups based on personalities or some pet doctrine (sometimes called a "hobby") or a preferred way of doing things. Those true believers who have waded into that sectarian quicksand are no less disciples of Christ than before, but they do need to repent of their exclusivity and again recognize others outside of their clans as being children of God.

**Dr. Rubel Shelly** has stated our disgraceful religious status quo about as clearly as anyone I have read. In his fine book, **I Just Want to Be a Christian** (revised edition, 1986, p. 29), he wrote:

"Over the centuries, the New Testament vision of a united church has been replaced by the present situation of denominationalism.

"The English word denominate means simply 'to give a name to.' Used in a religious context, a denomination is 'a party of religious people who are in agreement around a central tenet (s) of faith and who are distinguished from other groups by a distinguishing name.'

"People become denominational in exalting one religious theme and crystallizing around it and/or by the exclusive use of some name which serves to separate themselves from other people who seek to follow Christ after the New Testament order of things. Sectarian partisanship works to build the walls higher and higher with the passing of time" (Fair Use Domain).

Please allow me to illustrate our dilemma this way. Right now I am a card-holding resident of Bradenton, Florida. I am also a resident of Manatee County. Not only that, but I am also a resident of the state of Florida. I am also a passport-holding resident of the United States. One status does not negate the other.

Similarly, I grew up in and long worshipped with a group of believers whose three main distinctions were (1) our use of vocal music (singing), only, when we sing gospel songs and hymns in worship; (2) our observance of the Lord's Supper each and every Sunday; and (3) the fact that we almost exclusively use the name or title "Church of Christ" on our buildings, in our advertising and our normal conversations about "our" congregation.

Remember, I told you how as a young man I was so narrow-minded you could not see my head if you looked straight at me. Yep, almost that bad. For example, a couple of years after I graduated from high school, I decided to attend a Christian College up in Portland, Oregon. I talked a recent high school grad -- and a member of our congregation -- into going with me.

So, we packed everything we owned into my ol' 1955 Ford and headed up Highway 99. When Sunday morning rolled around, we were passing through a small-sized town in far northern California and decided we ought to stop for worship. Lo and behold, we drove near a building with "Church of Christ" on it. Eureka, we find a place!

Except, the minute we walked through the door, we heard somebody beating on a devilish piano. Right there in church building. So we frowned at each other and got the heck out of Dodge City. We made the decision that we would be better off not worshipping anywhere at all than worshiping with heathen. As it turns out, that was a congregation from our own Stone-Campbell faith-heritage. They were our piano-plunking cousins, as it were. It was pretty comfortable back then to be so young and yet know-it-all. We thought. Today, when I tell that story, it brings me closer to tears than to laughter.

Praise the Lord that now I recognize I am also in a similar fellowship with a much larger segment of God's people who are much like us but with a few variations. Those differences can put strains on much interchange between us. In addition, I sometimes help on joint community projects with a much wider and diverse group of people who also love God and claim Jesus as their Lord. We do not spend much time with these last folks and don't know them very well, which leads to distrust and isolation. But all of that does not mean that any of us is less a child of the King for any of those relationships. Friend, if you are God's child and I'm God's child then we are brothers and sisters whether we feel comfortable admitting it or not.

There is a humorous story about the late **Marshall Keeble**, a black evangelist based in Nashville. It was his customary greeting to say, "Hello, Brother Smith" (or whatever the name), no matter what sect or denomination the person was affiliated with. A few of the more conservative members of his congregation went to his office one day and confronted him about his egregiously liberal practice.

"How can you just go about the city calling people 'Brother' when you know they're a Baptist, a Methodist, a Presbyterian and so on?"

Keeble was a popular speaker before black and white audiences even in the days of segregation. He had a keen sense of humor. And he just smiled at this small group and said, "Well, brethren, it is like this. I figure when I say, 'Hello Brother' to a man that if I don't hit him in Christ, I'll hit him in Adam." And he continued with his little bit of ecumenicalism.

# What are you doing, for God's sake, to help tear down the walls dividing the people of God?

Another thing which is advocated among many peacemakers is for all followers of Christ to return to the custom of wearing only his name as his people.

As the early church developed, factions appeared because one group's favorite preacher was Paul and they wanted to call themselves "Paulites." Others favored the Christian orator Apollos and wanted to call themselves "Apollosites."

Looking back over centuries we today might be tempted to say that was a pretty doggoned silly thing for those first-century folks to do. Nobody with an ounce of spirituality would adopt a name of a mere man or a methodology or some act of obedience.

Really?

Well, that is just what happened all through church history. It plainly smacks of sectarianism and the party spirit. It unnecessary pushes members of the family of God into different man-made corrals than the universal body of Christ. And so we sincerely call upon Lutherans to adopt the name Christians and use it to identify themselves. We in love ask Methodists to give up that name and just give their religious affiliation as Christians or disciples of Christ. We encourage our Baptist friends and neighbors, likewise, to distance themselves from their man-made name and use that which honors the Son of God. Perhaps the Presbyterians, Quakers, Seventh Day Adventists, and the Episcopalians would follow suit.

I heard a really good bluegrass in concert a few years ago. The Bluegrass Etc band was so good that I bought one of their CDs, "Travelin' Band." From it, I transcribed a hilarious song titled, **"A Matter of Church Policy."** Each verse tells about some situation where church policy got in the way of essential matters which needed attention. Here is the first verse and the chorus. You will note, because you cannot miss it, the name of this fictional congregation.

1. A funny thing happened on the way to church last Sunday.
Billows of smoke came rolling from the door.
Well, I ran up to tell the leading deacons that something should be done,
Because the church was on fire for sure.

CHORUS:

And they said, "That's a point well-put and a timely suggestion.
We'll bring it up at the very next meeting of the board of deacons,
A week from Tuesday.
I don't know why, it's just church policy.
At the First-Naza-Metho-Bapti-Costal-Seventh-Day-Orthodox-
Lutherterian-Non-Denominational-Church-of-Our-Lady-of-the-Mind.

Pretty doggoned ridiculous.

Though I have Irish roots, I do not want to be called an Irish-American. Like so many early leaders in my faith-heritage, I also do not want to be known as a hyphenated Christian. I cringe when someone calls me a "Church of Christ-Christian" or even a "Church of Christ-minister." And I wish others were not so inclined to speak of Baptist-Christians, Methodist-Christians, Pentecostal-Christians and so forth. Why cannot we just refer to ourselves and graciously refer to others by the name above all names, Christian, and be satisfied with it?

A hundred years ago, one of the outspoken men in my own faith-heritage stated this case this way for using the name "Christian":

"The name 'Christian' is a name broad enough and great enough to include every being in the wide, wide world who accepts and obeys the teachings of the Lord Jesus Christ . Simply because one is obedient to Christ and wears the name 'Christian' is no indication he feels he has a copyright on that name. I would to God that every man who is a Christian should wear that name and no other to indicate his religion. One child of God does not need to be distinguished or separated from another child of God. God's children should be one in purpose, one in spirit, and one in life. They are not to be divided and contending over names as did the church at Corinth. Such division produced carnality, and carnality leads to death. I would like to be helpful in bringing all Christians to the point that they are willing to lose sight of human names and simply wear the name of Christ. – **J.C. McQuiddy**, "The Name 'Christian'," in the **Gospel Advocate** for Oct. 14, 1920, pp. 1003-1004 (Public Domain).

The big problem is those man-made names – when used exclusively to brand our fold of sheep in our little corner corrals of Christianity—produce harmful pride in that group and isolation from other believers. The whole evil mess tends to confuse and divide us from one another and, even worse, our divisions keep some truth seekers from accepting Jesus as their Lord.

After all, why in the world would they want to sit in a pew next to these bickering and nitpicking people who sure don't look or act like the joyous, peacemaking Jesus they all say they love? Shame on every one of us who has ever worn those sectarian glasses and seen others of God's people as our enemies or people to be converted to our opinions rather than as people of faith, justified by God and still loved by him in spite of our respective errors.

## Identifying Sectarianism

One of the giveaways of sectarianism rearing its ugly head is when a group selects a certain name for the body of Christ and insists on using that one to the exclusion of all other valid names or identifiers of the church of the Bible.

I would be less than transparent if I did not admit that my own religious group or faith-heritage has been and in some circles still is guilty of "denominating" (naming) a particular descriptive term, "The Church of Christ." Our fixation with that term is based on the single reference in Romans 16:16 in which Paul sent greetings to the brothers and sister in Rome with these words: "Holy embraces all around! All the churches of Christ send their warmest greetings!" (**The Message**)

This plural use of the warm description of Jesus' ownership of his people is only found once in the New Testament. It is never found in the singular form, while other descriptions are repeatedly used: "the church of God" (1 Corinthians 1:2), "the church of the Lord" (Acts 20:28), "the children of God" (Galatians 3:26), "the body of Christ" (Ephesians 4:12), etc.

However, the leaders in my faith-heritage after the Civil War latched onto that one term, "Church of Christ," and made it ours. And we get a case of righteous indignation and holy heartburn when we find anybody else using it without conforming to our "pattern" of idiosyncrasies. That is the title on the sign in front of 90 % of our group's church buildings. We "denominated" the term by our exclusive use of it. And to "denominate" something is a sign that a group is, in fact, a denomination. It is what it is, though most of us get high blood pressure and our tongues twisted in knots trying to defend that use.

The well-meaning folks in the Church of God, Assembly of God, Church of the Firstborn, etc., have erred in the same fashion by a sectarian, exclusive use of a valid and scriptural term.

The winds of change are blowing, however. Many of the mainline denominations in the U.S.A. now post web sites and signs outside their buildings which only say something like, "THE HILLS" in large print. But in the smaller print it may confess a denominational tag like "Presbyterian Church, U.S.A." or "United Methodist Church." The motive behind these games of smoke and mirrors often may be trying to attract people by hiding or downplaying their true colors and, thereby, postponing the revelation of their considerable denominational baggage. Or, and hopefully this is so at least in some cases, they are practicing simple Christianity. That often means the way forward is to go back . . . to the basics.

## Where God has a Child,
## We have a Brother

Wherever God has a child, I have a brother or a sister. We are family members, not robots, so very likely we will have differences of opinions and traditions. We must continue to love each other and seek maturity, while realistically knowing our family unity will always be based on diversity.

We stand united on the so-called "Seven Facts of Christian Unity" stated by Paul long ago: "Always be humble and gentle. Be patient and accept each other with love. You are joined together with peace through the Spirit. Do all you can to continue together in this way. Let peace hold you together. There is one body and one Spirit. And [one – SP] God called you to have one hope. There is one Lord, one faith, and one baptism" (Ephesians 4:2-5; **The Everyday Bible: New Century Version**).

Let's stop right here and list those precious "Ones" that bind us in Christian love with just a bit of elaboration.

(1) One body – God's spiritual family, also described as the body of Christ, the church of Christ, the church of God, the way, etc.

(2) One Spirit – the Great Counselor and Prayer Interpreter, the Holy Spirit who dwells within each Believer's heart.

(3) One God - the Creator and Supreme Commander of all we know, our Father God, Jehovah, Yahweh, or Elohim.

(4) One hope – our fact-based and heart-motivated optimism which looks forward to the return of Jesus and our ascension to heaven for eternity where we will live with the redeemed (saved) of all ages and continuously praise and serve God.

(5) One Lord – Jesus our Savior and King, the Messiah promised by the prophets in the Old Testament and descended to earth ; this seems to have been the only creed of the early Christians: "Jesus is Lord."

(6) One faith – our rock-solid belief in Jesus and his sacrificial work of salvation on the cross for us, our faith in the grace and love of God to shower us with spiritual blessings in Christ.

(7) One baptism – a symbolic public testimony to honor a person's having come to saving faith in God. In a very real sense, it is also an anointing of this new believer as a fellow priest in the "Royal Priesthood" where Jesus is our High Priest. It is a testimony that a person has been saved by grace and added to the fellowship of all believers everywhere.

When God adopts you into his world-wide family, you are in a close-knit fellowship of all saved people. Unlike Sunday morning on earth, in this spiritual family there is not one compound for the Methodists, another for the Baptists, a different one for the Catholics and another one for the Episcopalians and so on. Why?

Hold on to your bonnet, Aunt Emma, 'cause this may knock it right in the creek.

Fact: There ain't no Baptists in heaven.

Oh, my. But hold on, there is more.

There are no Methodists in God's spiritual family, either.

And no Catholics, no Pentecostals, no Seventh Day Adventists, no Church of Christ folks.

None. Zip. Nada.

So how is it that God's spiritual family, both on earth and in heaven, does not have a single Baptist, Methodist, Pentecostal, Seventh Day Adventist, or Church of Christ person?

The answer is in a foundational principle of simple Christianity:

> *There are no sectarian corrals (or compounds or campuses, in modern lingo) in the family of God. Not one. We are all just believers, born again Christians, washed in the blood of the Lamb. God sees each of us as his beloved and sanctified child, not as a card-carrying, bonified and certified member of a denomination. Not even when one is labled the Church of God, Assembly of God, or Church of Christ. God's heart is broken when his people slice and dice the body of Christ just to claim one little part of it was their very own.* --
> *Stan Paregien Sr.*

So in the case of baptized believers, our fellowship is in the world-wide family of God. We are not so much "Members," as that smacks of a business club or a Lions Club or the Red Hat Society where you pay your dues, show up once in a while and enjoy whatever benefits there are in that "membership."

Instead, we are part of the world-wide body (the community, the fellowship) of Christ. Our relationship with the Lord requires our finances, our generous good deeds, and our deep, abiding love. I have worshiped with all kinds of congregations, composed of blacks, Hispanics, whites, and mixed groups) in most states of the USA as well as in Mexico, Honduras, Costa Rica, Scotland, and Ireland. Even in that "Whole 'Nother Country" of Texas. His people are scattered around the world and God sees them only as his beloved children, not as sectarian Episcopalians, Methodists, Baptists, Pentecostals or whatever. We may slap sectarian name labels on each other's backs . . . but God never does.

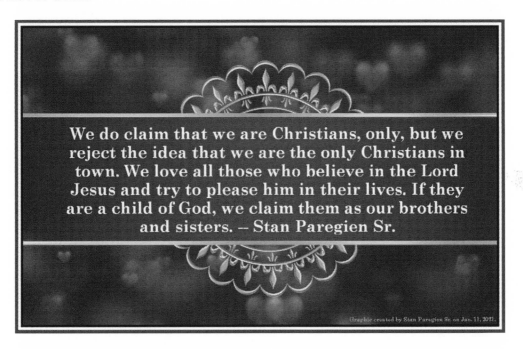

We do claim that we are Christians, only, but we reject the idea that we are the only Christians in town. We love all those who believe in the Lord Jesus and try to please him in their lives. If they are a child of God, we claim them as our brothers and sisters. – Stan Paregien Sr.

(Graphic created by Stan Paregien Sr. on Jan. 11, 2021.

Wherever in this vast world that God has a child, then I have a spiritual brother or a sister. And the "family traits" are many – such as deep love for God and his people, an eagerness born of gratitude to obey whatever our Father asks of us, and a peacemaker's determination to bless rather than judge the intentions and behaviors of others. After all, we are not in competition for God's approval.

However, the family traits which characterize God's spiritual children are also diverse. For one thing, we do not all look alike (thank God for that!). We are not an endless number of identical clones. Nor does our loving Father require us to think just alike on every point of scripture, every moral issue, or every ethical situation. We may be mistaken about a hundred doctrinal points and countless procedural details about how the family "ought" to work here on earth. We may all be flat wrong on a laundry list of ideas about what the return of the Lord Jesus (where, when, how, how long, etc.), but that does not take away our family relationship. We are in God's family, not because we have all the right answers but because we have the right DNA. Born again through the Spirit.

**Christian Unity in Diversity**

The following song by **Gloria and Bill Gaither**, written and copyrighted in 1970, describes the wonderful nature of that family bond:

> I'm so glad I'm a part of the family of God-
> I've been washed in the fountain, cleansed by His blood!
> Joint heirs with Jesus as we travel this sod;
> For I'm part of the family, the family of God.

You will notice we say "brother and sister" 'round here,
It's because we're a family and these are so near;
When one has a heartache, we all share the tears,
And rejoice in each victory in this family so dear.
(Fair Use Domain)

You see, friend, our hand of fellowship with another brother or sister in the family must never be based on anything other than the fact that God accepted them into his family on the same basis that he does us – our faith in the gospel news that (1) God the Father, God the Son (Jesus the Christ or Messiah) and the Holy Spirit have always existed; (2) God sent Jesus to this earth, to live as a human; (3) then at God's appointed time Jesus died upon the cross for our sins; (4) Jesus was raised from the dead; (5) Jesus ascended back to heaven; and (6) one day Jesus will come again to take the saved to heaven; and (7) to punish the wicked.

That being the case, we are bound not only to be civil toward each other but to be pro-active peacemakers engaged in loving and encouraging others. We do that even when they may refuse our goodwill because they are stuck in their sectarian quicksand.

Do you remember seeing those famous military recruiting posters from World War I and WW II with a likeness of "Uncle Sam" (representing the United States government and people) with the call to serve.

The gospel of Christ is not only an affirmation of the story of his life and mission, for it is also a ringing call for men and women of faith to visibly demonstrate their faith and love by their works and not just by their words. It is the invitation of the King of Kings to obey him and follow him, while you get more training so you can mature in Christ.

When the gospel story sinks in and you want to love God as he loves you, there comes the understanding that you as a believer must be prepared to follow his orders. And, oh, by the way. How many times does God have to state a command for it to apply to you?

I admire the attitude and actions of an older entertainer named **Connie Smith**. For decades, she won acclaim and made lots of money recording country-western songs. It is less known that she recorded many albums of gospel music. Several years ago, she married Nashville legend **Marty Stuart** – also a singer of country and gospel songs. They have each been inducted into the Country Music Hall of Fame.

Back in about 1976, when Peggy and I lived in Council Bluffs, Iowa, we went across the Missouri River to Omaha and saw Ms. Smith in a large country music concert. About half-way through her program, she stopped singing. Right then and there she said, "You folks need to know that I did not come all the way from Nashville just to sing country songs to you. I want to say that Jesus is my Lord and Savior, and he has been since I became a Christian long, long ago. He is still my rock and strength, and I highly recommend him to you." (Photo above is a PR photo. Fair Use Domain)

Those were not her exact words because, well, my memory today is just not what it never was. It is a fair gist of what she said that night. She spoke as a sincere friend, not in the least bit confrontational.

Well, someone else once said, "If the Bible said it, I believe it and that settles it." So if God gives a command only once or twice, that is plenty for the person who loves him and wants to please him. That is certainly true when it comes to baptism, isn't it?

However, please remember this: there is no power at all in the chemistry of the waters of baptism. If we are saved, it can only be because of faith in the sacrificial blood of Jesus, the atonement for our sins. The apostle Peter put it this way: "You know that you were ransomed from the futile ways inherited from your ancestors, not with perishable things like silver or gold, but with the precious blood of Christ, like that of a lamb without defect or blemish" (1 Peter 1:19; **New Revised Standard Version**).

In my own faith-heritage we somehow got bamboozled by well-meaning but largely uneducated preachers into believing two major errors.

# Error 1

The first error was in believing the satanical notion that God loved us so much that he sent us a "plan of salvation" which, if followed like a blueprint for a birdhouse, we could save ourselves. That was brainwashing at its worst. God did not send a plan. He loved us so very much he actually sent his son, Jesus the Christ, to do all the work for our salvation. Some of us need to have John 3:16 branded on our foreheads.

# Error 2

The second tragic error was in believing that we magically "contacted the saving blood of Christ" at the exact moment we were dipped under the surface of the baptismal waters.

Even today, some of my beloved people parrot the sentiment, "Let's call Bible things by Bible names." Okay, then where in the pages of the New Testament does it specifically talk about "contacting the blood of Christ through baptism?" It is not there. Zip. Nada.

# Error 3

There was another rhetorical deception by which our early preachers often used to get folks into the baptistry. The illustration went something like this: "If you love God and believe in Jesus, you need to repent of your sins and come forward right now to be baptized. Right now, while you are able and have the opportunity. If you miss this chance, you may die tonight and then your soul would go to hell.

"After all, getting saved is like a marriage ceremony. Say that Bubba and Sally have good intentions about getting married and have set the date for 7:00 pm on September 1st. But Bubba is driving his pickup to the church building for the wedding that evening and gets hit by a train and killed. There was no ceremony and, therefore, no marriage in the eyes of the state. It is the same thing with salvation. Acts 2:38 says you have to repent and be baptized for the remission of your sins. Therefore, if you are not baptized, you will be eternally lost. So come on and get it done before we leave the building."

These same leaders made it clear any unbaptized folks were just kindling wood headed for the fires of hell unless and until they were "plunged beneath that crimson flood." They left the impression that a miraculous process took place in the waters of baptism that provided our only hope of escaping eternity with the Devil and his evil crowd.

Those of about my age who were reared in that religious group know exactly what I'm talking about. Such preachers were decent men with honorable intentions who nevertheless spread terrible theology by saying such things.

We are not saved by or during the act of baptism but at the time of our faith-experience in Jesus and his act of sacrificial death upon the cross. He alone is our salvation. Period. Exclamation point.

The wonderful truth is this: We were saved by grace when by faith we lovingly accepted Christ as our Lord. That passion for pleasing God spills over into the act of repentance just as much as it does into the act of witnessing or participating in the Eucharist ceremony (communion or Lord's Supper) or into the act of being baptized. No more, no less.

Our living faith reflects the light of Jesus into the darkness around us. And so we testify in many ways, through countless acts, to our new status as children of God and even as his friends. Not one of these acts should be elevated more than God has ordained, for not one reaches the level of bestowing salvation to us. We should be happy to say that salvation is a God-thing, not a baptism-thing, and not a repentance-thing.

Of course, it is true that most of us see in baptism a highly symbolic reenactment of the death, burial, and resurrection of Jesus. It is a public testimony of our aim to please God by dying to the power of the Devil, and by burying our sinful ways of acting and thinking. In the act of testimonial baptism, we bear witness that we have previously had a faith-experience in which we were saved by God's grace. That moment came when we named Jesus as our Lord. And by water baptism, we also celebrate our new standing or status as part of the world-wide fellowship of all others who have been saved through the work of Jesus.

These facts are both the rock and mortar of the foundation upon which we all may stand, no matter what sectarian names we have adopted. Jesus made it clear he is the Shepherd of all of his sheep, that is, he is over all those world-wide who have come to love him, to obey him to the best of their understanding and to honor him as their Lord. That is the body, the fellowship, or the communion which all enjoy after we have been saved by God's grace through faith in Jesus as the Son of God.

That is where simple Christianity begins.

# Chapter 14

# Understanding the Priesthood
## of All Believers, Part 1

Most religions of the world have wound up having a select group of people called priests who, together, make up a priesthood. Often, they devote themselves fully to their special duties and are supported by the general people in that religious organization. They become, in essence, a professional class. That eventually happened with the nation of Israel.

To start with, though, the Old Testament depicts what might rightly be called "Family Priests." There was a time when the male head of the household or clan was able to make a blood-sacrifice to God. Abel sacrificed an offering to God, as did both Noah and Abraham.

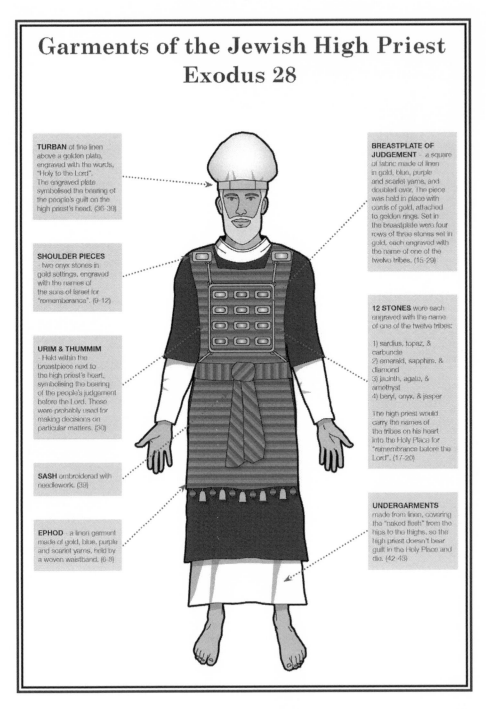

# Garments of the Jewish High Priest
## Exodus 28

**TURBAN** of fine linen above a golden plate, engraved with the words, "Holy to the Lord". The engraved plate symbolised the bearing of the people's guilt on the high priest's head. (36-39)

**SHOULDER PIECES** - two onyx stones in gold settings, engraved with the names of the sons of Israel for "rememberance". (9-12)

**URIM & THUMMIM** - Held within the breastpiece next to the high priest's heart, symbolising the bearing of the people's judgement before the Lord. These were probably used for making decisions on particular matters. (30)

**SASH** embroidered with needlework. (39)

**EPHOD** - a linen garment made of gold, blue, purple and scarlet yarns, held by a woven waistband. (6-8)

**BREASTPLATE OF JUDGEMENT** - a square of fabric made of linen in gold, blue, purple and scarlet yarns, and doubled over. The piece was held in place with cords of gold, attached to golden rings. Set in the breastplate were four rows of three stones set in gold, each engraved with the name of one of the twelve tribes. (15-29)

**12 STONES** were each engraved with the name of one of the twelve tribes:

1) sardius, topaz, & carbuncle
2) emerald, sapphire, & diamond
3) jacinth, agate, & amethyst
4) beryl, onyx, & jasper

The high priest would carry the names of the tribes on his heart into the Holy Place for "remembrance before the Lord". (17-20)

**UNDERGARMENTS** made from linen, covering the "naked flesh" from the hips to the thighs, so the high priest doesn't bear guilt in the Holy Place and die. (42-43)

The Jewish priesthood began by God appointing Aaron, the eloquent brother of stuttering Moses, as their first High Priest. There was even a fellow from Midian, a man named Jethro, who was considered a priest in his own right and who also engaged in a mutual sacrifice with the elders of Israel, with Aaron and with Moses (Exodus 18:12).

Later, following God's exact orders and specifications, Moses oversaw the building of a large and portable tabernacle for a place of worship. An ordinary Israelite would never see inside the walls of the tabernacle.

Again, by God's design, he ordered that Moses create a priesthood to offer sacrifices in the tabernacle in regard to the sins of the people. Moses ordained or set aside the entire tribe of Levi to serve as priests and their staff. The old saying is true: "All priests were Levites, but not all Levites were priests."

Moses appointed his brother, Aaron as the High Priest. God allowed only Aaron to enter into the mysterious "Holy of Holies" once each year for a special sacrifice. His sons and other Levitic priests offered the meat and blood of animals and birds as sacrifices to God. These priests were supported by special unspecified offerings from all the people, while the rest of the members of the tribe of Levi were supported by a tithe (10%) required of all the Israelites. (Numbers 18:20-24). See also see the books of Leviticus, Numbers and Deuteronomy for the qualifications of priests, requirements of their garments and rituals, and details of the tabernacle itself. Much later, Levitical priests served in the great Temple in Jerusalem built by Solomon.

## Qualification & Duties of the High Priest

The High Priest was appointed for life, and he was to keep himself holy and totally dedicated to his work (Leviticus 10:5, 9; 21:10-15; Numbers 18:7; 25:11-13; 35:25, 28; Nehemiah 12:10-11). He even had to wear a special headgear, a turban made of linen cloth and embedded with a gold placard inscribed with, "Holy to Yaweh" (God). He could not leave the immediate vicinity of the tabernacle (later, the Temple). When he sinned, he brought guilt and shame on all of Israel. Therefore the sacrifice was as valuable and as elaborate as that offered when the whole nation actually did sin (Leviticus 4:3-21).

The High Priest had to be a descendent of Aaron through the tribe of Levi (Exodus 29:29-30; Leviticus 16:32).

The High Priest was the only person who could enter the Holy of Holies area within the Tabernacle (later, the Temple). And he could do that only on the annual **Day of Atonement** (Leviticus 16:1-25; aka *Yom Kippur* in Hebrew). In Bible times, the word atonement was used in the sense of "covering up" or "covering over" one's sins with blood sacrifices (or incense or money) so God would turn away and not see those sins.

After the burnt sacrifices, the High Priest conducted a final and highly symbolic ritual. Two carefully selected goats were brought before him. He cast lots between them, with one goat thereby designated as a blood-offering. The sacrificial goat was killed and the body burnt, and the High Priest took its blood into the Holy of Holies and sprinkled it on the Mercy Seat. He did so to make atonement for the sins of all Jewish people. This "Mercy Seat" or "Throne of Mercy" was a heavy, rectangular plank of gold which lay on top of the mysterious Ark of the Covenant. There was an angel-like statue (a cherub) on each end of the slab, facing inwardly (Much larger ones were later installed in the magnificent Temple). That anointing with blood symbolized Israel's desire for peace with God.

Next, the High Priest turned his attention to the second goat. He symbolically placed his own sins, those of his family and the entire nation on this live goat. Then the regular priests took the goat outside the walls and turned it loose in the countryside to die. That is the origin of the word "**scapegoat**," one who takes the blame for another. God himself prescribed this whole process. The end result was a reconciliation of genuine fellowship between the two estranged parties, God and the individual and/or the nation of Israel. They were, again, "at-one-ment." The holy day is still celebrated by Jews on the 10th day of the Jewish calendar period of Tishri (our September-October).

The High Priest was supposed to identify with the people of Israel and to be gentle with them. The writer of Hebrews said Chapter 5: "1-3 Every high priest selected to represent men and women before God and offer sacrifices for their sins should be able to deal gently with their failings, since he knows what it's like from his own experience. But that also means that he has to offer sacrifices for his own sins as well as the peoples'

"4 No one elects himself to this honored position. He is called to it by God, as Aaron was" (Hebrews 5:1-4a, **The Message** – MSG).

The Holy Spirit-inspired writer of the book of Hebrews gave us many insights into how the Old Covenant played out in the worship and day-to-day lives of the Jewish people. Here are a few passages:

**Hebrews 9:1-10:**

"Now the first covenant had regulations for worship and also an earthly sanctuary. 2 A tabernacle was set up. In its first room were the lampstand and the table with its consecrated bread; this was called the Holy Place. 3 Behind the second curtain was a room called the Most Holy Place, 4 which had the golden altar of incense and the gold-covered ark of the covenant. This ark contained the gold jar of manna, Aaron's staff that had budded, and the stone tablets of the covenant. 5 Above the ark were the cherubim of the Glory, overshadowing the atonement cover. But we cannot discuss these things in detail now.

"6 When everything had been arranged like this, the priests entered regularly into the outer room to carry on their ministry. 7 But only the high priest entered the inner room, and that only once a year, and never without blood, which he offered for himself and for the sins the people had committed in ignorance. 8 The Holy Spirit was showing by this that the way into the Most Holy Place had not yet been disclosed as long as the first tabernacle was still functioning. 9 This is an illustration for the present time, indicating that the gifts and sacrifices being offered were not able to clear the conscience of the worshiper. 10 They are only a matter of food and drink and various ceremonial washings—external regulations applying until the time of the new order" (**New International Version** – NIV).

**NOTE**: By the first century, the office of High Priest had become politicized and extremely corrupt. The Romans used both force and various forms of bribery to get the High Priest to do their bidding. Likewise, the High Priest was not above using both bribery and force to achieve his own desires. During the adult life of Jesus, the High Priest was Joseph Caiaphas. He held the office from about 18 A.D. to 37 A.D. Caiaphas had inherited the office from his father-in-law, Annas, who had been High Priest himself from 6 A.D. to 14 A.D. And Annas was the real power behind Caiaphas, perhaps with a title like "High Priest Emeritus" to indicate his continued influence in what was usually a lifetime calling.

**Hebrews 10:1-31**

"The Law is like a picture of the good things to come. The Jewish religious leaders gave gifts on the altar in worship to God all the time year after year. Those gifts could not make the people who came to worship perfect. 2 If those gifts given to God could take away sins, the people who came to worship would no longer feel guilty of sin.

They would have given no more gifts. 3 When they gave the gifts year after year, it made them remember that they still had their sins. 4 The blood of animals cannot take away the sins of men.

"5 When Christ came to the world, He said to God, 'You do not want animals killed or gifts given in worship. You have made My body ready to give as a gift. 6 You are not pleased with animals that have been killed or burned and given as gifts on the altar to take away sin. 7 Then I said, 'I have come to do what You want, O God. It is written in the Law that I would.'

"8 Then Christ said, 'You do not want animals killed or gifts given in worship to you for sin. You are not pleased with them.' These things are done because the Law says they should be done. 9 Then He said, 'I have come to do what You want Me to do.' And this is what He did when He died on a cross. God did away with the Old Way of Worship and made a New Way of Worship. 10 Our sins are washed away and we are made clean because Christ gave His own body as a gift to God. He did this once for all time.

"11 All Jewish religious leaders stand every day killing animals and giving gifts on the altar. They give the same gifts over and over again. These gifts cannot take away sins. 12 But Christ gave Himself once for sins and that is good forever. After that He sat down at the right side of God. 13 He is waiting there for God to make of those who have hated Him a place to rest His feet. 14 And by one gift He has made perfect forever all those who are being set apart for God-like living.

"15 The Holy Spirit tells us this: First He says, 16 'This is the New Way of Worship that I will give them. When that day comes, says the Lord, I will put My Laws in their hearts. And I will write them in their minds.' Then He says, 17 'I will not remember their sins and wrong-doings anymore.' 18 No more gifts on the altar in worship are needed when our sins are forgiven.

"19 Christian brothers, now we know we can go into the Holiest Place of All because the blood of Jesus was given. 20 We now come to God by the new and living way. Christ made this way for us. He opened the curtain, which was His own body. 21 We have a great Religious Leader over the house of God. 22 And so let us come near to God with a true heart full of faith. Our hearts must be made clean from guilty feelings and our bodies washed with pure water. 23 Let us hold on to the hope we say we have and not be changed. We can trust God that He will do what He promised. 24 Let us help each other to love others and to do good. 25 Let us not stay away from church meetings. Some people are doing this all the time. Comfort each other as you see the day of His return coming near.

"26 If we keep on sinning because we want to after we have received and know the truth, there is no gift that will take away sins then. 27 Instead, we will stand before God and on that day He will judge us. And the hot fires of hell will burn up those who work against God. 28 Anyone who did not obey the Old Way of Worship died without loving-kindness when two or three men spoke against him. 29 How much more will a man have to be punished if he walks on and hates the Son of God? How much more will he be punished if he acts as if the blood of God's New Way of Worship is worth nothing? This New Way of Worship is God's way of making him holy. How much more will he be punished if he laughs at the Holy Spirit Who wanted to show him loving-favor? 30 For we know God said, 'I will pay back what is coming to them.' And, 'The Lord will judge His people.' 31 The very worst thing that can happen to a man is to fall into the hands of the living God!

(Hebrews 10:1-31, **New Life Version** – NLV)."

# Chapter 15

# Understanding the Priesthood
# of All Believers, Part 2

## Jesus as Our High Priest

God in his wisdom - and from the beginning of time - had plans for Jesus to serve as the Christian's holy High Priest and to be a mediator between believers and God. In order to do that, Jesus made the ultimate sacrifice for our sins.

Jesus began his public ministry in Israel in about 29A.D. From that moment to his death in 33 A.D., there was a constant drumbeat of clues that this young man would give his life in dedicated service to God's mission for him.

John the Baptist was one of the first to see and understand the sacrificial nature of his service. While getting as many people as he could to prepare for the coming of this Messiah, John the Baptist preached a baptism of repentance in anticipation of that coming. He preached, mainly, in the rural areas. We have this record of his awakening to what Jesus himself was preparing to do:

"29 The next day John saw Jesus coming toward him and said, 'Look! There is the Lamb of God who takes away the world's sin! 30 He is the one I was talking about when I said, 'Soon a man far greater than I am is coming, who existed long before me!' 31 I didn't know he was the one, but I am here baptizing with water in order to point him out to the nation of Israel.'

"32 Then John told about seeing the Holy Spirit in the form of a dove descending from heaven and resting upon Jesus.

"33 'I didn't know he was the one,' John said again, 'but at the time God sent me to baptize he told me, 'When you see the Holy Spirit descending and resting upon someone—he is the one you are looking for. He is the one who baptizes with the Holy Spirit.' 34 I saw it happen to this man, and I therefore testify that he is the Son of God.'

"35 The following day as John was standing with two of his disciples, 36 Jesus walked by. John looked at him intently and then declared, 'See! There is the Lamb of God!'

"37 Then John's two disciples turned and followed Jesus.

"38 Jesus looked around and saw them following. 'What do you want?' he asked them.

"'Sir,' they replied, 'where do you live?'

"39 'Come and see,' he said. So they went with him to the place where he was staying and were with him from about four o'clock that afternoon until the evening. 40 (One of these men was Andrew, Simon Peter's brother.)

"41 Andrew then went to find his brother Peter and told him, 'We have found the Messiah!' 42 And he brought Peter to meet Jesus" (Gospel of John 1:29-42, **The Living Bible** - TLB).

John the Baptist declared that Jesus of Nazareth was "the lamb of God" and Andrew told Peter that Jesus was the longed-for Messiah. Both statements were references to the poetic verses found in the Old Testament in Isaiah 53. Those men who wrote the New Testament often quoted and alluded to the words in Isaiah as being primarily about Israel but secondarily as prophecies that apply to Jesus the Christ (Messiah).

The parallels between the young servant in Isaiah 53 and the life of Jesus are certainly plain, and you may want to study them in depth at a later time. Here is Isaiah 53 in modern English:

"2-6 The servant grew up before God—a scrawny seedling,
a scrubby plant in a parched field.
There was nothing attractive about him,
nothing to cause us to take a second look.

He was looked down on and passed over,
a man who suffered, who knew pain firsthand.
One look at him and people turned away.
We looked down on him, thought he was scum.
But the fact is, it was our pains he carried—
our disfigurements, all the things wrong with us.
We thought he brought it on himself,
that God was punishing him for his own failures.
But it was our sins that did that to him,
that ripped and tore and crushed him—our sins!
He took the punishment, and that made us whole.
Through his bruises we get healed.
We're all like sheep who've wandered off and gotten lost.
We've all done our own thing, gone our own way.
And God has piled all our sins, everything we've done wrong,
on him, on him.

"7-9 He was beaten, he was tortured,
but he didn't say a word.
Like a lamb taken to be slaughtered
and like a sheep being sheared,
he took it all in silence.
Justice miscarried, and he was led off—
and did anyone really know what was happening?
He died without a thought for his own welfare,
beaten bloody for the sins of my people.
They buried him with the wicked,
threw him in a grave with a rich man,
Even though he'd never hurt a soul
or said one word that wasn't true.

"10 Still, it's what God had in mind all along,
to crush him with pain.
The plan was that he give himself as an offering for sin
so that he'd see life come from it—life, life, and more life.
And God's plan will deeply prosper through him.

"11-12 Out of that terrible travail of soul,

226

he'll see that it's worth it and be glad he did it.
Through what he experienced, my righteous one, my servant,
will make many 'righteous ones,'
as he himself carries the burden of their sins.
Therefore I'll reward him extravagantly—
the best of everything, the highest honors—
Because he looked death in the face and didn't flinch,
because he embraced the company of the lowest.
He took on his own shoulders the sin of the many,
he took up the cause of all the black sheep"
(Isaiah 53:2-12, **The Message** – MSG).

**Jesus voluntarily endured death threats, beatings, mock trials, crucifixion on a Roman cross, and a slow and painful death**. Looking back toward the crucifixion and resurrection, the writer of Hebrews said of our Lord in 2:9-18: "9 For a short time Jesus was made lower than the angels, but now we see him wearing a crown of glory and honor because he suffered and died. Because of God's grace, Jesus died for everyone.

"10 God—the one who made all things and for whose glory all things exist—wanted many people to be his children and share his glory. So he did what he needed to do. He made perfect the one who leads those people to salvation. **He made Jesus a perfect Savior through his suffering** [emphasis mine, SP].

"11 Jesus, the one who makes people holy, and those who are made holy are from the same family. So he is not ashamed to call them his brothers and sisters. 12 He says,

'God, I will tell my brothers and sisters about you.
Before all your people I will sing your praises.'

"13 He also says, 'I will trust in God.' And he says, 'I am here, and with me are the children God has given me.'

"14 These children are people with physical bodies. So Jesus himself became like them and had the same experiences they have. **Jesus did this so that, by dying, he could destroy the one who has the power of death—the devil** [emphasis mine, SP]. 15 Jesus became like these people and died so that he could free them. They were like slaves all their lives because of their fear of death. 16 Clearly, it is not angels that Jesus helps. He helps the people who are from Abraham. 17 For this reason, Jesus had to be made like us, his brothers and sisters, in every way. **He became like people so that he could be their merciful and faithful high priest in service to God** [emphasis mine, SP]. Then he could bring forgiveness for the people's sins. 18 And now he can help those who are tempted. He is able to help because he himself suffered and was tempted" (Hebrews 2:9-18, ERV).

**Jesus voluntarily took upon himself the weight and shame of our sin, and literally became a blood-sacrifice in our place to secure our atonement with God.** That is called a "substitutionary sacrifice."

Paul wrote, "God has a way to make people right, and it has nothing to do with the law. He has now shown us that new way, which the law and the prophets told us about. 22 God makes people right through their faith in Jesus Christ. He does this for all who believe in Christ. Everyone is the same. 23 All have sinned and are not good enough to share God's divine greatness. 24 They are made right with God by his grace. This is a free gift. They are made right with God by being made free from sin through Jesus Christ. 25-26 God gave Jesus as a way to forgive people's sins through their faith in him. God can forgive them because the blood sacrifice of Jesus pays for their sins. God gave Jesus to show that he always does what is right and fair. He was right in the past when he was patient and did not punish people for their sins. And in our own time he still does what is right. God worked all this out in a way that allows him to judge people fairly and still make right any person who has faith in Jesus" (Romans 3:21-26, ERV).

The apostle Paul further wrote, "While we were God's enemies, he made friends with us through his Son's death. And the fact that we are now God's friends makes it even more certain that he will save us through his Son's life" (Romans 5:10, ERV).

You see, Jesus voluntarily became sin for us when we could not help ourselves. He who was God and from heaven was sinless (without sin), but he became sin for us.

And Jesus voluntarily substituted himself for everyone else, including you.

Like Israel's first High Priest, Aaron, Jesus prays for God's family and acts as an advocate for us. That is where his priesthood is far superior to Aaron's. The Old Covenant motivated people by "fear and trembling," but the New Covenant draws people by the love and kindness of God. Aaron was set apart from common people, while Jesus reveled in associating with and blessing the commoners. The Bible says Jesus in his human/God role on earth was tempted in all ways we are but never did sin.

He was blameless and pure and holy. And because he is our elder brother and advocate, we can approach the throne of God boldly with great confidence that he welcomes us . . . because of Jesus (see Hebrews 4:14-16).

One artist's conception of the death of Jesus

**Jesus voluntarily sacrificed himself to both fulfill the Old Covenant as well as to establish the New Covenant of God with all people.** The apostle Paul explained it this way in Romans 3, referring to the Old Covenant with Moses simply as "the law":

"27 So do we have any reason to boast about ourselves? No reason at all. And why not? Because we are depending on the way of faith, not on what we have done in following the law. 28 I mean we are made right with God through faith, not through what we have done to follow the law. This is what we believe. 29 God is not only the God of the Jews. He is also the God of those who are not Jews. 30 There is only one God. He will make Jews right with him by their faith, and he will also make non-Jews right with him through their faith. 31 So do we destroy the law by following the way of faith? Not at all! In fact, faith causes us to be what the law actually wants" (Romans 3:27-31, ERV).

The emphasis in the whole book of Hebrews is on how the Old Covenant was nailed to the cross of Christ and the far superior New Covenant is offered to everyone. Here are some selected passages with that theme:

### Hebrews 4:14-16

"14 Seeing then that we have a great High Priest who has passed through the heavens, Jesus the Son of God, let us hold fast our confession. 15 For we do not have a High Priest who cannot sympathize with our weaknesses, but was in all points tempted as we are, yet without sin. 16 Let us therefore come boldly to the throne of grace, that we may obtain mercy and find grace to help in time of need" (**New King James Version** – NKJV).

### Hebrews 5:5-11

"5 So also Christ did not glorify Himself to become High Priest, but it was He who said to Him:

'You are My Son,
Today I have begotten You.'

"6 As He also says in another place:

'You are a priest forever
According to the order of Melchizedek';

"7 who, in the days of His flesh, when He had offered up prayers and supplications, with vehement cries and tears to Him who was able to save Him from death, and was heard because of His godly fear, 8 though He was a Son, yet He learned obedience by the things which He suffered. 9 And having been perfected, He became the author of eternal salvation to all who obey Him, 10 called by God as High Priest 'according to the order of Melchizedek,' 11 of whom we have much to say, and hard to explain, since you have become dull of hearing" (Hebrews 5:5-11, **New King James Version** – NKJV).

This man named Melchizedek is a mysterious person. In Genesis 14, he was said to be both the King and the Priest of Salem (likely an ancient part of present-day Jerusalem). On one occasion, Abram was returning with the spoils of a battle with his enemy. Melchizedek met him in the countryside, gave him wine and bread, and then pronounced a blessed on both Abram and on God. The Hebrew text is unclear as to whether Abram gave a tithe (normally about 10%) of his spoils to Melchizedek or whether it was actually Melchizedek who gave some tribute to Abram. Melchizedek is also mentioned in Psalm 110:4.

## Hebrews 7:11-28

"11 Therefore, if perfection were through the Levitical priesthood (for under it the people received the law), what further need was there that another priest should rise according to the order of Melchizedek, and not be called according to the order of Aaron? 12 For the priesthood being changed, of necessity there is also a change of the law. 13 For He of whom these things are spoken belongs to another tribe, from which no man has officiated at the altar.

"14 For it is evident that our Lord arose from Judah, of which tribe Moses spoke nothing concerning priesthood. 15 And it is yet far more evident if, in the likeness of Melchizedek, there arises another priest 16 who has come, not according to the law of a fleshly commandment, but according to the power of an endless life. 17 For He testifies:

> 'You are a priest forever
> According to the order of Melchizedek.'

"18 For on the one hand there is an annulling of the former commandment because of its weakness and unprofitableness, 19 for the law [of Moses, SP] made nothing perfect; on the other hand, there is the bringing in of a better hope, through which we draw near to God.

"20 And inasmuch as He was not made priest without an oath 21 (for they have become priests without an oath, but He with an oath by Him who said to Him:

> 'The Lord has sworn
> And will not relent,
> 'You are a priest forever
> According to the order of Melchizedek'),

"22 by so much more Jesus has become a surety of a better covenant.

"23 Also there were many priests, because they were prevented by death from continuing. 24 But He, because He continues forever, has an unchangeable priesthood. 25 Therefore He is also able to save to the uttermost those who come to God through Him, since He always lives to make intercession for them.

"26 For such a High Priest was fitting for us, who is holy, harmless, undefiled, separate from sinners, and has become higher than the heavens; 27 who does not need daily, as those high priests, to offer up sacrifices, first for His own sins and then for the people's, for this He did once for all when He offered up Himself. 28 For the law appoints as high priests men who have weakness, but the word of the oath, which came after the law, appoints the Son who has been perfected forever" (**New King James Version** – NKJV).

**NOTE:** Normally, the priests were selected from the men in the tribe of Levi who were at least 30 years of age. Then the High Priest was chosen from that select group to serve his entire life. When a High Priest died or was incapacitated, they again selected from the large pool of Levitic priests. This was not the case with Jesus, however, as he was from the tribe of Judah. And he was divinely appointed by God as the new and eternal High Priest for all who confess faith in him as our Lord and as the Son of God.

**Hebrews 8:1-13**

"8 1-2 In essence, we have just such a high priest: authoritative right alongside God, conducting worship in the one true sanctuary built by God.

"3-5 The assigned task of a high priest is to offer both gifts and sacrifices, and it's no different with **the priesthood of Jesus** [emphasis mine, SP]. If he were limited to earth, he wouldn't even be a priest. We wouldn't need him since there are plenty of priests who offer the gifts designated in the law. These priests provide only a hint of what goes on in the true sanctuary of heaven, which Moses caught a glimpse of as he was about to set up the tent-shrine. It was then that God said, "Be careful to do it exactly as you saw it on the Mountain."

"6-13 But **Jesus' priestly work far surpasses what these other priests do** [emphasis mine, SP], since he's working from a far better plan. If the first plan—the old covenant—had worked out, a second wouldn't have been needed. But we know the first was found wanting, because God said,

> Heads up! The days are coming
> when I'll set up a new plan
> for dealing with Israel and Judah.
> I'll throw out the old plan
> I set up with their ancestors
> when I led them by the hand out of Egypt.
> They didn't keep their part of the bargain,
> so I looked away and let it go.
> This new plan I'm making with Israel
> isn't going to be written on paper,
> isn't going to be chiseled in stone;
> This time I'm writing out the plan in them,
> carving it on the lining of their hearts.
> I'll be their God,
> they'll be my people.
> They won't go to school to learn about me,
> or buy a book called 'God in Five Easy Lessons.'
> They'll all get to know me firsthand,
> the little and the big, the small and the great.
> They'll get to know me by being kindly forgiven,
> with the slate of their sins forever wiped clean.

"By coming up with a new plan, a new covenant between God and his people, God put the old plan on the shelf. And there it stays, gathering dust" (Hebrews 8:1-13, **The Message** - MSG).

## Hebrews 9:1-28

"Now even the first covenant had regulations for worship and an earthly sanctuary. 2 For a tent was constructed, the first one, in which were the lampstand, the table, and the bread of the Presence; this is called the Holy Place. 3 Behind the second curtain was a tent called the Holy of Holies. 4 In it stood the golden altar of incense and the ark of the covenant overlaid on all sides with gold, in which there were a golden urn holding the manna, and Aaron's rod that budded, and the tablets of the covenant; 5

above it were the cherubim of glory overshadowing the mercy seat. Of these things we cannot speak now in detail.

"6 Such preparations having been made, the priests go continually into the first tent to carry out their ritual duties; 7 but only the high priest goes into the second, and he but once a year, and not without taking the blood that he offers for himself and for the sins committed unintentionally by the people.

"8 By this the Holy Spirit indicates that the way into the sanctuary has not yet been disclosed as long as the first tent is still standing. 9 This is a symbol of the present time, during which gifts and sacrifices are offered that cannot perfect the conscience of the worshiper, 10 but deal only with food and drink and various baptisms, regulations for the body imposed until the time comes to set things right.

"11 But when Christ came as a high priest of the good things that have come, then through the greater and perfect tent (not made with hands, that is, not of this creation), 12 **he entered once for all into the Holy Place, not with the blood of goats and calves, but with his own blood, thus obtaining eternal redemption** [emphasis mine, SP]. 13 For if the blood of goats and bulls, with the sprinkling of the ashes of a heifer, sanctifies those who have been defiled so that their flesh is purified, 14 how much more will the blood of Christ, who through the eternal Spirit offered himself without blemish to God, purify our conscience from dead works to worship the living God!

"15 For this reason **he is the mediator of a new covenant** [emphasis mine, SP], so that those who are called may receive the promised eternal inheritance, because a death has occurred that redeems them from the transgressions under the first covenant. 16 Where a will is involved, the death of the one who made it must be established. 17 For a will takes effect only at death, since it is not in force as long as the one who made it is alive. 18 Hence not even the first covenant was inaugurated without blood. 19 For when every commandment had been told to all the people by Moses in accordance with the law, he took the blood of calves and goats, with water and scarlet wool and hyssop, and sprinkled both the scroll itself and all the people, 20 saying, "This is the blood of the covenant that God has ordained for you." 21 And in the same way he sprinkled with the blood both the tent and all the vessels used in worship. 22 Indeed, under the law almost everything is purified with blood, and without the shedding of blood there is no forgiveness of sins.

"23 Thus it was necessary for the sketches of the heavenly things to be purified with these rites, but the heavenly things themselves need better sacrifices than these. 24 For Christ did not enter a sanctuary made by human hands, a mere copy of the true one, but **he entered into heaven itself, now to appear in the presence of God on our behalf** [emphasis mine, SP]. 25 Nor was it to offer himself again and again, as the high priest enters the Holy Place year after year with blood that is not his own; 26 for then he would have had to suffer again and again since the foundation of the world. But as it is, he has appeared once for all at the end of the age to remove sin by the sacrifice of himself. 27 And just as it is appointed for mortals to die once, and after that the judgment, 28 so Christ, having been offered once to bear the sins of many, will appear a second time, not to deal with sin, but to save those who are eagerly waiting for him" (Hebrews 9:1-28, **New Revised Standard Version** – NRSV).

Jesus came to teach us the simple yet profound truth that God is love. The apostle John is an intriguing Bible character. He and his brother James were fishermen by trade. They were athletic, intelligent and . . . well, . . . often spoke before their minds were fully engaged. In other words, they were a lot like most of us in their early age.

However, John's intimate walk with Jesus had a dramatic effective on him. In time, John became the peacemaker among the early Christians. He was so effective he became known as the apostle of love. Here is just part of what he wrote on that topic:

"7 Dear friends, we should love each other, because love comes from God. Everyone who loves has become God's child. And so everyone who loves knows God. 8 **Anyone who does not love does not know God, because God is love** [emphasis mine, SP]. 9 This is how God showed his love to us: He sent his only Son into the world to give us life through him. 10 True love is God's love for us, not our love for God. He sent his Son as the way to take away our sins.

"11 That is how much God loved us, dear friends! So we also must love each other. 12 No one has ever seen God. But if we love each other, God lives in us. If we love each other, God's love has reached its goal—it is made perfect in us.

"13 We know that we live in God and God lives in us. We know this because he gave us his Spirit. 14 We have seen that the Father sent his Son to be the Savior of the world, and this is what we tell people now. 15 **Anyone who says, 'I believe that Jesus is the Son of God,' is a person who lives in God, and God lives in that person. 16**

235

**So we know the love that God has for us, and we trust that love** [emphasis mine, SP].

"God is love. Everyone who lives in love lives in God, and God lives in them. 17 If God's love is made perfect in us, we can be without fear on the day when God judges the world. We will be without fear, because in this world we are like Jesus. 18 Where God's love is, there is no fear, because God's perfect love takes away fear. It is his punishment that makes a person fear. So his love is not made perfect in the one who is afraid.

"19 We love because God first loved us. 20 If we say we love God but hate any of our brothers or sisters in his family, we are liars. If we don't love someone we have seen, how can we love God? We have never even seen him. 21 God gave us this command: If we love God, we must also love each other as brothers and sisters" (1 John 4:7-21, ERV).

The late Bible scholar, **William Barclay**, nailed it when he talked about how Jesus himself guarantees the validity and longevity of this agreement between men and God:

"Jesus is the surety of a new and a better covenant, a new kind of relationship between man and God. The difference is this – the old covenant was based on law and justice and obedience; the new covenant is based on love and on the perfect sacrifice of Jesus Christ. The old covenant was based on man's achievement; the new covenant is based on God's love" (**The Letter to the Hebrews**, p. 81; Fair Use Domain).

Those are important insights into the differences between the Old Covenant (i.e., the 10 Commandments) and the New Covenant (love for God, for others, and doing good words motivated by love). Please take just a moment to read the above paragraph, again, and give it some thought.

The whole aim of religion, any kind of religion, is to bridge the gap between God and mankind. It is an effort to reconcile the holy with the unholy, the worthy from the unworthy. Jesus alone, having experienced as a man/God the struggles humans face, is the only one who can stand as both our Savior and our Advocate with the Father. He is our great High Priest and will be forever more.

# Chapter 16

## Understanding the Priesthood
## of All Believers, Part 3

[NOTE: The priesthood of all believers is also called "the royal priesthood." Both are also related to the concept of mutual ministry.]

There is an ol' **Bob Wills** country song titled, "Time changes everything." There's a heck of lot of truth in that song. It goes too far, of course, because some things – like the love of God – do not ever change.

However, in most things and organizations when a human is in control, things can go south (i.e., wrong) in a heartbeat. It took longer than a heartbeat for the simple organization of the early Christian church to take a long walk on a short pier. It took a few decades for weeds to sprout up in our garden, but grow they did. And little by little, the concept of freedom in Christ was replaced with smooth words from folks grabbing like crazy for power and prestige.

Sometimes people are lazy or indifferent or just spiritually illiterate when it comes to standing up to loud and pushy people who advocate ill-conceived changes. They are inclined to "just get along" as best they can. It is a recipe for disaster.

Eventually, local and totally independent congregations were taken over by aggressive authoritarians miles away. Then enforcers were appointed to act as Chief Muckymucks over multiple congregations. Then districts and state lines were carved out and assigned to other change agents with bigger titles.

That happened on a large scale. So let's just take the Roman Catholic Church and their development in electing one man as their head. They gave him the title of "Pope" (Latin for *papa*). Pope Number 1, they assert, was none other than the apostle Peter. They elected him Pope of Rome prior to 67 A.D., they say. Okay, and their count is now up to 260 people who have filled the papal shoes. Francis I, the current Pope, took office in 2013 (all of this was taken directly from *Catholic Online* at www.catholic.org/pope on Aug. 25, 2020).

Alright, for the sake of discussion, let's just say that by 200 A.D., there were certain groups already obsessed with the concentration of power over the lives and worship activities of ordinary Christians. By 1500 A.D., the trickle of water leaking from the dam had burst wide open and flooded the civilized world with complex organizations and centralized leadership.

Yikes. It was really bad. But there was hope on the horizon.

The concept often called **"The Priesthood of All Believers"** developed early in the 16th century. It was a direct protest against the Catholic priesthood in which the clergy stood between the people and God, often as more of a barrier than a conduit. The priesthood of all believers argued that all Christians were equal in stature and importance in God's eyes. Therefore, they certain did not have to have a priest acting as a gatekeeper or even a mediator. It was a dramatic bid for a large amount of democracy in religious activities.

Generally, the leaders of this liberation movement were Catholic reformer **Martin Luther**, Bible translator **William Tyndale**, and theologian **John Calvin**. In his book published in 1520, Luther renounced the Catholic doctrine that living Christians fell into one of two categories: they were either spiritual or they were secular. He took the position that all baptized believers were, in fact, not only spiritual but also priests themselves (based on 1 Peter 2:9 and Revelation 5:10). He also argued that all Christians were ministers involved in ministry.

Here are some benefits of sharing in this simple priesthood of all believers:

# # 1

**First, the believer – each and every believer – has direct access to God.** That means we may have a personal, vertical relationship with God. We may pray directly to God without having to have any human being monitor us or judge us. We do not have to read a prayer that someone else has written. We may pour out to him our love for him and our praise for him, as well as our most intimate concerns and needs.

As with other aspects of life, the Bible is always frank and right to the point. That is also a quality which most of the people mentioned in the Bible reflected time and again. Each expressed his or her personal hopes, needs, fears, joy, and failures. Yes, even failures. I remember reading a book years ago with the intriguing title, **Failure: The Way to Success**. And it was right on target. We are all prone to mistakes, to spurts and sputters. God knows it, so we may as well admit it to each other. No one gets to any position of responsibility without leaving a trail of experimental experiences sprinkled with misfires and flops.

In the Old Testament, we see prayers being said in intimate and brutally honest ways. Remember Abraham praying fervently for God to spare the evil people of Sodom (Genesis). Moses repeated prayed through his tears for God to forgive his rebellious people (Exodus 32:10-13). Job even prayed earnestly for his friends who really weren't very friendly or helpful at all (Job 42:8-20). Think of all the times that David praised God in his prayers, but also questioned God's actions and severely criticized his enemies. Those prayers were not always politically correct, but they were genuinely from the heart.

In the New Testament, Jesus emphasized the value of prayer that is improvised, informal, personal and most of all sincere and honest. Early in his minister, Jesus spoke these words of warning and encouragement regarding prayer, as recorded in Matthew 6:

"5 'Whenever you pray, do not be like the hypocrites. They love to stand and pray in the synagogues and on the street corners so that they may be seen by people. Amen I tell you: They have received their reward. 6 But whenever you pray, go into your private room, close your door, and pray to your Father who is unseen. And your Father, who sees what others cannot see, will reward you.

"7 'And when you pray, do not babble like the heathen, since they think that they will be heard because of their many words. 8 However do not be like them, because your Father knows what you need before you ask him. 9 Therefore pray like this: 'Our Father in heaven, hallowed be your name. 10 Your kingdom come. Your will be done on earth as it is in heaven. 11 Give us today our daily bread. 12 Forgive us our debts, as we also forgive our debtors. 13 Lead us not into temptation, but deliver us from evil.'

"14 'Indeed if you forgive people when they sin against you, your heavenly Father will also forgive you. 15 But if you do not forgive people their sins, your Father will not forgive your sins'" (Matthew 6:5-15; **Evangelical Heritage Version** – EHV).

# # 2

**Second, the believer also has as his mediator or advocate with God the Lord Jesus Christ himself**. The term mediator is only found five times in the New Testament and not a single time in the Old Testament. Yet the concept for which it stands is an important doctrine in both Testaments. That idea is seen when someone acts as a go-between, arbiter, or intermediary between two different parties with the goal of keeping peace or achieving peace.

In the Old Testament, Moses repeatedly was certainly an advocate for the Israelites before God, and he was the conduit of information from God to the people. The word "mediator" was applied to him in Galatians 3:19.

In the New Testament, "mediator" or "mediation" often referred to the process of salvation under the New Covenant. In those scriptures, it is clear that the mediator can only be one who is sinless himself and, therefore, can identify with and reason with God about his concern for **justice**. That person must also be able to identify with and communicate with sinners who stand empty-handed and in need of mercy or **grace**. Jesus filled that role because he was tempted in every way we are, yet without sin. The apostle John wrote about Jesus being our advocate in these words:

"1 My dear children, I write this letter to you so that you will not sin. But if anyone sins, we have Jesus Christ to help us. He always did what was right, so he is **able to defend us before God the Father** [emphasis mine, SP]. 2 Jesus is the way our sins are taken away. And he is the way all people can have their sins taken away too" (1 John 2:1-2; ERV).

Here is exactly how Jesus prayed to God the Father when he was nearing his execution. It is found in John 17:

"1 When Jesus had spoken these words, he lifted up his eyes to heaven, and said, 'Father, the hour has come; glorify your Son that the Son may glorify you, 2 since you have given him authority over all flesh, to give eternal life to all whom you have given him. 3 And this is eternal life, that they know you the only true God, and Jesus Christ whom you have sent. 4 I glorified you on earth, having accomplished the work that you gave me to do. 5 And now, Father, glorify me in your own presence with the glory that I had with you before the world existed.

"6 'I have manifested your name to the people whom you gave me out of the world. Yours they were, and you gave them to me, and they have kept your word. 7 Now they know that everything that you have given me is from you. 8 For I have given them the words that you gave me, and they have received them and have come to know in truth that I came from you; and they have believed that you sent me. 9 I am praying for them. I am not praying for the world but for those whom you have given me, for they are yours. 10 All mine are yours, and yours are mine, and I am glorified in them. 11 And I am no longer in the world, but they are in the world, and I am coming to you. **Holy Father, keep them in your name, which you have given me, that they may be one, even as we are one** [emphasis mine, SP].

"12 'While I was with them, I kept them in your name, which you have given me. I have guarded them, and not one of them has been lost except the son of destruction, that the Scripture might be fulfilled. 13 But now I am coming to you, and these things I speak in the world, that they may have my joy fulfilled in themselves. 14 I have given them your word, and the world has hated them because they are not of the world, just as I am not of the world. 15 I do not ask that you take them out of the world, but that you keep them from the evil one. 16 They are not of the world, just as I am not of the world. 17 Sanctify them in the truth; your word is truth. 18 As you sent me into the world, so I have sent them into the world. 19 And for their sake I consecrate myself, that they also may be sanctified in truth.

"20 '**I do not ask for these only, but also for those who will believe in me through their word, 21 that they may all be one, just as you, Father, are in me, and I in you, that they also may be in us, so that the world may believe that you have sent me. 22 The glory that you have given me I have given to them, that they may be one even as we are one, 23 I in them and you in me, that they may become perfectly one, so that the world may know that you sent me and loved them even as you loved me** [emphasis mine, SP].

"24 'Father, I desire that they also, whom you have given me, may be with me where I am, to see my glory that you have given me because you loved me before the

241

foundation of the world. 25 O righteous Father, even though the world does not know you, I know you, and these know that you have sent me. 26 I made known to them your name, and I will continue to make it known, that the love with which you have loved me may be in them, and I in them' (John 17:1-26; **English Standard Version Anglicised** – ESVUK)."

Part of the reason the gospel is such wonderful news is that it is offered to everyone, regardless of race or nationality or social standing. In the case or ordinary Jewish people in the first century, **William Barclay** gives a vivid description of how they were ostracized by the elite Pharisees and Sadducees. Here is how Jesus changed the playing field through the universality of the New Covenant:

"All men would know God from the least to the greatest. That was something quite new. In the ordinary life of the Jews there was a complete cleavage. On the one hand there were the Pharisees and the orthodox who kept the law; on the other hand there were what were contemptuously called 'The People of the Land,' the ordinary people who did not fully observe the details of the ceremonial law. They were completely despised. It was forbidden to have any fellowship with them; to marry one's daughter to one of them was worse than to throw her to a wild beast; it was forbidden, as far as it was possible, to have any trade or business dealings with them. To the rigid observers of the law the ordinary people were beyond the pale. But in the new covenant these breaches would no longer exist. All men, wise and simple, great and small, would know the Lord. The doors which had been shut were thrown wide open" (**The Letter to the Hebrews**, pp. 92-93).

# # 3

**Third, each and every believer has the freedom to discover and use his special gifts in ways that honor God and bless those who are both outside and inside the household of God.** We have not only that freedom but that responsibility before our Maker. Paul made that same point in Romans 12:

"So then, my friends, because of God's great mercy to us I appeal to you: **Offer yourselves as a living sacrifice to God, dedicated to his service and pleasing to him** [that is what a priest does – emphasis mine, SP]. This is the true worship that you should offer. 2 Do not conform yourselves to the standards of this world, but let God transform you inwardly by a complete change of your mind. Then you will be able to know the will of God—what is good and is pleasing to him and is perfect.

"3 And because of God's gracious gift to me I say to every one of you: Do not think of yourself more highly than you should. Instead, be modest in your thinking, and judge yourself according to the amount of faith that God has given you. 4 We have many parts in the one body, and all these parts have different functions. 5 In the same way, though we are many, we are one body in union with Christ, and we are all joined to each other as different parts of one body. 6 So we are to use our different gifts in accordance with the grace that God has given us. If our gift is to speak God's message, we should do it according to the faith that we have; 7 if it is to serve, we should serve; if it is to teach, we should teach; 8 if it is to encourage others, we should do so. Whoever shares with others should do it generously; whoever has authority should work hard; whoever shows kindness to others should do it cheerfully" (Romans 12:1-7, **Good News Translation** – GNT).

In his first letter to the believers in Corinth, Greece, Paul talked frankly about their need to get organized so that each Christian would be encouraged to use his particular talent or gift to the glory of God and to the advancement of his kingdom. Listen to Paul's words in I Corinthians 12, where he urges them to practice unity through diversity – even in terms of the diversity of gifts given to each person:

> "Unity is oneness of purpose, not sameness of persons."
>
> - TONY EVANS -

"1 Now concerning what comes from the Spirit: brothers, I do not want you to be unaware. 2 You know that when you were pagans, you used to be led off to the idols that could not speak. 3 Therefore I am informing you that no one speaking by the Spirit of God says, 'Jesus is cursed,' and no one can say, 'Jesus is Lord,' except by the Holy Spirit.

"4 Now there are different gifts, but the same Spirit. 5 There are different ministries, but the same Lord. 6 And there are different activities, but the same God activates each gift in each person. 7 A demonstration of the Spirit is given to each person to produce what is beneficial:

> "8 to one is given a message of wisdom
> through the Spirit,
> to another, a message of knowledge
> by the same Spirit,
> 9 to another, faith by the same Spirit,
> to another, gifts of healing by the one Spirit,

10 to another, the performing of miracles,
to another, prophecy,
to another, distinguishing between spirits,
to another, different kinds of languages,
to another, interpretation of languages.

"11 But one and the same Spirit is active in all these, distributing to each person as He wills.

"12 For as the body is one and has many parts, and all the parts of that body, though many, are one body—so also is Christ. 13 For we were all baptized by one Spirit into one body—whether Jews or Greeks, whether slaves or free—and we were all made to drink of one Spirit. 14 So the body is not one part but many. 15 If the foot should say, 'Because I'm not a hand, I don't belong to the body,' in spite of this it still belongs to the body. 16 And if the ear should say, 'Because I'm not an eye, I don't belong to the body,' in spite of this it still belongs to the body. 17 If the whole body were an eye, where would the hearing be? If the whole body were an ear, where would the sense of smell be? 18 But now God has placed each one of the parts in one body just as He wanted. 19 And if they were all the same part, where would the body be? 20 Now there are many parts, yet one body.

"21 So the eye cannot say to the hand, 'I don't need you!' Or again, the head can't say to the feet, 'I don't need you!' 22 But even more, those parts of the body that seem to be weaker are necessary. 23 And those parts of the body that we think to be less honorable, we clothe these with greater honor, and our unpresentable parts have a better presentation. 24 But our presentable parts have no need of clothing. Instead, God has put the body together, giving greater honor to the less honorable, 25 so that there would be no division in the body, but that the members would have the same concern for each other. 26 So if one member suffers, all the members suffer with it; if one member is honored, all the members rejoice with it.

"27 Now you are the body of Christ, and individual members of it. 28 And God has placed these in the church:

first apostles, second prophets,
third teachers, next miracles,
then gifts of healing, helping,
managing, various kinds of languages.

29 Are all apostles? Are all prophets?
Are all teachers? Do all do miracles?
30 Do all have gifts of healing?
Do all speak in other languages?
Do all interpret?

(I Corinthians 12:1-30, **Holman Christian**
Standard Bible – HCSB)

# # 4

**Fourth, all believers are to accept all other children of God as their own brothers and sisters in the faith.** We are to fight discrimination and sectarianism whenever and wherever we find it. We will make no test of fellowship where God has not done so.

When a woman hears the gospel message and accepts Jesus as the Son of God, the Lord God himself adds her to the community of faith. Her salvation by grace through faith in the work of Jesus made her a child of our heavenly Father. That is the identical path we took as we were also made children of God. It is that spiritual bloodline or DNA or kinship which makes all such people brothers and sisters in the family of God.

Please hear and understand the following truths about the church, God's worldwide family.

**We all became children in the family by hearing the same gospel, believing the same facts about Jesus, and accepting the same wonderful grace of our Father.** That was how we were inducted (or adopted) into the same family with the same benefits. We were each saved by our respective faith in Jesus, not by our good works, not by our good looks, not because of our race or our IQ, and not by the amount of loot in our bank account. We stand united on the facts of the gospel.

**Love is the essence of our relationship in God's large family.** God loved us enough to watch his Son nailed to a Roman cross, not because of the Son's sins but to pay our outstanding debt of sin. Jesus loved us enough to leave the Father for a time and became a human on earth. He loved us enough to teach us about God's nature and to be wrongly executed for our sins. And because they first loved us, we love them back. We love our Father sincerely and deeply, and we want to please him and honor him. We love our elder brother, Jesus, and long for him to return to take us to the greatest family reunion ever held. And we love and cherish every single one of our brothers and sisters in this wonderful spiritual family.

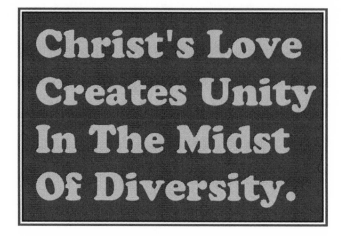

If you want to pick out a true Christian from a lineup, look for the one who is happy walking in the grace and love of God. Look for the one who eagerly submits to the leading of the Holy Spirit which is living within him or her (Romans 8:14). And, above all, look for the one who demonstrates his or her genuine love for God. See how he or she loves all of God's children (Romans 12:10). And see how he or she even loves those who are enemies (Romans 12:14, 17-18; 13:8-10) .

> *We allow our dear brothers and sisters the same freedoms in Christ which we cherish. We value our right to think for ourselves. We value the right to hold our own opinions regarding many points of apostolic doctrine. Just as we would resist a brother or sister forcing his or her interpretations of doctrinal facts upon us, we must not insist that others accept our opinions as law. -- Stan Paregien Sr.*
>
> *Graphic created by Stan Paregien Sr on Dec. 6, 2020*

A dictatorial rule by one human over another does not sit well with most of us. In fact, Samuel Butler (1612-1680) stated the usual end to such treatment back in this poem *Hudibras* (Part III, Canto iii, lines 547-550):

## He that complies against his will
## Is of his own opinion still.

If we freely allow, even encourage, different opinions about how we "do church," then we will have a rich (and maybe curious) diversity of practices. Some independent congregations (yes, a first century concept) will sing mostly the old sacred "high church" hymns, while others will mostly feature praise songs and still others may prefer mostly Christian cowboy songs or maybe Christian rock. Probably not many of us really want our congregational singing to return to Gregorian chants (popular in the first century, by the way).

In that regard, some honestly believe *a cappella* music (without instrumental accompaniment) is alone God-approved. Others draw closer to God by the sound of a string quartet, and others prefer an acoustic guitar, fiddle and weeping steel guitar. Some enjoy organ music while others find it boring.

There will be traditionalists who hold to reading the **King James Version** of the Bible, while others prefer something like the middle-of-the-road **New International Version** and still others will cherish the modernish **Good News Translation** or **The Message**. We can and do practice unity in diversity regarding many of our behaviors and opinions.

When we each were saved by faith, we are in the same family because we each love the same Lord Jesus and we came to the family through our new birth. We don't boot a brother Gus right out of the family because we disagree about how to best observed the Lord's Supper. We don't disown sister Suzie because she is wrong (in our view) about exactly when the Lord will come again.

**God did not appoint any of us as a judge (or judge and jury), but calls for us to encourage one another rather than stirring up descension**. The apostle Paul wrestled with these problems during his ministry, and all of us who have been Christians for 10 years or more have seen them. So it is important for us to get this thing right.

Below are Paul's Spirit-inspired solutions to differences of opinion on moral dilemmas. In all of these passages, the specific dilemmas don't mean much to us today. Some Grecian Christians grew up with idolatry running rampant, where meat that had been offered to various idols and pagan gods were sold and eaten in the pagan temples. Or sold for home consumption. The problem was that some of these Christians literally could not stomach, literally or spiritually, eating "idolatrous meat." Many other Christians saw it as no problem at all, since there are no other gods and it did not affect the meat itself. There was the big fly in the ointment.

So Paul, led by the Holy Spirit, presented answers for those specific problems. However, there is a generalized wisdom there which can be applied to moral issues of any kind in any age. Paul, if he were us, might have made a hardline, individualistic ruling that these "weak" folks needed to be quiet and catch up with the rest of us. He could have, but he did not.

What the apostle does is to look at the situation through **communal** glasses. Yes, for some individuals with no scruples about idolatrous food, it would be fine for them to eat the meat. But, hey, we are not in this thing as the Lone Ranger. We are in the family of God and we must never, ever do harm to a brother or sister – not even to a stubborn, ill-informed one. Not even if we don't exercise our freedom and feel our style is kinda cramped by it.

The problem we often face is the fantasy that it is nobody else's business what we do. That is not only wrong, but also dumb. Dumb, dumb, double-dumb. We are not in the Lions Club, the Chamber of Commerce or the Red Hats Society. We are in the household of God and are his redeemed-by-grace children. We just cannot go around acting like immature children and whining, "Well, I wanna do it my way." We need to wake up and get over that selfishness.

What you do and what I do can set off ripples that produce real social consequences. We need to make sure what happens to others is helpful, not harmful. Or as Paul wrote in big letters: "'Everything is permissible,' but not everything is beneficial. 'Everything is permissible,' but not everything builds up. No one is to seek his own good, but the good of the other person" (1 Corinthians 23-24; **Holman Christian Standard Bible** – HCSB; see also 1 Corinthians 14:1-21).

**1 Corinthians 8:1-13** ("Protecting the Weak")

"8 Now concerning things sacrificed to idols, we know that we all have knowledge. Knowledge puffs up, but love builds up. 2 If anyone supposes that he knows something, he does not yet know the way he ought to know. 3 But if anyone loves God, this person has been known by him.

"4 So, concerning the eating of food from idol sacrifices, we know that an idol is not anything real in the world and that there is no God but one. 5 Indeed, even if there are so-called 'gods,' whether in the heavens or on earth (as in fact there are many 'gods' and many 'lords'), 6 nevertheless for us there is one God—the Father, from whom all things exist and we exist for him—and one Lord—Jesus Christ, through whom all things exist and we exist through him.

"7 However, that knowledge is not in everyone. Instead some, who are still affected by their former habit with the idol, eat the food as something sacrificed to an idol, and their conscience, being weak, is defiled.

"8 Food will not bring us closer to God. We do not lack anything if we do not eat, nor are we better off if we do. 9 And be careful that this right of yours does not somehow become a stumbling block to the weak. 10 For if someone sees you, a person who has knowledge, dining in an idol's temple, will not the conscience of this man, weak as he is, be emboldened to eat food from an idol sacrifice? 11 You see, the weak person is being destroyed by your knowledge—the brother for whose sake Christ died! 12 And **when you sin in this way against your brothers and wound their weak conscience, you sin against Christ** [emphasis mine, SP]. 13 Therefore, if food causes my brother to sin, I will never eat meat again, so that I do not cause my brother to sin" (**Evangelical Heritage Version** – EHV).

## 1 Corinthians 10:23-11:1 ("Christian Liberty")

''23-24 Looking at it one way, you could say, 'Anything goes. Because of God's immense generosity and grace, we don't have to dissect and scrutinize every action to see if it will pass muster.' But the point is not to just get by. We want to live well, but our foremost efforts should be to help others live well.

"25-28 With that as a base to work from, common sense can take you the rest of the way. Eat anything sold at the butcher shop, for instance; you don't have to run an 'idolatry test' on every item. 'The earth,' after all, 'is God's, and everything in it.' That 'everything' certainly includes the leg of lamb in the butcher shop. If a nonbeliever invites you to dinner and you feel like going, go ahead and enjoy yourself; eat everything placed before you. It would be both bad manners and bad spirituality to cross-examine your host on the ethical purity of each course as it is served. On the other hand, if he goes out of his way to tell you that this or that was sacrificed to god or goddess so-and-so, you should pass. Even though you may be indifferent as to where it came from, he isn't, and you don't want to send mixed messages to him about who you are worshiping.

"29-30 But, except for these special cases, I'm not going to walk around on eggshells worrying about what small-minded people might say; I'm going to stride free and easy, knowing what our large-minded Master has already said. If I eat what is served to me, grateful to God for what is on the table, how can I worry about what someone will say? I thanked God for it and he blessed it!

"31-33 So eat your meals heartily, not worrying about what others say about you—you're eating to God's glory, after all, not to please them. As a matter of fact, do everything that way, heartily and freely to God's glory. At the same time, **don't be callous in your exercise of freedom, thoughtlessly stepping on the toes of those who aren't as free as you are** [emphasis mine, SP]. I try my best to be considerate of everyone's feelings in all these matters; I hope you will be, too.

"11 1-2 It pleases me that you continue to remember and honor me by keeping up the traditions of the faith I taught you. All actual authority stems from Christ" (**The Message** – MSG).

**Romans 14:1-12** ("The Law of Liberty")

"1 Accept anyone who is weak in faith, but don't argue about doubtful issues. 2 One person believes he may eat anything, but one who is weak eats only vegetables. 3 One who eats must not look down on one who does not eat, and one who does not eat must not criticize one who does, because God has accepted him. 4 Who are you to criticize another's household slave? Before his own Lord he stands or falls. And he will stand. For the Lord is able to make him stand.

"5 One person considers one day to be above another day. Someone else considers every day to be the same. Each one must be fully convinced in his own mind. 6 Whoever observes the day, observes it for the honor of the Lord. Whoever eats, eats for the Lord, since he gives thanks to God; and whoever does not eat, it is for the Lord that he does not eat it, yet he thanks God. 7 For none of us lives to himself, and no one dies to himself. 8 If we live, we live for the Lord; and if we die, we die for the Lord. Therefore, whether we live or die, we belong to the Lord. 9 Christ died and came to life for this: that He might rule over both the dead and the living. 10 But you, why do you criticize your brother? Or you, why do you look down on your brother? For we will all stand before the tribunal of God. 11 For it is written:

'As I live, says the Lord,
every knee will bow to Me,
and every tongue will give praise to God.'

"12 So then, each of us will give an account of himself to God" (**Holman Christian Standard Bible** – HCSB).

Christian Love Unites Us as One in Purpose

**Romans 14:13-23** ("The Law of Love")

"13 Therefore let us not pass judgment on one another any longer, but rather decide never to put a stumbling block or hindrance in the way of a brother. 14 I know and am persuaded in the Lord Jesus that nothing is unclean in itself, but it is unclean for anyone who thinks it unclean. 15 For if your brother is grieved by what you eat, you are no longer walking in love. By what you eat, do not destroy the one for whom Christ died. 16 So do not let what you regard as good be spoken of as evil. 17 For the kingdom of God is not a matter of eating and drinking but of righteousness and peace and joy in the Holy Spirit. 18 Whoever thus serves Christ is acceptable to God and approved by men. 19 So then **let us pursue what makes for peace and for mutual upbuilding** [emphasis mine, SP].

"20 Do not, for the sake of food, destroy the work of God. Everything is indeed clean, but it is wrong for anyone to make another stumble by what he eats. 21 It is good not to eat meat or drink wine or do anything that causes your brother to stumble. 22 The faith that you have, keep between yourself and God. Blessed is the one who has no reason to pass judgment on himself for what he approves. 23 But whoever has doubts is condemned if he eats, because the eating is not from faith. For whatever does not proceed from faith is sin" (**<u>English Standard Version</u>** – ESV).

**Romans 15:1-7** ("Accepting Each Other as Christ Accepted Us")

"1 Now we who are strong [in our convictions and faith] ought to [patiently] put up with the weaknesses of those who are not strong, and not just please ourselves. 2 Let each one of us [make it a practice to] please his neighbor for his good, to build him up spiritually. 3 For even Christ did not please Himself; but as it is written [in Scripture], 'The reproaches of those who reproached You (the Father) fell on Me (the Son).' 4 For whatever was written in earlier times was written for our instruction, so that through endurance and the encouragement of the Scriptures we might have hope and overflow with confidence in His promises. 5 Now may the God who gives endurance and who supplies encouragement grant that you be of the same mind with one another according to Christ Jesus, 6 so that with one accord you may with one voice glorify and praise and honor the God and Father of our Lord Jesus Christ.

"7 Therefore, **[continue to] accept and welcome one another, just as Christ has accepted and welcomed us** [emphasis mine, SP] to the glory of [our great] God" (**<u>Amplified Bible</u>** – AMP).

# # 5

**Fifth, all members of God's priesthood are to be advocates for acceptance of the "New Covenant" of salvation by grace through faith.** And in so doing, we refuse to bind or to be bound by any creed outside of that New Covenant. We further refuse to bind on others or to be bound by personal opinions which add to, subtract from, or are different from that covenant.

Remember, the Covenant God made with Israel was made while they were camped around the foot of Mt. Sinai (aka Horeb). The Old Covenant was a two-party agreement between God and the nation of Israel. The provisions or stipulations of the actual Covenant were few and clear. There were only ten stipulations God presented and to which Israel agreed to comply. We call those simple-to-understand stipulations "the 10 Commandments."

Later, in about 1406 B.C., Moses in Deuteronomy 4:10-13 reminded his people of what took place back at Mt. Sinai: "10 Remember the day you stood at Mount Horeb. The Lord your God was there. He said to me, 'Bring the people to me to hear my words. I want them to learn to have respect for me as long as they live in the land. I want them to teach my words to their children.' 11 You came near and stood at the foot of the mountain. It blazed with fire that reached as high as the very heavens. There were black clouds and deep darkness. 12 Then the Lord spoke to you out of the fire. You heard the sound of his words. But you didn't see any shape or form. You only heard a voice. 13 **He announced his covenant to you. That covenant is the Ten Commandments. He commanded you to obey them. Then he wrote them down on two stone tablets** [emphasis mine, SP]" (**New International Reader's Version** – NIRV).

The Ten Commandments were the sum and total of the Covenant given by God to the people of Israel. That story is told in Exodus 20. Therefore, the previous material only applied to the "fathers" (Noah and Abram), including all of Genesis and in the first 18 chapters of Exodus. And the next 37 books after Genesis and Exodus, were not a part of this Covenant. Yes, those later documents – histories, poems, songs, and prophecies – often referred to the Old Covenant. But it is vital to remember they were not the Covenant themselves.

One may speak of the 39 books of the "Old Testament" but it should be remembered only those few verses in Exodus 20 actually comprise the Mosaic Covenant. Those commands established God's relationship with his beloved Nation. He wanted them to be holy as he is holy.

This Mosaic Covenant would constantly keep before Israel the basic precept that there is only one true God. It would also act as a custodian or a guardian to eventually bring them to the Messiah (Jesus; Galatians 3:24). It was based on law and the law-keeping way of living, thereby enabling the Nation to determine what was sinful and what was not (Romans 7:7).

253

Out of that foundation of the Ten Commandments, God dictated to Moses many other rules, laws, and rituals (Deuteronomy 5:31; Romans 9:4). Though not part of the Covenant, these things help to regulate and guide the Nation in this new relationship with God. Much later, the rabbinical scholars determined those 10 commandments and related spinoff laws totaled a whopping 613 laws people should obey. All of that eventually became stumbling blocks to the people. For if one is living under and by a legalistic system and mentality, one must obey each and every law perfectly.

Let's be crystal clear here: Never think for a moment that the Lord God of the universe somehow messed up and strapped the nation of Israel with a faulty, imperfect law. In and of itself, the heavenly legislation was fine. It was up to code. In fact, it was perfectly . . . well, perfect.

The problem was that the people of Israel were not perfect. They were sinful and rebellious, and could never keep this perfect law perfectly. That was the insurmountable problem.

"So," one might reasonably ask, "Why the heck did God add such a code of law to the simple agreement he had given Abraham?"

The apostle Paul answered that question a few years ago. Well, nearly 2,000 years ago to be exact. Here is what he said, over in **Galatians 3:5-29 and 4:1-7**:

"Chapter 3 - 2 Let me ask you this one question: Did you receive the Holy Spirit by obeying the law of Moses? Of course not! You received the Spirit because you believed the message you heard about Christ. 3 How foolish can you be? After starting your new lives in the Spirit, why are you now trying to become perfect by your own human effort? 4 Have you experienced so much for nothing? Surely it was not in vain, was it?

"5 I ask you again, does God give you the Holy Spirit and work miracles among you because you obey the law? Of course not! It is because you believe the message you heard about Christ.

"6 In the same way, 'Abraham believed God, and God counted him as righteous because of his faith. 7 The real children of Abraham, then, are those who put their faith in God.

"8 What's more, the Scriptures looked forward to this time when God would make the Gentiles right in his sight because of their faith. God proclaimed this good news to Abraham long ago when he said, 'All nations will be blessed through you.' 9 So all who put their faith in Christ share the same blessing Abraham received because of his faith.

"10 But those who depend on the law to make them right with God are under his curse, for the Scriptures say, 'Cursed is everyone who does not observe and obey all the commands that are written in God's Book of the Law.' 11 So it is clear that no one can be made right with God by trying to keep the law. For the Scriptures say, 'It is through faith that a righteous person has life.' 12 This way of faith is very different from the way of law, which says, 'It is through obeying the law that a person has life.'

"13 But Christ has rescued us from the curse pronounced by the law. When he was hung on the cross, he took upon himself the curse for our wrongdoing. For it is written in the Scriptures, 'Cursed is everyone who is hung on a tree.' 14 Through Christ Jesus, God has blessed the Gentiles with the same blessing he promised to Abraham, so that we who are believers might receive the promised Holy Spirit through faith.

"15 Dear brothers and sisters, here's an example from everyday life. Just as no one can set aside or amend an irrevocable agreement, so it is in this case. 16 God gave the promises to Abraham and his child. And notice that the Scripture doesn't say 'to his children,' as if it meant many descendants. Rather, it says 'to his child'—and that, of course, means Christ. 17 This is what I am trying to say: The agreement God made with Abraham could not be canceled 430 years later when God gave the law to Moses. God would be breaking his promise. 18 For if the inheritance could be received by keeping the law, then it would not be the result of accepting God's promise. But God graciously gave it to Abraham as a promise.

"19 **Why, then, was the law given? It was given alongside the promise to show people their sins** [emphasis mine, SP]. But the law was designed to last only until the coming of the child who was promised. God gave his law through angels to Moses, who was the mediator between God and the people. 20 Now a mediator is helpful if more than one party must reach an agreement. But God, who is one, did not use a mediator when he gave his promise to Abraham.

"21 Is there a conflict, then, between God's law and God's promises? Absolutely not! If the law could give us new life, we could be made right with God by obeying it. 22

But the Scriptures declare that we are all prisoners of sin, so we receive God's promise of freedom only by believing in Jesus Christ.

"23 Before the way of faith in Christ was available to us, we were placed under guard by the law. We were kept in protective custody, so to speak, until the way of faith was revealed.

"24 Let me put it another way. **The law was our guardian until Christ came; it protected us until we could be made right with God through faith. 25 And now that the way of faith has come, we no longer need the law as our guardian** [emphasis mine, SP].

"26 For you are all children of God through faith in Christ Jesus. 27 And all who have been united with Christ in baptism have put on Christ, like putting on new clothes. 28 There is no longer Jew or Gentile, slave or free, male and female. For you are all one in Christ Jesus. 29 And now that you belong to Christ, you are the true children of Abraham. You are his heirs, and God's promise to Abraham belongs to you.

"Chapter 4 – 1 Think of it this way. If a father dies and leaves an inheritance for his young children, those children are not much better off than slaves until they grow up, even though they actually own everything their father had. 2 They have to obey their guardians until they reach whatever age their father set. 3 And that's the way it was with us before Christ came. We were like children; we were slaves to the basic spiritual principles of this world.

"4 But when the right time came, God sent his Son, born of a woman, subject to the law. 5 God sent him to buy freedom for us who were slaves to the law, so that he could adopt us as his very own children. 6 And because we are his children, God has sent the Spirit of his Son into our hearts, prompting us to call out, 'Abba, Father.' 7 Now you are no longer a slave but God's own child. And since you are his child, God has made you his heir" (**New Living Translation** – NLT).

It seems to me that one thing which would it made it hard to accept the Old Covenant was the fact it was forced on male children. Under the Mosaic law, male babies were inducted into the Jewish religion without their consent and certainly with no understanding. Each male baby was taken before a priest on his 8th day of life and, without his consent or understanding, he was involuntarily circumcised. The baby had no say about it, so could neither consent to it nor object to it. That symbol of God's covenant with them put that tiny male child into a covenant with God that he knew absolutely nothing about and had no feeling about it in his heart at all. There was no commitment from the child, only a desire by the parents to obey the law as they understood it.

After the day of the boy's circumcision, it became the heavy responsibility of the parents, priests, and teachers to explain why they did such a thing. They were expected to indoctrinate the boy child with Jewish laws, rules, and rituals to get him ready for his coming of age **Bar Mitzvah** ("son of commandment") at the age of 13. He was then considered an adult and responsible for his own decisions. The parents of girls were expected to give similar instructions to them so they would be ready for their **Bat Mitzvah** ("daughter of commandment") at either age 12 or 13 (depending on the preference of the sect of Judaism they were identified with).

Once these respective ceremonies were completed, each child was considered as full member of the community and personally responsible for their actions. They were obligated to follow the 613 laws of the Torah without question.

However, many of these Jewish young people did privately question why their parents imposed their brand of religion on them as defenseless and largely clueless children. They resented the forced aspect of the practice, something most outsiders would call abusive.

Question: Does not that same principle apply to "infant baptism" in many Christian churches? In such cases, infants are baptized absolutely without their knowledge or consent. And there is naturally some parental pressure applied as the child ages to get them to conform to what their particular denomination believes is right and true.

There was a who man who preached in Kentucky and surrounding areas with great success between 1820 and 1865. His name was John Smith and his nickname was "Raccoon." Though he has little formal education, he spoke with eloquence and he was widely known for his keen sense of humor. One day **John "Raccoon" Smith** was baptizing more than a dozen adult believers in a river. He noticed a Methodist preacher watching him with interest. So Raccoon John Smith walked over to the preacher, took him by the arm and headed to the river with him. "What are you doing?" the preacher said. Raccoon replied, "Sir, I am going to baptize you in the river." The wide-eyed preacher said, "But I don't want to do that!" And John Smith said, "No, and I expect all those babies you baptize don't want to do that, either. But you don't give them a choice." It was quite a "show and tell" moment.

Well, in the end, the Old Covenant could not justify anyone because it lured people to those sins which were forbidden (Romans 3:20; 7:7-8). It was powerless to make people good, it just made them long for personal goodness. The Mosaic Law was all about legal justice, with no room for mercy (Romans 7:11). The Old Covenant was an external code written on stone, while the New is internal and written on the hearts of believers.

The "principle of Law," being inflexible and heartless, is the direct opposite of the "principle of Faith." A person trying his best to earn his salvation by law-keeping soon finds himself sinking in the quicksand of doubt and hypocrisy. Despite his effort, he is never sure he has dotted all the "I's" and crossed all the "T's." His constant, gnawing fear is that he doesn't know enough about the "pattern" of codes and doesn't do enough for the judge who knows all.

## Freedom in the New Covenant

Living by the principle of Faith is a whole different matter. Instead of being motivated by fear, living by faith gives us the certainty of right-standing with God. We don't depend on our performance of and knowledge of the rules, because we have place our faith in the Ruler. We trust in the righteousness of the perfect sacrifice, thanks to Jesus.

We know exactly where the line between lost and saved is, because we in faith have crossed it. The apostle John, in 1 John 3:14, said, "We know we have passed from death into life. We know this because we love the Christians. The person who does not love has not passed from death into life" (**New Life Version** – NLV).

And in 1 John 5:1-5, he says: "1 The person who believes that Jesus is the Christ is a child of God. The person who loves the Father loves His children also. 2 This is the way we know we love God's children. It is when we love God and obey His Word. 3 Loving God means to obey His Word, and His Word is not hard to obey. 4 Every child of God has power over the sins of the world. The way we have power over the sins of the world is by our faith. 5 Who could have power over the world except by believing that Jesus is the Son of God?" (NLV)

The documents in the New Testament speak of the **New Covenant** but they are **not** that covenant. Please read that sentence again.

The New Covenant between God and each individual cannot be chiseled onto tables of stone like the old one. The New Covenant cannot be printed and then sandwiched between covers of a book, but it can be imprinted and engraved on our minds. It was not written on paper, papyrus, or even on space age materials. This covenant is also stoneless because it was not written on stone tablets like the old one.

Under the Mosaic Law, the tablets of stone containing the Covenant with Israel were placed in a fancy container called the Ark of the Covenant. It was holy to the people and to the priests. They never got to see the tablets or touch them because the Ark of the Covenant, containing the Ten Commandments, was securely kept in the Holy of Holies in both the Tabernacle and much later in the first Temple in Jerusalem. The Ark of the Covenant, along with the tablets, disappeared in about 587 B.C. Scholars seem to think that the Babylonians destroyed it. The Ark never appeared in the second Temple.

Instead, the New Covenant is written on our hearts by the Holy Spirit himself. While God's glory, his **Shekinah**, formerly rested over the Ark . . . now his code of love, grace and knowledge is present in the heart of each Christian. Instead of God temporarily residing in a Tabernacle or a fancy Temple, he now lives in the temple of our earthly bodies. That makes our inner man a sort of holy of holies for Jehovah, the one and only true God. And the Holy Spirit also occupies our hearts and bodies.

The New Covenant is primarily about changing our **motivation**. Why do we do what we do? Shame? Social pressures? Political pressures? Selfishness? Oppressive guilt? Fear? Desire to impress someone or to hurt someone?

When we invite the Holy Spirit to take up residence in the temple of our body, we open ourselves up to a complete renovation and transformation of our motivation. When we are really "in Christ" and Christ and the Holy Spirit are really "in us," we better fasten our seat belts because it is going to be an exhilarating journey of faith.

Fear, that shadowy figure always ready to point an accusing finger at us, has been put on the "down" escalator and love is rushing toward us on the "up" escalator. We no longer worry about living up to somebody else's standards. Nor do we verbally beat-up on others who don't pay much attention to what we think they should do. Instead, we stand completely bathed in the righteousness of Jesus, his righteousness and not our own. God first loved us, even when we were u-g-l-y. Coyote ugly. So we are now motivated to love him back with that same unconditional love.

We soon find that not only has our motivation changed, but our behavior is on the way to making us a mirror image of our Lord Jesus. Grace reaches down and picks us up from the gutter, but never leaves us hopeless. As long as we are walking in the Light, we don't have to be in any man's spotlight. We are free to serve and do good in the name of Jesus and never give a thought as to who is going to get the glory or credit.

When we have the Holy Spirit dwelling in our hearts and encouraging us, we don't have to have the applause of the crowd. We are released from the guilt and condemnation from our past shameful behavior, and can come out from the corner in which we're hiding. Our past sins are forgiven and our future is secure by the grace of God.

Please pay attention to what the aged apostle John said about security, motivation and behavior in 1 John 3:1-3:

"See what sort of love the Father has given to us: that we should be called children of God, and we are! Because of this the world does not know us: because it did not know him. 2 Dear friends, now we are children of God, and what we will be has not yet been revealed. We know that whenever he is revealed we will be like him, because we will see him just as he is. 3 And everyone who has this hope in him purifies himself, just as that one is pure" (**Lexham English Bible** – LEB).

Make no mistake about it, the freedom-giving New Covenant -- based on grace-accepting and not by law-keeping -- is a far higher standard than the Old. We are careful, now, to be as consistent as possible in living for Jesus. We would rather be offended than to offend. We seek to be genuine peacemakers where once we would have been agitators. We are free to practice unity in diversity rather than being divisive sectarians.

We are patient where once we were pushy. We are hospitable with those whom we once despised as heretics and false teachers. We gladly show kindness where once we were rough and thoughtless. We are free to encourage others in their Christian walk, even though they may disagree with us on many doctrinal matters. We are free to allow God to be the judge of others, while we are merely sympathetic fruit inspectors. Remember, our loving God is always merciful, fair, and just.

The Mosaic Covenant of law was in reality a legal constitution for a physical people, the whole Nation of Israel in a certain earthly place, the land of Israel. On the other hand, the New Covenant of grace was specifically for a spiritual kingdom composed of all of the redeemed from all the lands of the world. Be sure to understand that though the old legalistic code is dead and gone, we are still subject to the authority of the one true God – and gladly so.

His will is that we love him back, that we love our neighbors and everyone we meet, and that we do good wherever we go. That sums up what Jesus did on this ol' earth, and we are to do the same.

Can you remember that? Of course you can. You don't have to hire a lawyer to put it down in legalese on paper. You don't have to hire anybody to tattoo that idea across your forehead. And you don't have to hire a skilled person to chiseled it in big letters on your front driveway. That is at the heart of the New Covenant, and you can remember it in your own heart.

Does what I just said sound way too good to be true? Well, then, believe it from the pen of the apostle Paul. He stated the same thing in Romans 13:8-10:

"8 Don't owe anyone anything, with the exception of love to one another—that is a debt which never ends—because the person who loves others has fulfilled the law. 9 The commands given to you in the Scriptures — do not commit adultery, do not murder, do not take what is not yours, do not covet — and any other command you have heard are summarized in God's instruction: 'Love your neighbor as yourself.' 10 Does love hurt anyone? Absolutely not. In fact, love achieves everything the law requires.

"Believers are not to have any obligation of any kind. Borrowed money and granted favors always come with strings attached. How many lives and families have been ruined by debts and deals made in haste! There is only one obligation Paul allows, and that is love. When we share God's care and compassion with others, we fulfill His law whether we realize it or not. Fundamentally, God's law has always been about love" (**The Voice** – VOICE).

Jeremiah often preached themes related to the coming Messiah, and related to stopping the Israelites from quarreling among themselves Here is a quote from the prophet Jeremiah, as found in Jeremiah 31:31-34, that is quoted in the New Testament as applying to the New Covenant:

"31 "Behold, the days are coming, declares the Lord, when **I will make a new covenant with the house of Israel and the house of Judah** [emphasis mine, SP], 32 not like the covenant that I made with their fathers on the day when I took them by the hand to bring them out of the land of Egypt, my covenant that they broke, though I was their husband, declares the Lord. 33 **For this is the covenant that I will make with the house of Israel after those days, declares the Lord: I will put my law within them, and I will write it on their hearts. And I will be their God, and they shall be my people. 34 And no longer shall each one teach his neighbor and each his brother, saying, 'Know the Lord,' for they shall all know me, from the least of them to the greatest** [emphasis mine, SP], declares the Lord. For I will forgive their iniquity, and I will remember their sin no more."

Unlike the Old Covenant, membership in the New Covenant is preceded by personally acquiring a knowledge and understanding of the basics of the gospel of Jesus Christ. It was also preceded by a personal development of faith or trust in Jesus as Lord and a personal love for him. It was also preceded by a desire to change the direction of one's life, to repent from a life of selfishness and sin. That dramatic shift of dedication and commitment was an absolute prerequisite before one could be baptized.

The Old Covenant was an agreement between God and the whole Nation of Israel. A male Jew back in the first century felt he was God's child because he was circumcised and part of the Nation of Israel.

The New Covenant, however, features God making agreements with individuals, with each of us through his Holy Spirit. So we belong to a covenant people today because we personally belong to God. For example, I entered into an agreement with God in which he promised his grace and forgiveness when by faith I accepted the atoning sacrifice of Jesus on the cross and I agreed to live for him. That made me a beloved, justified and fully accepted member of the body (church) of Jesus Christ and a child of God.

Our relationship with each other is primarily depended upon our individual relationship with Jesus the Christ. And remember, we draw close to God by grace through our faith in the substitutionary sacrifice of Jesus on the cross for us. Faith in the **gospel** puts us into God's family and makes us one with all his other children who have done the same thing. Therefore, our relationship with each other is not conditioned upon whether we agree or disagree about the vast and often complex statements of **doctrine** taking up most of the space in the last 23 documents of the New Testament.

If we are walking by grace and motivated by love, does that mean we no longer have any responsibility when it comes to God's commands? Of course not. We trust and obey, not out of fear or guilt, but out of a deep desire to please our heavenly Father in every way we can. We do not obey in order to win God's love, but because he loved us first. We read the documents of John, Peter, Paul, James , etc., as love letters to the redeemed. And we honor and obey as best we can the spirit their corrections and edification. But we must not view them as collections of legal codes.

After all, we do not want to slip back into the error of expecting ourselves or anyone else to have a perfect understanding of and perfect behavior regarding doctrinal matters. If that error should happen, we will be centering our faith in our IQ, our particular method of interpretation, our ability to apply logic to abstract matters, and our impeccable performance or behavior. Sorry, but I don't know anyone who meets that high standard, except perhaps for my wife and I . . . and I'm not too sure about her (joke, joke).

This New Covenant was made possible through the atoning death of Jesus. The apostle Luke, recalling the final supper with Jesus and his disciples in an upper room, said: "In the same way, after the supper He took the cup, saying, 'This cup is the new covenant in My blood, which is poured out for you.' (Luke 22:20 – **New International Version – NIV)"**

The writer of Hebrews said, "Because of this oath, Jesus has become the guarantee of a better covenant (Hebrews 7:22 - NIV)." And the Hebrews author also said: "How much more, then, will the blood of Christ, who through the eternal Spirit offered Himself unblemished to God, cleanse our consciences from acts that lead to death, so that we may serve the living God! For this reason Christ is the mediator of a new covenant, that those who are called may receive the promised eternal inheritance— now that He has died as a ransom to set them free from the sins committed under the first covenant" (Hebrews 9:14-15 – NIV)

The New Covenant has no provision for blind faith or forced obedience. The history books around the world are filled with sad disclosures of how over-enthusiastic religionists compelled native peoples by sword and spear to kneel and confess belief in Christ whether they understood anything or not. Evangelicals who were biblically illiterate or those who were flat-out charlatans often pressured ignorant people and mentally challenged persons to submit to baptism. Worst of all, priests and leaders in many faith groups took innocent babies and forcibly "christened" them by sprinkling water on them or pouring water on them to signify their conversion to the church.

Yet each of these people did not understand what was going on, did not make any real confession of faith, did not repent of anything, and did not volunteer to be baptized. Such sham practices were . . . and are today . . . contrary to the scriptures and bring shame on the whole body of Christ. We can and must do better, regardless of man-created creed books and rule books. Let's go back to Bible basics, back to Christianity 101.

**G.R. Beasley-Murray** was a highly respected Bible scholar. Several years ago, he wrote this about the ritual baptism of infants:

"Whereas most Christian people since the third century A.D. have assumed with question that infant baptism was instituted by the apostles, there has been quite a revolution in New Testament scholarship during the present century. It is common knowledge that most critical scholars who work in the field of New Testament studies agree that there is no evidence in the New Testament writings for the practice of infant baptism in the primitive church" (**Baptism Today and Tomorrow**, p. 114; Fair Use Domain).

One who carefully reads the conversion experiences in Acts will be struck by the fact that all who were baptized were adults (say, using the Jewish standard, age 13 or above) who were of sufficient capacity to understand the gospel story and to make up their own minds whether to accept Jesus as Lord and to commit to the responsibilities of living for him. Then, as soon as possible, they were baptized (likely, a total immersion) as a symbol or testimony of their union with Christ through faith. The Bible way was simple, straight, narrow, and without exceptions.

We sum up this point with a quote from Jesus in John 6. There he points out that people come to him because God the Father draws them by his word and the leading of the Holy Spirit. Then those who reflect on the truths of the gospel story are led to a deep trust or faith in Jesus as Lord. That is the way to salvation and to eternal life. Jesus said:

"44 The Father is the One who sent me. No one can come to me unless the Father draws him to me, and I will raise that person up on the last day. 45 It is written in the prophets, 'They will all be taught by God [Isaiah 54:13].' Everyone who listens to the Father and learns from him comes to me. 46 ·No one has [or Not that anyone has] seen the Father except the One who is from God; only he has seen the Father. 47 ·I tell you the truth [Literally, Truly, truly I say to you], whoever believes has eternal life" (John 6:44-47; **The Expanded Bible** – EXB).

Jim Woodruff, in his book **The Aroma of Christ**, pointed out how our New Covenant with God is far superior to the Old one because it emphasizes the Spirit of Christ as being the powerful dynamic which motivates our service in the priesthood of all believers.

Please allow me to share with you about two whole pages from Woodruff's book. In those two pages he points the spotlight on two inspirational incidents which happened when he worked in New Zealand. These two events opened his mind, changed his heart, and thereafter made his ministry much more Christ-centered. Here are Jim's moving words:

"A young Christian woman . . . had been a Christian only a short time when she came to me, the American evangelist, and said in despair, 'I am not going to make it.' 'Not going to make what?' I asked. 'All this,' she said, pointing out all the duties of the Christian contained in the letters to the churches. 'I'll never be able to do all these things,' she said despondently.

"Though I had been a Christian for many years (and an evangelist for nearly as many), I had no answer for her. She turned and walked away. But not for long. Only a few days passed before she came running to me, exclaiming, 'I've found it! I've found it!' Again, she took me by surprise. 'Found what?' I asked. She excitedly burst forth with this profound, life-changing observation: **'I have found in the gospels the power to do what is in the letters'** [emphasis mine, SP]

**"She had discovered the key to triumphant living and successful ministry. She, on her own, had seen the Lord in the gospels, and had thus discovered the power of the Christian life. Beholding the glory of the Lord, she had begun a lifetime of being transformed into his very likeness** [emphasis mine, SP].

"A year passed before I experienced this principle validated in my own life – at least to the degree that I could appropriate it to my ministry. It occurred as I was preparing to preach in a three-week campaign being sponsored in New Zealand by a group of American Christians. I had accepted reluctantly the assignment to preach for the campaign, for I knew it would require months of intensive preparation. But having accepted it, I went to work on it.

"The preparation that followed took me through nine months of in-depth study of the life of Jesus Christ; something, strange as it may seem, I had never done before. And it changed my entire ministry. I discovered the same truth the young woman had discovered a year earlier; the power is in the gospels. I saw, as I had never seen before, the power of the personality and teachings of Jesus and the meaning of his death and resurrection. I stood before him in wonder and amazement, and my preaching began to show it.

"With increasing clarity, I began to see that Jesus himself is the attracting power that draws people to God. I understood, perhaps for the first time in my life, what Jesus meant when he said, 'And I, when I am lifted up, will draw all men to myself' (John 12:32). In preparing to preach to others, I myself was irresistibly drawn to him. He was the magnet and I the metal down to him. Spirit upon spirit was finally a reality.

"Having thus come to see the beauty of the Lord, I gradually became aware of the principle that I now recognize as the dynamic of the new covenant and the factor that qualifies all those who serve as ministers of that covenant. That is:

### *"A person comes to be like what he loves, and grows to be like what he worships.*

"Luther's observation startles as it enlightens: 'That upon which your soul relies and in which your heart delights is your god.' And every person comes to be like his god, regardless of who the god may be.

"**Thus when one has so seen the Lord Jesus that he loves him and keeps his attention and longings focused on him, he actually comes to be like Jesus. For the magnet which, in turn, attracts other pieces of metal. So Christ not only draws us, but as long as we are in union with him, he transforms us into his own likeness so that we, in turn, may draw others to him. Herein is our sufficiency. Herein God qualifies us to be ministers of the new covenant** [emphasis mine, SP]" (pp. 72-74. Fair Use Domain).

Finally, here in a modern translation are several scriptures highlighting the freedom, insight and growth which flow from rejoicing in the New Covenant. And they conclude with the basic point made by Jim Woodruff, above. The Lord Jesus himself draws us to him, supercharges us, and sends us out to share that knowledge and energy with others. Here it is:

"12 Since this new way gives us such confidence, we can be very bold. 13 We are not like Moses, who put a veil over his face so the people of Israel would not see the glory, even though it was destined to fade away. 14 But the people's minds were hardened, and to this day whenever the old covenant is being read, the same veil covers their minds so they cannot understand the truth. And this veil can be removed only by believing in Christ. 15 Yes, even today when they read Moses' writings, their hearts are covered with that veil, and they do not understand.

"16 But whenever someone turns to the Lord, the veil is taken away. 17 For the Lord is the Spirit, and wherever the Spirit of the Lord is, there is freedom. 18 So all of us who have had that veil removed can see and reflect the glory of the Lord. And **the Lord— who is the Spirit—makes us more and more like him as we are changed into his glorious image** [emphasis mine, SP]" (2 Corinthians 3:12-18; **<u>New Living Translation</u>** – NLT).

## A Summary of the New Covenant

The New Covenant is simple enough that a normal person of about 13 years of age can easily understand and accept. This new agreement replaced the old Mosaic Covenant. It did away with a law-keeping method of trying to relate to God. The new way depends on the loving grace of God to draw us close to him and help us see Jesus as both human and divine and as the Son of God.

In this New Covenant, God promises to forgive our sins and save us for eternity when we act on our faith by confessing Jesus publicly, by repenting of our sinful way of life, and by accepting Jesus as Lord. That faith-experience is usually followed as soon as possible by believer's baptism, which is another act of faith. It is a symbolic and public testimonial to the person's recent salvation. The new believer receives the indwelling of the Holy Spirit, and an array of other blessings. Our part of this conditional covenant is to keep God's commandments, to love God, our neighbors, and others. In imitation of Jesus, we are to live at peace with others so much as it depends on us, and we are to go about doing good works because we are saved.

The foundation of New Covenant is the principle of love. Someone long ago said that he gave everyone the permission to do whatever they wanted to him, so long as they really loved him. Well, when you really love someone, you want to please that person. You want to bless that person. You want to honor and serve that person. And you never in any way want to harm or bring shame to that person. The same is true when you love God and his children. Love is the motivation for everything we do.

Many years back, W. Carl Ketcherside did a wonderful job of summing up our New Covenant with God. In his book, **The Death of the Custodian: The Case of the Missing Tutor** (p. 92), he wrote:

"The new covenant has been inscribed on the walls of the heart. It has not been written with ink but with the Spirit. **It does not consist of a compilation of legal propositions, but of one word: love!** [emphasis mine, SP] Correctly understood, that word involves all that law was intended to accomplish but could not. It lifts man out of the very domain of law. It places him in a realm where he can bear the fruits of the Spirit (Galatians 5:13-26)" [Fair Use Domain]

# # 6

**Sixth, all believers involved in any ministry should display the same virtues which marked the ministry of Jesus.** Those characteristics include kindness, patience, humility, truthfulness, genuine love for all people, hospitality, service as needed, gladly suffering persecution or even death for God and his people. We are thus motivated by our knowledge that God loved us first. In this way, we prove our desire to love him back and to give him all the honor.

Those ideas at first baffled disciples James and John. They were ambitious, really anxious to be important men in the early church. Jesus taught them a hard lesson, but he changed them for the good. Here is what Jesus told them when they revealed their arrogant plan:

"35 Then James and John, sons of Zebedee, came to Jesus and said, 'Teacher, we want to ask you to do something for us.'

"36 Jesus asked, 'What do you want me to do for you?'

"37 The sons answered, 'Let us share the great honor you will have as king. Let one of us sit at your right side and the other at your left.'

"38 Jesus said, 'You don't understand what you are asking. Can you drink from the cup that I must drink from? Can you be baptized with the same baptism that I must go through?'

"39 The sons answered, 'Yes, we can!'

"Jesus said to the sons, 'It is true that you will drink from the cup that I drink from. And you will be baptized with the same baptism that I must go through. 40 But it is not for me to say who will sit at my right or my left. God has prepared those places for the ones he chooses.'

"41 When the other ten followers heard this, they were angry with James and John. 42 Jesus called all the followers together. He said, 'The non-Jewish people have men they call rulers. You know that those rulers love to show their power over the people. And their important leaders love to use all their authority over the people. 43 But it should not be that way with you. Whoever wants to be your leader must be your servant. 44 Whoever wants to be first must serve the rest of you like a slave. 45 Follow my example: Even the Son of Man did not come for people to serve him. He came to serve others and to give his life to save many people'" (Mark 10:34-45, ERV).

In the above scriptures, Jesus used the phrases "you will drink from the cup that I drink from" and "you will be baptized with the same baptism that I must go through" to make it clear these two young hotshots that – just like their Lord – they would go through intense hardships and suffering for the cause of the kingdom. In essence, he told them to stand strong in their discipleship before they worried about leadership.

Standing strong as God's people is another way to look more like the Lord we love. He suffered much and we may be called to do so as well. The apostle Peter knew much himself suffering and he encourages us with these words:

"21b Christ suffered for us, leaving us an example, that you should follow His steps:

> 22 'He committed no sin,
> nor was deceit found in His mouth.'

"23 When He was reviled, He did not revile back; when He suffered, He did not threaten, but He entrusted Himself to Him who judges righteously. 24 He Himself bore our sins in His own body on the tree, that we, being dead to sins, should live unto righteousness. 'By His wounds you were healed.' 25 For you were as sheep going astray, but now have been returned to the Shepherd and Guardian of your souls" (1 Peter 2:221b – 25; **The Modern English Version** – MEV).

Paul, in 1 Corinthians 12 discussed many of the wonderful spiritual gifts which God gives. And then in the 13th chapter he told them something even better than the gift of preaching, or the gift of prophesying, or the gift of physical healing. That super-gift is none other than love in the believer's heart and actions.

On the night of his betrayal, Jesus told his inner disciples to draw closer to each other than ever before. He said, "Now I am giving you a new command—love one another. Just as I have loved you, so you must love one another. This is how all men will know that you are my disciples, because you have such love for one another" (John 13:34-35; **J.B. Phillips New Testament** – PHILLIPS).

The apostle John added even more words of clarity about how we as "Christians" (i.e., "little Christs"), must mirror our Lord:

"3 If we obey what God has told us to do, then we are sure that we know him. 4 If we say we know God but do not obey his commands, we are lying. The truth is not in us. 5 But when we obey God's teaching, his love is truly working in us. This is how we know that we are living in him. 6 **If we say we live in God, we must live the way Jesus lived** [emphasis mine, SP]" (1 John 3-6; ERV).

The apostle Paul reminds us in Romans 13 that we must focus on love, not as only an emotional response but as an intellectual platform from which we do good to all people and no harm to anyone:

"8 Owe no one anything, except to love each other, for the one who loves another has fulfilled the law. 9 For the commandments, 'You shall not commit adultery, You shall not murder, You shall not steal, You shall not covet', and any other commandment, are summed up in this word: 'You shall love your neighbor as yourself.' 10 Love does no wrong to a neighbor; therefore love is the fulfilling of the law" (Romans 13:8-10; **English Standard Version Anglicised** – ESVUK).

# # 7

**Seventh, all believers are to be ambassadors for Jesus Christ, our High Priest.** When we perform our proper roles as ambassadors for and priests under Jesus Christ, we may do away our all-too common professional ministerial caste system. We no longer need to tolerate hireling "Ministers" who expect to be treated a whole lot better than any other of our fellow/ordinary men and women in the general priesthood of all believers.

We no longer have to depend on a single man or small team to "do church" for us. We no longer have to sit in a pew and listen to only messages developed by one person and run through his interpretative filtration process, with never a question or comment entertained from the congregation. We will no longer have to give them special titles. We no longer have to pay the Clergy of Churchianity a salary, benefits, and homage.

> *We, the people and the heart of our local mutual ministry, will encourage and teach and train one another to accomplish the mission of our independent congregation. We and our own leaders selected from among us (often called elders or presbyters and the deacons) will direct our own affairs according to our understanding of the New Covenant and the leading of the Holy Spirit. We will not be browbeaten by people outside of our congregation, not by influential editors of religious magazines, nor by well-known administrators of Christian universities, and not by arrogant and/or power-grabbing preachers. -- Stan Paregien Sr.*

Graphic created by Stan Paregien Sr on Dec. 6, 2020

The apostle Paul put it pretty simply when he explained to the early disciples that this in-bred, Holy Spirit-inspired desire to tell others the good news of Jesus is a God-thing:

"18 All this is from God. Through Christ, God made peace between himself and us. And God gave us the work of bringing people into peace with him. 19 I mean that God was in Christ, making peace between the world and himself. In Christ, God did not hold people guilty for their sins. And he gave us this message of peace to tell people. 20 So we have been sent to speak for Christ. It is like God is calling to people through us. We speak for Christ when we beg you to be at peace with God" (2 Corinthians 5:18-20, ERV).

Paul's description of men and women who boldly speak to others about Jesus is close to poetry. Think of your favorite fragrant flower - maybe a rose, a gardenia, an orange blossom or lavender – and of yourself as a commissioned witness as you read these words:

"14 But thanks be to God, who always leads us in triumphal procession in Christ, and who reveals the fragrance of the knowledge of him through us in every place. 15 For **we are the aroma of Christ to God** [emphasis mine, SP] among those who are being saved and among those who are perishing, 16 to those on the one hand an odor from death to death, and to those on the other hand a fragrance from life to life. And who is qualified for these things? 17 For we are not like the majority who peddle the word of God, but as from pure motives—but as from God—we speak before God in Christ" (2 Corinthians 2:14-17 – **Lexham English Bible** – LEB).

Here are the words of praise given to the first century Christians by the apostle Peter himself. Remember as you read these words, they also apply to every believer testifying for Christ right now. Peter wrote in 1 Peter 2:2-16:

"2-3 Now that you realize how kind the Lord has been to you, put away all evil, deception, envy, and fraud. Long to grow up into the fullness of your salvation; cry for this as a baby cries for his milk.

"4 Come to Christ, who is the living Foundation of Rock upon which God builds; though men have spurned him, he is very precious to God who has chosen him above all others.

"5 And now **you have become living building-stones** [emphasis mine, SP] for God's use in building his house. **What's more, you are his holy priests** [emphasis mine, SP]; so come to him — you who are acceptable to him because of Jesus Christ — and offer to God those things that please him. 6 As the Scriptures express it, 'See, I am sending Christ to be the carefully chosen, precious Cornerstone of my church, and I will never disappoint those who trust in him.'

"7 Yes, he is very precious to you who believe; and to those who reject him, well— 'The same Stone that was rejected by the builders has become the Cornerstone, the most honored and important part of the building.' 8 And the Scriptures also say, 'He is the Stone that some will stumble over, and the Rock that will make them fall.' They will stumble because they will not listen to God's Word nor obey it, and so this punishment must follow — that they will fall.

"9 But you are not like that, for you have been chosen by God himself — **you are priests of the King, you are holy and pure, you are God's very own** [emphasis mine, SP] — all this so that you may show to others how God called you out of the darkness into his wonderful light. 10 Once you were less than nothing; now you are God's own. Once you knew very little of God's kindness; now your very lives have been changed by it.

"11 Dear brothers, you are only visitors here. Since your real home is in heaven, I beg you to keep away from the evil pleasures of this world; they are not for you, for they fight against your very souls.

"12 Be careful how you behave among your unsaved neighbors; for then, even if they are suspicious of you and talk against you, they will end up praising God for your good works when Christ returns.

"13 For the Lord's sake, obey every law of your government: those of the king as head of the state, 14 and those of the king's officers, for he has sent them to punish all who do wrong, and to honor those who do right.

"15 It is God's will that your good lives should silence those who foolishly condemn the Gospel without knowing what it can do for them, having never experienced its power. 16 You are free from the law, but that doesn't mean you are free to do wrong. Live as those who are free to do only God's will at all times" (1 Peter 2:2-16, **The Living Bible** – TLB).

Anyone who becomes a Christian is also expected to be an active minister in the priesthood of all believers and in mutual ministry. Little of that working witness for Christ is done inside a church building. Most often, it is done in someone's home or place of business, at a school or a nursing home or hospital or funeral parlor. Sometimes it is done in in a garden, a rescue mission for the homeless, or inside a jail house or a smoke-filled bar. Yes, mark it down: Ministry is often messy and sometimes even dangerous.

In 2 Corinthians 4, the apostle Paul has some frank, truthful and mostly encouraging words regarding our mutual ministry and priesthood. Right off he says "Hey, folks, God has graced us with work to do and we're not gonna give up. We have good news to share and we're gonna plant the plain truth." There is a lot of good stuff here:

"1 **So because of God's mercy, we have work to do. He has given it to us. And we don't give up** [emphasis mine, SP]. 2 Instead, we have given up doing secret and shameful things. **We don't twist God's word. In fact, we do just the opposite. We present the truth plainly** [emphasis mine, SP]. In the sight of God, we make our appeal to everyone's sense of what is right and wrong. 3 Suppose our good news is covered with a veil. Then it is veiled to those who are dying. 4 The god of this world has blinded the minds of those who don't believe. They can't see the light of the good news that makes Christ's glory clear. **Christ is the likeness of God. 5 The message we preach is not about ourselves. Our message is about Jesus Christ. We say that he is Lord** [emphasis mine, SP]. And we say that we serve you because of Jesus. 6 God said, 'Let light shine out of darkness.' (Genesis 1:3) He made his light shine in our hearts. His light gives us the light to know God's glory. His glory is shown in the face of Christ.

"7 **Treasure is kept in clay jars. In the same way, we have the treasure of the good news in these earthly bodies of ours. That shows that the mighty power of the good news comes from God** [emphasis mine, SP]. It doesn't come from us. 8 We are pushed hard from all sides. But we are not beaten down. We are bewildered. But that doesn't make us lose hope. 9 Others make us suffer. But God does not desert us. We are knocked down. But we are not knocked out. 10 We always carry around the death of Jesus in our bodies. In that way, the life of Jesus can be shown in our bodies. 11 **We who are alive are always in danger of death because we are serving Jesus. This happens so that his life can also be shown in our earthly bodies** [emphasis mine, SP]. 12 Death is at work in us. But life is at work in you.

"13 It is written, 'I believed, and so I have spoken.' (Psalm 116:10) We have that same spirit of faith. So we also believe and speak. 14 We know that God raised the Lord Jesus from the dead. And he will also raise us up with Jesus. And he will present both you and us to himself. 15 All this is for your benefit. God's grace is reaching more and more people. So they will become more and more thankful. They will give glory to God.

"16 **We don't give up. Our bodies are becoming weaker and weaker. But our spirits are being renewed day by day** [emphasis mine, SP]. 17 Our troubles are small. They last only for a short time. But they are earning for us a glory that will last forever. It is greater than all our troubles. 18 So we don't spend all our time looking at what we can see. Instead, we look at what we can't see. That's because what can be seen lasts only a short time. But what can't be seen will last forever" (**New International Readers Version** – NIRV).

Jim Woodruff, in his book **The Aroma of Christ**, reminds us that we cannot attract people to Christ if we do not emit that heavenly fragrance. He said there are two main factors in our being the aroma of Christ.

First, each of us must be brave enough to be authentic in the eyes of unbelievers. Jim said, "It is just that simple. We are to be a people of sincerity first, last, and always" (page 46; Fair Use Domain).

Frankly, most of us are trained to present ourselves as "Super Saints." We never admit our sins, though the Bible encourages us to confess our faults one to another. Of course, if you are perfect, then you have an out. Nope, not at all. We need to get rid of the complex Max Davis sang about long ago in his country music song, "Lord, It's Hard to be Humble (When You're Perfect in Every Way)." Yes, indeed.

Second, each of us must recognize and use our God-given authority. Our spirit of love-driven evangelism is energized by the words of Jesus to the apostles (and by extension, to all believers today):

"18 All authority in heaven and on earth has been given to me. 19 Therefore go and gather disciples from all nations by baptizing them in the name of the Father and of the Son and of the Holy Spirit, 20 and by teaching them to keep all the instructions I have given you. And surely I am with you always until the end of the age" (Matthew 28:18b – 20; **Evangelical Heritage Version** – EHV).

Those three verses are often referred to as the "marching orders" for God's army of believers. Commenting on them, **William Barclay** in his book **The Letter to the Hebrews** tells this powerful story going back to biblical times:

"The ambassador is clothed with all the authority of the king who sends him. On one occasion the king of Syria, **Antiochus Epiphanes**, invaded Egypt. Rome desired to stop him and sent an envoy called **Popillius** to tell him to abandon his projected mission. Popillius caught up with Antiochus on the borders of Egypt and they talked of this and that for they had known each other in Rome. Popillius had not the vestige of an army with him, not even a guard.

"Finally, Antiochus asked him why he had come. Quietly Popillius told him that he had come to tell him that Rome wished him to abandon the invasion and go home. 'I will consider it,' said Antiochus. Popillius smiled a little grimly; and he took his staff and drew a circle in the earth around Antiochus. 'Consider it,' he said, 'and come to your decision before you leave that circle.' Antiochus thought for a few seconds and then said: 'Very well, I will go home.'

"Popillus himself had not the slightest force available – but behind him was all the power of Rome. So Jesus came from God and all God's grace and mercy and love and power were in his ***apostolos***' [the Greek word for ambassador or one who is sent with a purpose and authority – SP]" (pp. 30-31; Fair Use Domain).

**Jimmy Allen** was not only a respected Bible professor at Harding University (Searcy, AR), but he was a noted evangelist. He is dead, now, but for several years, he preached for area-wide revivals in convention centers drawing thousands of people each night. He explained, in an interview conducted by a reporter for ***Christian Chronicle*** magazine in 2010, that sharing the story of Jesus with any and everyone just always seemed natural to him. He said:

"From the day I became a Christian at Harding, I knew the Gospel was too good for me to keep my mouth shut. I've shared the Gospel wherever I go – with hitchhikers, in a restaurant, or on an airplane. Seems to me like this is what Christians are supposed to be doing" (Fair Use Domain).

Yep, that is pure truth. An early missionary to the people of Japan, **John Moody McCaleb** (1861-1953), put that thought into the lyrics of his song:

### The Gospel is For All
#### by J.M. McCaleb

Of one the Lord has made the race
Through one has come the fall.
Where sin has gone must go His grace.
The gospel is for all.

The blessed gospel is for all,
The gospel is for all.
Where sin has gone must go His grace.
The gospel is for all.

Do not say the heathen are at home,
So beyond we have no call.
For why should we be blessed alone?
The gospel is for all.

We freely received, so we freely give.
From every land they call.
If we don't tell, they may never hear.
The gospel is for all.

Similarly, a female missionary nurse from England wrote two songs about the joy Christians have in introducing people to the one who has changed our life. That missionary, **Katherine Hankey** (January 12, 1834 – May 9, 1911), was working in Africa when she became very sick. She had to stay in her bed for many days of rest and recover. The year was1866, just one year after the Civil War ended in the United States.

She lay there day after day. Finally, she regained enough strength to sit up. And then after a while, she was well enough to put down her thoughts on paper. She wrote two separate epic poems about the life of Jesus. A Christian friend, **Dr. W.H. Doane**, in 1867 selected verses from each of those two parts of her poems and created two songs from them. Later, they were set to music by a man named **William G. Fischer**. Here are those songs, each of them dearly loved by Christians around the world:

### Tell Me the Story of Jesus
By Katherine Hankey

1
Tell me the old, old story
Of unseen things above,
Of Jesus and His glory,
Of Jesus and His love.

Tell me the story simply,
As to a little child,
For I am weak and weary,
And helpless and defiled.

Refrain:

Tell me the old, old story.
Tell me the old, old story.
Tell me the old, old story
Of Jesus and His love.
(Refrain after each verse)

2

Tell me the story slowly,
That I may take it in,
That wonderful redemption,
God's remedy for sin.

Tell me the story often,
For I forget so soon;
The early dew of morning
Has passed away at noon.

3

Tell me the story softly,
With earnest tones and grave.
Remember I'm the sinner
Whom Jesus came to save.

Tell me the story always,
If you would really be,
In any time of trouble,
A comforter to me.

4

Tell me the same old story
When you have cause to fear
That this world's empty glory
Is costing me too dear.

Yes, and when that world's glory
Is dawning on my soul,
Tell me the old, old story:
Christ Jesus makes us whole.

## I Love to Tell the Story
By Katherine Hankey
(Slight updates by Stan Paregien Sr.)

I love to tell the story
Of unseen things above
Of Jesus and his glory
Of Jesus and his love

I love to tell the story
Because I know it is true
It satisfies my longings
As nothing else can do.

I love to tell the story
It will be my theme in glory.
To tell the old, old story
Of Jesus and his love.

I love to tell the story,
For those who know it best,
Seem hungering and thirsting
To hear it like the rest.

And when in scenes of glory
I sing the new, new song
It will be my theme in glory.
To tell the old, old story
Of Jesus and his love.

In this great ministry of the Master, our aim is not just the exchange of intellectual data or information. It is always a good things to make the gospel story available to people who are searching for direction in their lives.

However, our real goal and hope is that these people may undergo a complete transformation. It is very akin to having a heart transplant. Our goal includes a whole process of things. It begins with the person receiving the word, then believing it, and then responding favorably by coming to faith in Jesus and accepting God's gracious offer of salvation. Then comes their confession to anyone who will listen that Jesus is

Lord of their lives, and living that out by repenting of their sins and committing to living for Jesus. That is soon reinforced by their undergoing another act of faith – a testimonial baptism.

The word **Sanctification** is a $50-dollar theological term that is hard to work into coffee shop conversations. Or anywhere. What it means, in basic terms, is a process of becoming "holy" or having the quality of "holiness." As you learn more about the love of Jesus, you will be transformed by God according to his timetable. He will mold you and form you like potter's clay to where you mirror Jesus. And that is the goal, to be more like our Lord. It is not just a flip of a switch, but a process of dedication, occasional repentance, and more growth.

The concept is that every day, as you mature in your faith, the Holy Spirit living in you will improve your decision making skills. When you are new in the faith, you are operating on a "child-like" level where your only perceived choices may be between something that is between "Awful" and "Not So Bad." As you grow stronger maybe you choices have improved to that between "Okay" and "Better." Later, as you grow in knowledge and in spiritual IQ, your choices are then largely between "Much Better" and "Good." Eventually, you get to the place where your perceived choices are between "Good" and "Excellent." Ask the Lord to help you with your decision-making skills each and every day.

Once a messenger has delivered the message (the gospel) to a person, then it becomes that individual's responsibility to accept it or to reject it. The messenger certainly may pray for the receiver to accept Jesus, but there is no room for arm-twisting or brow-beating. The gift of eternal life is free to the receiver because Jesus himself paid the price. Now the receiver may freely accept or reject it, with certain consequences either way. But the messenger may rejoice that he or she has done his job in delivering the seed of life (the gospel) to an unbeliever. Now he can say, as Paul did in Acts 20:26, he has told him all he needs to know about Jesus in order to be saved and that is the end of his responsibility.

The late **Jimmy Lovell** was a family friend of ours. He was a retired executive from a large corporation. But he was a Christian with a passion for the unsaved. He never retired from that. He established a magazine named ***Action*** in order to motivate and educate other people on how to present the basic gospel to their unbelieving friends, neighbors, and family. One of his favorite sayings, though I don't think he originated it, was this: **"No one has the right to hear the gospel twice before everyone hears it once."** That is a challenge to each of us.

We want to be more like Jesus every single day. More joyful. Kinder to everyone, but particularly to the poor and those living in defeat. More hospitable. More teachable. More outspoken with the gospel. More courageous in standing up against evil and for justice. More spontaneous in following the leading of the Holy Spirit. More aware of opportunities for doing good. Consistency in our speech and actions. More faithful to our promises, both to God and to our friends.

Pretend I'm whispering in your ear about something that must really be important. I know a secret technique which can help us move faster toward the goal of being more like Jesus.

So . . . can you keep a secret?

Okay, come closer and I'll "'splain to you" as **Desi Arnaz** often said to his wife on the old TV show, "I Love Lucy."

I call this the "Erasure" technique. You probably have a calendar on which you note future appointments or events, and the calendar is divided into sections for each day of the year. You pencil in notes as needed. That's fine in that context. But the way our minds often work is that we further dissect our lives into nice, neat sections, compartments or boxes. There is our "work time box," our "leisure time box," our "family time box," and our "religious or church time" box. And we're pretty darned good at compartmentalizing those various parts of our lives..

**Buzzzzzzzz**.

That's the print way of indicating that a warning buzzer just sounded off.

The practice of compartmentalization is a real drag on our becoming more like Jesus. It subjective suggests that it is great to discuss Jesus and his work on Sundays became that is in our "religious time" box, and it also urges us to keep it there. So we find ourselves reluctant to mention the good news of Jesus to our co-workers during "our work time box" or during our fishing trip with two other families. So the idea here is that we use our king-sized imaginary erasure to snuff out the artificial lines we're drawn between our various activities.

Jesus never displayed or even hinted at a nice, neat dividing line between his ministry and his life. It was all the same. His life was his ministry and his ministry his life. So if we are to better model ourselves after our Lord, we must see no wall or line between our lives and our ministries for God.

Jim Woodruff put it this way, "Until we recognize our life as our ministry and our ministry as our life we will not become the grassroots movement needed in the world today; we will not be the salt of the earth, the city on a hill. But those whose life is their ministry and whose ministry is their life are the aroma of Christ and are spreading the fragrance of the knowledge of him everywhere" (**The Aroma of Christ**, p. 119; Fair Use Domain).

When you discover some bad news, you are probably tempted to just keep it to yourself. But when you discover something that represents extremely good new, the first impulse should be to share it with as many people as possible. An Old Testament proverb states, "Good news from a faraway place is like a cool drink of water when you are hot and thirsty" (Proverbs 25:25, ERV).

That is really all that the word "evangelize" means. It is a central idea in the lives of Christians because they want to share the joy they found.

It is not a new idea, for it started in the manger of baby Jesus in Bethlehem hundreds of years ago. Jesus was born into a Jewish family, plus he lived and died as an orthodox Jew.

In case haven't read the Christmas story closely in a long time, here is the text in

Luke 2:8-20:

"8 That night, some shepherds were out in the fields near Bethlehem watching their sheep. 9An angel of the Lord appeared to them, and the glory of the Lord was shining around them. The shepherds were very afraid.

"10 The angel said to them, "Don't be afraid. I have some very good news for you—news that will make everyone happy. 11Today your Savior was born in David's town. He is the Messiah, the Lord. 12This is how you will know him: You will find a baby wrapped in pieces of cloth and lying in a feeding box."

"13 Then a huge army of angels from heaven joined the first angel, and they were all praising God, saying,

"14 "Praise God in heaven, and on earth let there be peace to the people who please him."

"15 The angels left the shepherds and went back to heaven. The shepherds said to each other, "Let's go to Bethlehem and see this great event the Lord has told us about."

"16 So they went running and found Mary and Joseph. And there was the baby, lying in the feeding box. 17When they saw the baby, they told what the angels said about this child. 18Everyone was surprised when they heard what the shepherds told them. 19Mary continued to think about these things, trying to understand them. 20The shepherds went back to their sheep, praising God and thanking him for everything they had seen and heard. It was just as the angel had told them."

Here is the sequence of events as they relate to evangelism:

First, an angel of the Lord announced to the shepherds that he/she had **"very good news"** for them. The angel just couldn't keep that good news about Jesus to himself.

Second, the shepherds believed the message but they wanted to verify it for themselves. God is never threatened or angered when we ask even the tough questions of him.

Third, the shepherds shared with Mary and Joseph the details of the good news revealed to them by the angels. Good news is always worth sharing, time and time again.

Fourth, the shepherds returned to their pasture and their sheep but kept "praising God and thanking him for everything they had seen and heard." Sharing good news and repeating it always has God's seal of approval.

The apostle Paul explained it this way: "So faith comes from hearing the **Good News**. And people hear the **Good News** when someone tells them about Christ" (Romans 10:17, ERV).

Jesus himself is recorded as saying (Mark 16:15): "Go everywhere in the world. Tell the Good News to everyone."

It is recorded in in Luke 4:44, "Then Jesus told the Good News in the synagogues in Judea." There you have Jesus, a Jew himself, witnessing or sharing good news about himself with the other Jews.

In the New Testament was known as Philip the Evangelist. Acts 8:35 (ERV) tells us about how he encountered an Ethiopian government official out in the desert. They met and stopped. The man was a Jew and on his way to Jerusalem to observed a Jewish feast. "Philip began to speak. He started with this same Scripture and told the man the Good News about Jesus."

In Acts 10:36, we have the apostle Peter talking to a group of truth-seekers who already favored the Jewish religion. "God has spoken to the people of Israel. He sent them the Good News that peace has come through Jesus Christ, the Lord of all people."

In Acts 15:7 (ERV), the apostle Peter – another Jew who had become a Christian – said, "My brothers, I am sure you remember what happened in the early days. God chose me from among you to tell the Good News to those who are not Jewish. It was from me that they heard the Good News and believed."

Even back in the Old Testament, there are examples of sharing good news with others. The author of Palm 68:11 said, "My Lord gave the command, and many people went to tell the good news."

It is written in 1 Chronicles 16:23 (ERV): "Let the whole world sing to the Lord! Tell the good news every day about how he saves us."

The writer of Psalm 40:9 penned, "I told the good news of victory to the people in the assembly. And, Lord, you know that I will never stop telling that good news."

The prophet Isaiah said to his Jewish brethren (Isaiah 40:9): "Zion, you have good news to tell. Go up on a high mountain and shout the good news. Jerusalem, you have good news to tell. Don't be afraid; speak loudly. Tell this news to all the cities of Judah: 'Look, here is your God!'"

The first century Christian history, Dr. Luke (himself an evangelist), recorded in his Book of Acts (5:42, ERV): "The apostles did not stop teaching the people. They continued to tell the Good News – that Jesus is the Messiah. They did this every day in the Temple area and in people's homes."

Let's stop here for a moment.

We must emphasize that when we share the Good News, we need to examine our hearts and make sure that we have right motives and right attitudes. We are not trying to force anyone to listen. We don't hold a bullhorn to their ears and shout them down. Paul touched on this theme when he said, "When we encourage people to believe the Good News, it's not out of wrong motives. We are not trying to trick or fool anyone" (1 Thessalonians 2:3, ERV).

Evangelism should be preceded by a prayer for God's assistance and a prayer for the Holy Spirit to draw people to the message. We must constantly examine our own attitudes so that we are speaking the truth out of genuine love for the listener.

Finally, let's remind one another of why we share. Paul wrote, "I am proud of the Good News, because it is the power God uses to save everyone who believes – to save the Jews first, and now to save those who are not Jews" (Romans 1:16, ERV).

# Conclusion

My hope and prayer is that those who have not yet accepted Jesus as Lord and Savior will do so. Now. And shown your commitment and new relationship by testimonial baptism and walking close to God.

For those Believers who have strayed from the Way, repent and reconnect with God's people. You don't need to be baptized, again, ever. When you believed, God declared you just in his sight. You never lose that status as a born again child of God.

For all of us, I pray we each may grow in God's grace and in the joy of our salvation. Each of us is to spread the aroma of Christ "by spreading the fragrance of the knowledge of him everywhere." Amen.

NOTE: This will likely be my last book of my thoughts about the Bible, about the current state of Christianity, and such. I see in front of me an hourglass the size of a gallon of milk. And I see a heck of a lot more sand in the bottom than left at the top. Such is life. My memory and my stamina and my most-everything-else is just not like it was even five years ago.

It is true, as my perceptive friend Perry Cotham noted in his Foreword, that I consider this book my spiritual legacy. It contains a lot of concepts and truths that might have kept me in the full-time ministry, had anyone shared them. Instead, I had to search them out over the years and test them on my own. My life is better for it, and my prayer is for each reader who completes it to feel the same. That will be my reward.

**A REQUEST: If this helped you, please consider gifting a copy (either the paperback or the eBook) to a person searching for direction, or to a new Christian, or to a person in his or her first few years of ministry. Thanks.**

Colored by Peggy Paregien on July 12, 2020

May you be *blessed* by the LORD, the Maker of *heaven and earth.*

Psalm 115:15

# Chapter 17

# Resources for Simple Christianity

Allen, Jimmy. **Re-Baptism? What One Must Know to Be Born Again.** West Monroe, LA.: Howard Publishing Co., 1991.

Babcock, Margaret A. **New Growth in God's Garden: Transforming Congregations through Mutual Ministry**. Washington, D.C. LeaderResources, 2012.

Barclay, William. **The Letter to the Hebrews**. Revised Edition. Philadelphia, PA: The Saint Andrew Press, 1976. First edition in Scotland in 1955.

Barclay, William. **The Letter to the Romans**. Edinburgh, Scotland: The Saint Andrew Press, 1955 and 1957. Then printed without a change in the date by the Westminster Press in Philadelphia, PA.

Baxter, Batsell Barrett. **Family of God: A Study of the New Testament Church**. Nashville, TN: Gospel Advocate Company, 1980. Dr. Baxter was head of the Bible Department at Lipscomb University in Nashville for decades. During much of that time he was the featured speaker for the internationally broadcasted "Herald of Truth" radio and TV programs. In addition, he was the highly respected preacher for the large Hillsboro Church of Christ. He was my major Bible teacher during my years at Lipscomb, and he was a congenial and soft-spoken disciple. Having said that, I included his book here only because it is a prime example of our denomination's very traditional understanding of the church and related matters. I simply recommend it as a reference for how things were previous to 2000, not as a model or template for how they should be today.

Beasley-Murray, G.R. **Baptism in the New Testament.** Grand Rapids, Mich.: William B. Eerdmans Publishing Co., 1962.

Beasley-Murray, G.R. **Baptism Today and Tomorrow**. New York: St. Martin's Press, 1966.

Campbell, Alexander. **A Debate on Christian Baptism between John Walker (Presbyterian) and Alexander Campbell (Christian)**. Pittsburg, PA: Eichbaum & Johnston, Publishers, 1822.

**Common English Version**. Wheaton, IL: Crossway Bibles, 2001.

**Contemporary English Version.** Philadelphia, PA: American Bible Society, 1995.

**English Standard Version**.

Fenhagen, James C. **Mutual Ministry: New Vitality for the Local Church**. Seabury Press, 1st Edition. 1977

Fosdick, Harry Emerson. **A Guide to Understanding the Bible**. New York: Harper and Brothers Publishers, 1938.

Fudge, Edward William. "Balancing Baptism." *Restoration Review*, Volume 28, Number 3, March 1986.

_____. **The Fire That Consumes: A Biblical and Historical Study of the Doctrine of Final Punishment**. Eugene, Oregon: Cascade Books, 3rd Edition, 2011.

Fudge, Edward William. "Why Bother to Preach." In his *gracEmail* newsletter dated Aug. 7, 2016.

Garrett, Leroy. "The Promises of Baptism." In his late-life newsletter: *"Soldier On!" – An Occasional Essay,"* Number 411. Aug. 23, 2012.

_____. "Is Baptism 'An Outward Sign

of an Inward Grace'?" in *Soldier On: An Occasional Essay*, #484, May 15, 2015).

Goad, Steven Clark. **A Unity Cordial**. Belleville, Ontario, Canada: Guardian Books, 2001.

Goff, Bob. **Love Does: Discover a Secretly Incredible Life in an Ordinary World**. Nashville, TN: Nelson Books, 2012. He is a law professor at Pepperdine University.

Hicks, John Mark. "Are We Saved by Grace Alone?" Professor at Lipscomb University in Nashville. This lecture was originally given at Harding University and appeared in published form as "Saved by Grace, **Harding University Lectureship Book** The theme was Ephesians. Searcy, Arkansas:1994.

Hook, Cecil. **Free in Christ**. New Braunfels, TX: Self-published by Cecil Hook, 1988. 4th Printing. Out-of-print, but used copies may be available online.

**Holy Bible: Easy-to-Read Version**. Fort Worth, Texas: World Bible Translation Center, Inc., 1996.

Jeremiah, David. **The God You May Not Know: Take the Journey from Knowing About God to Knowing God**. San Diego, CA: Turning Point for God, 2018.

_____. **The Jesus You May Not Know**. San Diego, CA: Turning Point for God, 2020.

Kaiser, Walter C. and Moisés Silva. **An Introduction to Biblical Hermeneutics: The Search for Meaning**. Grand Rapids, MI: Zondervan Academic, 1994.

Ketcherside, W. Carl. "Baptism and Brethren." *Mission Messenger*, 1973 (Vol. 35, Issue 6), page 66-75.

Ketcherside, W. Carl. "More About Baptism." *Mission Messenger*, 1973 (Vol. 35, Issue 6), pp. 81-94.

Ketcherside, W. Carl. **Pilgrimage of Joy**. Joplin, MO: College Press Publishing, 1991.

Knowles, Victor. **Together in Christ: More Than a Dream**. Joplin, MO: College Press Publishing Co., 2006.

**Lexham English Bible** LEB. Logos Bible Software, 2012.

Lockhart, Clinton. **Principles of Interpretation**. Delight, Arkansas: Gospel Light Publishing Company, Revised Edition, 1915.

Lucado, Max. "Baptism: The Demonstration of Devotion." On Dec. 29, 2020, I found that article his web site, Max Lucado.com (maxlucado.com/baptism-the-demonstration-of-devotion/).

Manning, Brennan. **The Ragamuffin Gospel**. No city cited. Copyrighted by Brennan Manning, 1990.

Maxey, Al. " Building Biblical Hermeneutists." *Reflections* #53

Maxey, Al. "Pre-Plunge Pronouncements." **Reflections** – Issue 326 – Nov. 16, 2007.

_____. "Preterism and Eternal Punishment." *Reflections* - Issue #721 - June 5, 2017.

_____. "Twenty Questions About Baptism." *Reflections* (online blog) - Issue 642 – Dec. 19, 2014.

McKnight, Scot. **A Fellowship of Differents**. Grand Rapids, MI: Zondervan, 2014.

Moser, K.C. **The Gist of Romans. Delight, Arkansas: An Exposition of the Principal Doctrines of the Epistle to the Romans**. Revised edition, 1958 (originally published in 1957).

_____. **The Way of Salvation: Being an Exposition of God's Method of Justification Through Christ**. Delight, Arkansas: Gospel Light Publishing Company, 1932.

Neighbour Jr., Ralph W. with Lorna Jenkins. **Where Do We Go from Here? A Guidebook for the Cell Group Church**. Houston, TX: Torch Publications, 1990.

**The New American Bible: Catholic**. (NAB). Washington, D.C.: Libreria Editrice Vaticana, 2003. It is the official Catholic version of the Bible in the United States, approved by the Vatican and the United States Conference of Catholic Bishops. It is written in modern English. The books of the Apocrypha are included in the Old Testament.

**New Living Translation: Life Application Study Bible**. 2nd Edition. Wheaton, ILL.: Tyndale House Publishers, Inc., 1996, 2004.

Osborne, Grant R. **The Hermeneutical Spiral: A Comprehensive Introduction to Biblical Interpretation**. Downers Grove, IL: IVP Academic. Originally published in 1991. Revised and expanded edition published in 2006.

Paregien, Stan. **The Day Jesus Died**. Bradenton, FL: Revised Edition, 2011. Printed by Amazon KDP. Distributed by Amazon and other fine retailers.

Paregien, Stan. **The Gospel of Jesus in Simple English**. Bradenton, FL: Published by Paregien Enterprises as a paperback in Jan., 2020. Distributed by Amazon and other fine retailers. Published by Paregien Enterprises as an eBook through Smashwords.com in Jan., 2020 and is available for free in several different formats (epub, PDF, etc.).

Paregien, Stan. Editor. **Thoughts on Unity**. St. Louis, MO: Mission Messenger, 1971. Currently only available as an eBook.

Peterson, Eugene H. **The Message: The Bible in Contemporary Language. Colorado Springs, CO**.: NavPress, 2002.

Phillips, J.B. **New Testament in Modern English**. First published in England in 1958. Revised edition in 1996 and published in New York City by Touchstone Books, a division of Simon and Simon. Phillips was a minister in the Church of England (Anglican).

Rainer, Thom S. and Eric Geiger. **Simple Church: Returning to God's Process for Making Disciples**. Nashville, TN: B&H Publishing Group, 2006.

Ridenour, Fritz. Editor. **How to Be a Christian Without Being Religious**. Glendale, CA: Regal Books, a Division of G/L Publications, 1967. The Book of Romans with the text from The Paraphrased New Testament and illustrated . . . and hilarious. Amazingly, was of Aug., 2020, it is still in print and Mr. Ridenour is still alive. However, Regal Books was sold to Baker Publishing Group in Ada, Michigan.

Rowland, Robert H. **"I Permit Not a Woman . . . " to Remain Shackled**. Newport, Oregon: Lighthouse Publishing Co., 1991. The late author was a personal friend of ours. He preached in Alaska in the early 1950s, served as president of Columbia Christian College (Portland, OR) in the late 1950's and the 1960's, then became the Director of the American Citizenship Center that was located on the campus of Oklahoma Christian University in Oklahoma City, OK. This book was Bob's ground-breaking study and effort to free Christian women from overly restrictive traditions in today's congregations.

Shelburne, Gene. **The Quest for Unity: An Appeal for Oneness Among All Believers in Christ**. Siloam Springs, AR: Leafwood Publishers, 2004.

Sheler, Jeffery L. **Is the Bible True? How Modern Debates and Discoveries Affirm the Essences of the Scriptures**. New York City, NY: Harper/Collins Publishers, 1999.

Shelly, Rubel. **I Just Want to Be a Christian**. Nashville, TN: 20th Century Christian, Revised Edition, 1986.

Shelly, Rubel and James E. Moore. **A Debate: Four Propositions Discussing Immersion, Sprinkling, Baptism of Infants, Baptism of Penitent Believers**. 1975

**The Holy Bible: New King James Version**. Nashville, Tenn.: Thomas Nelson Publishers, 1984.

**Today's English Version: The Good News Bible**. New York: American Bible Society, 1992.

Warren, Rick. **Rick Warren's Bible Study Methods: 12 Ways You Can Unlock God's Word**. Grand Rapids, Mich.: Zondervan, 1981, 2006.

Woodruff, James S. **The Aroma of Christ**. Revised. Foreword by F.F. Bruce. Searcy, AR: Distributed by The Bible House, 1992. Printed by Gospel Light Publishing Co., in Delight, AR. This paperback is an in-depth study of 2 Corinthians 2:15 through 6:1. It promotes the development of grassroots ministry, and it aims at transforming followers of Christ into ambassadors.

# Chapter 18

# Other Books by Stan Paregien

Here is a chronological list of his books available online at several retailers and in a range of formats. Just do a computer search for "Books by Paregien" to find them.

Book 1:

## The Day Jesus Died

Originally published in 1970 in Austin, TX by the Firm Foundation Publishing House (Reuel Lemmons, Editor). It contained 18 essays on such topics as "The Problem of Unbelief," "The Peace of God," "The Day Jesus Died," and "The Importance of Truth." Stan had preached this material as sermons, then made them into essays. Revised in 2011 and published via Smashwords.com as an eBook. Totally revised and with dozens of new graphics, then printed in Aug. of 2019 as a "Revised Version" paperback through Amazon.

Book 2:

## Thoughts on Unity

First published as a hardback in 1971 in St. Louis, MO by W. Carl Ketcherside, editor and publisher of **Mission Messenger** magazine. It was out of print for decades, then in about 2013, the Ketcherside family made it available in the Kindle format on Amazon for only 99 cents. Stan saw his book as an effort to get Christian people to work closer together, especially those within the various factions of the Church of Christ, Christian Church and Disciples of Christ.

Book 3:

## Twenty-six Lessons on the Gospel of John

This 200-page paperback book is the only one of Stan's books which is not available to English speaking people. It was published in 1977 in Joplin, MO., by Don DeWelt and his College Press. It is a brief introduction to the entire Gospel of John. A church leader in India, a physician by trade, translated this book into one of India's many dialects and published it there in 2016. Stan is considering writing a new and expanded version in the future.

Book 4:

## Guy W. Logsdon: Award-winning Folklorist

Published as an eBook in 2013 and distributed by Smashwords.com to many fine retailers. Biography of the late Guy W. Logsdon, a native of Ada, OK., who lived most of his adult life in Tulsa. He earned a doctorate at the University of Illinois and became the head librarian and folklore professor at the University of Tulsa. He was recognized as a leading authority on Woody Guthrie's life and music, Bob Wills' life and music, Western Swing in general, and old-time cowboy music.

Book 5:

## Clara Luper: Civil Rights Pioneer

Published as an eBook on Jan. 9, 2012. Oklahoma schoolteacher Clara Luper courageously began early in her career a life-long battle against racism. She walked in the March on Selma, AL and the March on Washington, DC. She made local and national news in 1958 when she organized a small group of teenagers (including her own children) and led them in a sit-in at a drugstore diner which did not serve Black people. They persisted, day after day, and were successful.

Book 6:

## Jim Shoulders: King of the Rodeo Cowboys

This biography was published as an eBook in 2013. It is a biography of the amazing life and rodeo career of the legendary Oklahoma cowboy Jim Shoulders. Shoulders was tough as a boot, mentally and physically, until the day he died. That is how he won an astounding 16 world championships in rodeo competition.

Book 7:

## Rootin' Tootin' Cowboy Poetry

Published as an eBook in 2012. This 159-page eBook contains 100 of Stan's original Western/cowboy poems.

Book 8:

## Woody Guthrie: His Life, Music & Myth

Published as an eBook in 2012 . It contains 342 pages It is a carefully researched biography of the life, music and myth of famed singer-songwriter Woody Guthrie (a native of Okemah, OK).

Book 9:

## Oklahoma Almanac of Facts & Humor,
## Part 1: Achille to Nowata

Foreword by the **Honorable George Nye, former Governor of Oklahoma**. Travel guide of Oklahoma's 77 counties, plus a dash of history, and lots of humor and photos. Volume 1 of 2. Published as an eBook on May 21, 2013.

Book 10:

## Oklahoma Almanac of Facts & Humor,
## Part 2: Okarche to Zafra

Volume 2 of 2. Published as an eBook in 2013. Foreword by the Honorable George Nye, former Governor of Oklahoma. Travel guide of Oklahoma's 77 counties, plus a dash of history, and lots of humor and photos.

Book 11:

## The Austin Chronicles, Book 1:
## Boggy Depot Shootout

A Western novel about the Austin family. ISBN: 9781310788215 Published as an eBook on Feb. 25, 2014. *Boggy Depot Shootout* is the first in a series of novels about the Austin family and how they coped with the unique challenges of living in the West just after the end of America's Civil War in 1865. The main character in this book is young Daniel Austin, a Confederate veteran. Their trials climax with a shootout at Boggy Depot, Indian Territory.

Book 12:

## The Austin Chronicles, Book 2:
## The Abilene Trail

A Western novel about the Austin family. ISBN: 9781311101624 Published as an eBook on March 24, 2014. *The Abilene Trail* is the second in a series of novels about the Austin family and how they coped with the unique challenges of living in the West. Here in Book 2, Daniel Austin, his younger brother David and their uncle Frank Austin start an adventure traveling from Arkansas northwest toward wild and beautiful Oregon.

Book 13:

## A Rainy Day Reader:
## 100 Poems for Your Enjoyment

Stan's original, general poetry. ISBN: 9781310912474 125 pages. Published as an eBook on April 3, 2014. Poetry, humor. This eBook contains 100 of his general poems.

Book 14:

## The Cajun Cowdog:
## 15 Cowboy Stories for Adults

"G-rated" for reading level age 10 and up. ISBN: 9781311267405 Published as an eBook on April 16, 2014. Humor, storytelling, Americana, cowboy culture. It is a collection of 15 of Stan Paregien's best cowboy stories. They are "for adults" only in the sense that the stories are probably above the reading levels of most children under 12.

Book 15:

## Cowboy Earmuffs:
## 15 Cowboy Stories for Adults

"G-rated" for reading level age 10 and up. ISBN: 9781311267405 Published as an eBook on April 16, 2014. Humor, storytelling, Americana, cowboy culture.

Book 16:

## Manatee County, Florida: Facts, Folks & Photos

ISBN: 9781370532858 Published as an eBook on May 5, 2017. It is a combination of one part travel guide for the beaches and other attractions in Manatee County, one part who's who of today's leaders and yesterday's heroes and heroines, one part family photo album, and one part a history book containing over 450 photos and 470 biographical sketches. It is written in a conversational style with touches of wit, wisdom, mystery and spice.

Book 17:

## S. Omar Barker: Las Vegas, NM's Legendary Cowboy Poet

Published as 8 X 10" paperback in August, 2019. Stan started researching this talented writer and author in 1994. And it "only" took him 25 years to complete the book. It tells the story of the writing team of husband-wife Omar and Elsa Barker, plus much about the people and culture of San Miguel County. It is 349 pages long, with 165 photos and graphics plus 52 poems. It is available from Amazon.com both as a full-color 8 X 10" paperback and in the far less expensive but still full-color eBook version. Texas cowboy singer and TV personality **Red Steagal**l wrote the Foreword, while Wyoming rancher and author **Rhonda Sedgwick Stearns** wrote the Introduction.

Book 18:

## The Day Jesus Died (Revised Edition).

ISBN-13: 978-1799145066

Published in August, 2019 as a Print-On-Demand 6 X 9" paperback through Amazon's KDP company and distributed to other fine retailers by them. Essays on such topics as "The Problem of Unbelief," "The Peace of God," "The Day Jesus Died," and "The Importance of Truth."

Book 19

## Big Book of Manatee County, Florida: Amazing Facts & Photos.

ISBN-13: 978-1699013083 This 389-page paperback is in in 8.5 X 11" format, in full color and on premium paper. It is a combination of one part travel guide for the beaches and other attractions in Manatee County, one part who's who of today's leaders and yesterday's heroes and heroines, one part family photo album, and one part a history book containing over 450 photos and 470 biographical sketches. It is written in a conversational style with touches of wit, wisdom, mystery and spice.

Book 20

## The Gospel of Jesus in Simple English.

It is a brief introduction to the background of and life of Jesus Christ. It presents the basics of the Gospel in plain, simple language. It is conversational, consumer-friendly and non-sectarian or non-denominational. All that the author wishes to do is to present the love that God has for you and everyone else, with hopes that you will respond favorably.

**ISBN: 9781370758555 – 118 pages. The eBook version** of this book became available on Jan. 18, 2020 at Smashwords.com. There is no charge; it is free. You may download any or all of the eight (8) different formats as often as you want. And you may order them as gifts and have them sent directly to anyone with an email address, all around the world. It is a simple way to introduce people to our Savior. We hope many of you will include a link to this book in your email's "signature" information for the bottom of every email you send. Another way to witness to others would be to mention in on your blog or Twitter account. We encourage congregations to make this a part of their evangelism effort. The link is **smashwords.com/books/view/1000752** to get your free copy.

**ISBN: 9798601749725 – 145 pages.** This is the **paperback version**. It is in a convenient 6 X 9" format and in full color. Christians may want to keep a copy on display at their home or office as a "discussion starter" with interested people. Also, makes a great birthday gift or Christmas gift. Friends, this is my 20th book. It is more important to me than the other 19 put together. When I received my first printed copy, I was so amazed and thankful it turned out so beautifully. And I'm glad the message I wanted to convey about Jesus to searchers is now available.

Book 21

**Big Book of Cowboy Stories**

This 8 X 10" paperback book came out in 2020. ISBN: 9798609642202. This beautifully illustrated book contains 40 of Stan's best cowboy stories. He began performing these and others in 1991 and retired in 2019. Published in Feb., 2020.

Also available as an eBook. ISBN: 9780463466520. All of the photos in the eBook are in color.

Book 22

**Big Book of Cowboy Poetry**

ISBN: 9798616888457. This big paperback book (277 pages; 8 X 10") of Stan's cowboy poems covers ranch romances, hard-nosed bankers, Old West con men, hard-working and hard living cowboys and the folks that love 'em. There are a total of 203 hand-picked from Stan's storehouse of cowboy poems.

It is available as an eBook. ISBN: 9780463252611. Published in Feb., 2020. Color photos.

Book 23

**Partners in Rhyme: Repeat Offenders of Literary Rules**

ISBN-13: 979-8630230867 This 199 page 6 X 9" paperback book was accepted by Amazon's KDP company on March 28, 2020. It is also available as an eBook. The book is a spirited romp in the poetic pasture by two old guys who still enjoy kicking up their heels. That would be the dynamic duo of long-time friends **Stan Paregien and Don Betts**, both of Manatee County, Florida. Their funny, sad, witty, and sometimes weird poetry jumps off every page.

The cover itself shouts out, "This ain't your Grandma's poetry book." No, it is not. Not by a long shot. It was written by two certified common guys for other common folks. The poems deal with the issues, stresses and pleasures of daily living. Part 1 is filled with "Patriotic Poems." Part 2, "Inspirational & Religious Poems." Part 3, "Poems of the Genus Cowboicus Poeticus," which being interpreted means "Cowboy Poetry." Part 4, "Americana, Floridianna & Such." Part 5, "Fun Poems with Few Redeeming Virtues." Part 6, "Odds and Ends and Such," has Stan's bio, Don's bio, and info on some of Stan's other books

Book 24

**The Paregien Family from 1816 to 1940**.

Bradenton, FL: April 5, 2020 as both a paperback and as an eBook by Amazon KDP. ISBN: B086PLBFG2.

Stan Paregien began collecting family history and photos in about 1970. He and his wife, Peggy, became frequent visitors to county court houses, history centers, and cemeteries in Illinois, Missouri, Arkansas, Oklahoma, and Texas. Then, as he acquired home computers and better access to internet resources, he spent countless hours of the day and night doing genealogical research far and wide.

He published his work in 1974. That was a 118 page collection titled, **A Paregien History**. Thirty-two years after that, having collected a mass of information and photos, he self-published **Paregien Family History: 1816 to 2006**. It contained a massive 676 pages with hundreds of photos, with a full index. That version is only available from the author on a DVD.

Fourteen years after the 2006 book, Stan published **The Paregien Family from 1816 to 1940: Plus the Paregine, Peargin & Pearigen Lines**. It is a complete reorganization of the material and ends in 1940. It has 238 pages and lots of photos. This is no run-of-the-mill genealogical book with bare facts. The author, a master writer and storyteller, shares the context behind the facts. He puts muscle and skin and faces on those bare bones. The names mentioned here come through as hardy men and women, each with many virtues and at least a few flaws. The author helps today's readers understand these ancestors had the same human needs that we feel today

Book 25 – The one you have in your hands.

# Chapter 19

## Stan Paregien's Bio

Stan Paregien was born in Wapanucka (Johnston County), Oklahoma. He and his parents, Harold and Evelyn (Cauthen) Paregien, moved to Ventura County, CA less than a year after he was born. He is a graduate of Fillmore Union High School in Fillmore, CA. He received his B.A. in Speech Communication (minors in history and Bible) from Lipscomb University in Nashville, TN. He received his M.A. in Speech Communication from the University of New Mexico in Albuquerque. He also completed all 60 hours of the course work toward a Ph.D. at the University of Oklahoma in Norman.

He describes himself as a storyteller. For nearly 30 years, he was active in performing his original stories and poetry (mostly of the cowboy variety) in venues from Florida to California and from Montana to Texas.

Over the years, Stan Paregien worked as a minister; salesperson; newspaper reporter, photographer and editor; director of mental health facilities in Texas and Oklahoma; and as a radio talk show host. At the heart of each of those professions was the art of storytelling.

Stan became a member of the Western Writers of America in 1986 and, from 1988 to 1992, served as both historian and publicist of that professional group of writers. In

1988 he earned the prestigious "Stirrup Award" from WWA for a series of articles he wrote profiling several Western writers. Though that organization, he was able to get to known and rub elbows with such legendary writers as Bill Gulick, Dee Brown, Jeanne Williams, Max Evans, Leon C. Metz, Robert J. Conley, Don Coldsmith, Jory and Charlotte Sherman, Jim Bob Tinsley, J.T. Edson, and Dusty Richards. That was a dream come true for this ol' country boy.

Paregien began writing cowboy poetry and stories in 1990 while living in Snyder (Scurry County), TX. It was **Alvin Davis**, founder of the National Cowboy Poetry Seminar & Celebration, who first encouraged him to start performing cowboy poetry. And it was **Rudy Gonzales**, a cowboy poet up in Idaho, who also gave him a helpful shove up that trail.

A few years after retiring, Stan and Peggy moved from Edmond, OK to Bradenton, FL (on the Gulf side, south of Tampa). Since that time in 2013, Stan had spent a lot of time writing poetry and books on different subjects. As he nears 80, he refuses to box in any book project with a **deadline.** "I like to tell inquirers that at my age the word 'deadline' has some really negative connotations. Truth is, there are a lot more important issues in life that any old manuscript. Not that I fear dying, for I do not. My wife and I have been walking with the good Lord for over 60 years, so we are packed and ready to go home whenever he calls. I sincerely hope you can say the same."

END.

Made in the USA
Monee, IL
01 February 2021